# Blood on the Lens

# Blood on the Lens

## Trauma and Anxiety in American Found Footage Horror Cinema

Shellie McMurdo

Edinburgh University Press is one of the leading university presses in the UK. We publish academic books and journals in our selected subject areas across the humanities and social sciences, combining cutting-edge scholarship with high editorial and production values to produce academic works of lasting importance. For more information visit our website: edinburghuniversitypress.com

© Shellie McMurdo, 2023, 2024

Edinburgh University Press Ltd
The Tun – Holyrood Road
12 (2f) Jackson's Entry
Edinburgh EH8 8PJ

First published in hardback by Edinburgh University Press 2023

Typeset in 12 on 14pt Arno Pro by
Cheshire Typesetting Ltd, Cuddington, Cheshire

A CIP record for this book is available from the British Library

ISBN 978 1 4744 8208 0 (hardback)
ISBN 978 1 4744 8209 7 (paperback)
ISBN 978 1 4744 8210 3 (webready PDF)
ISBN 978 1 4744 8211 0 (epub)

The right of Shellie McMurdo to be identified as author of this work has been asserted in accordance with the Copyright, Designs and Patents Act 1988 and the Copyright and Related Rights Regulations 2003 (SI No. 2498).

# Contents

| | |
|---|---|
| List of Figures | ix |
| Acknowledgements | xi |
| 1 Found footage horror: a cinema of absences | 1 |
|     Why found footage horror? | 3 |
|     Defining found footage horror | 6 |
|     Finding found footage horror | 10 |
|     Found footage horror and trauma | 13 |
|     Structure | 18 |

**Part I**

| | |
|---|---|
| 2 Found footage horror and documentary conventions | 25 |
|     'You must admit, it's exceptional footage!': documentary modes and styles within found footage horror | 27 |
|     'The camera can see, and what the camera sees the audience sees': documentary truth and the camera as a tool of veracity | 31 |
|     'Tape everything, you hear me? Tape everything!': the limitations of the camera, absence as authenticity and the failed documentary project | 33 |
|     Conclusion | 40 |
| 3 Found footage horror and historical trauma | 43 |
|     'Whatever happens, this story needs to be told': are there limits to traumatic representation? | 45 |

'I don't want to get any more involved': the (post)
   allegorical moment and the Jonestown Death Tape                48
'We go there so you don't have to': the *Vice* aesthetic and
   the importance of witnessing                                   51
'You have a great responsibility': accidental and
   endangered – failing objectivity, crisis reporting and
   trauma tourism in *The Sacrament*                              56
Why Jonestown, why now? The Othering of the
   Jonestown dead and *The Sacrament* as traumatic space          58
Conclusion                                                        63

4 Found footage horror and televisual actualities                 67
   'I don't think either of us are going to want you alive for
      the things I'm going to do to you': making a murder
      documentary with *The Poughkeepsie Tapes*                   68
   'I wonder what was on those tapes': the mythology of
      *The Poughkeepsie Tapes*                                    74
   'Edited strictly for time': the look of the real in
      *Grave Encounters*                                          77
   'Be a fucking professional and stay in character':
      performing the real, participation and privilege in
      *Grave Encounters*                                          81
   'People are going to want to see this': the ever present
      threat of a haunted landscape                               84
   Conclusion                                                     87


## Part II

5 Found footage horror, 9/11 and a culture of fear                93
   Horror with a message(?)                                       96
   Searching the wreckage: the paranoid landscape of
      post-9/11 America                                           98
   Fear on screen: cinema and horror post-9/11 – a brief
      overview                                                   100
   A new visual language of terror: bystander footage and the
      (un)believability of continuing to tape                    104
   Conclusion                                                    107

| | |
|---|---|
| 6 'They're going to let us die': trust in found footage horror | 111 |
|     'They're not going to let us out of here alive, are they?': inadvertent witnesses | 113 |
|     'I signed up for brave and courageous': the heroic firefighter in *Quarantine* and *9/11* | 117 |
|     'Turn it off!': editing and crisis censorship | 120 |
|     'Hit her again': the camera as a tool in found footage horror | 123 |
|     Conclusion | 125 |
| 7 'What if they're not even listening?': truth in found footage horror | 129 |
|     'There's a little thing called the first amendment?': the found footage truth teller | 131 |
|     'With an underlying threat of social satire': editing | 134 |
|     'We need to keep this in perspective': on being collateral damage in post-9/11 found footage horror | 140 |
|     Conclusion | 144 |

## Part III

| | |
|---|---|
| 8 Death in digital: found footage horror and the internet | 149 |
|     Ghosts in the machines: new media/new horror | 151 |
|     'Is it real?': internet-based paratexts and found footage horror | 158 |
|     Conclusion | 165 |
| 9 'You have committed a fatal error': social media horrors | 169 |
|     'It's the internet, you should have expected something like this': real death, the internet and *The Den* | 171 |
|     'What you've done here will live forever': the haunted (social) media of *Unfriended* | 177 |
|     'If you're not documenting yourself, it's simple. You don't exist': content, identity and audiences in *Spree* | 184 |
|     Conclusion | 190 |
| 10 The footage yet to be found | 193 |

| | |
|---|---|
| Bibliography | 203 |
| Found Footage Filmography and Other Media | 231 |
| Filmography | 235 |
| Index | 239 |

# Figures

| | | |
|---|---|---|
| 3.1 | Images of marginalised death in *The Sacrament* | 50 |
| 3.2 | 'Haute hobo chic' Sam Turner in *The Sacrament*... | 54 |
| 3.3 | ... and Shane Smith of *Vice* | 54 |
| 4.1 | The physical presence of *The Poughkeepsie Tapes* | 71 |
| 4.2 | VHS decay underlines the illicit nature of the tapes... and their overuse | 73 |
| 4.3 | A ghost hunting show gone horribly wrong: Sasha's blood on the lens in *Grave Encounters* | 80 |
| 6.1 | Getting to know Jake and Fletcher in *Quarantine* | 119 |
| 6.2 | The fallen firefighter takes on a new resonance in post-9/11 found footage horror | 123 |
| 6.3 | The camera as a tool in found footage horror: the bludgeoning of Elise in *Quarantine* | 124 |
| 7.1 | *The Bay* contains a vast array of varied footage, including a police dashcam | 132 |
| 7.2 | 'They changed it....': tensions around editing arise for the students of *Diary of the Dead* as they watch the recut Channel 10 footage | 135 |
| 7.3 | *The Conspiracy* repeatedly forefronts 9/11 | 140 |
| 7.4 | Aaron becomes obsessed with Terrence's research in *The Conspiracy* | 142 |
| 9.1 | The pay-per-view torture website in *The Den* includes categories for 'axe play', 'blow torch' and other niche interests | 175 |
| 9.2 | Ken's death in *Unfriended*, the horror emphasised by violent glitching, is witnessed digitally by his friends | 179 |
| 9.3 | Content, content, content: a triumphant Jessie with a dead Kurt | 188 |

9.4  Hyperconnectivity: screens upon screens and constant comments in *Spree* 189
10.1 Haunting images: the found photography of *Savageland* 195

# Acknowledgements

This book has been just over eight years in the making, and that's if we are not counting the many years that I watched every found footage horror film I could get my grubby hands on without any clue about what I could do with that obsession. I want to thank a variety of people from the bottom of my heart for their support before, during, and after the creation of this piece of work: without you, this wouldn't have been possible.

First of all, I give very grateful thanks to Gillian Leslie, Sam Johnson and Richard Strachan at Edinburgh University Press. You have made the experience of producing this monograph an absolute delight and I'm very honoured to have been able to publish this book through such an esteemed press, and in the company of so much fabulous horror scholarship. Thanks also go to my peer reviewers for their kind and encouraging comments on the proposal for this book and their suggestions for improving it. Enormous thanks are due to Stacey Abbott and Iain Robert Smith, who supervised the doctoral thesis this book grew out of. Stacey and Iain always had a kind word when I was at low points, and great suggestions when I was at my highest. They were everything I could have hoped they would be and I'm acutely aware how lucky I have been to have had them as my supervisory team and to now count them among my friends.

I maintain the belief that people who study horror are the sweetest, kindest, and most generous kind of people there are. With that in mind, special thanks are due to Kate Egan, Char Baker, Wickham Clayton, Jaymes Fox, Johnny Walker, Steve Jones, Xavier Aldana Reyes, Dawn Keetley, Kendall Phillips, Alison Peirse, Jon Towlson, Caitlin Shaw, David Church, Martin Barker, Lindsay Hallam, Deborah Jermyn, Kieran Foster, Steen Christiansen, Pete Turner, Caitlin Duffy, and Joe Ondrak. These people have shared their work, their thoughts, and their time with me and

I'll always be in their debt. Also, a massive thanks to Sarah Appleton, Chris Holden, and Josh Saco – who made me feel like my scattered thoughts on the subgenre were interesting outside of the academy.

Extra special thanks go to my monster squad, who have been my best friends and greatest peers over the past few years: Craig Ian Mann (an ever patient sounding board and encouraging voice), Laura Mee (an amazing scholar and selfless friend), Stella Gaynor (a founding member of the horror girl gang), and Tom Watson (who shares with me a love of very violent films and very brootal music). Extra super special thanks go to Laura, who dragged me kicking and screaming through the last few months of writing this book and fielded what must have seemed like endless panicked phone calls and text messages, cheers mate – I owe you!

I give huge snogs and thanks to my girls, my best friend Emily – who has supported and encouraged me for well over a decade, humoured my rants about horror films, and nourished my soul with documentary recommendations and murder trips – and Julie, who is the Disney princess counterpart to my grim, goth, self.

Last but most definitely not least, I give thanks to my family. My mum, who sat through an obscene amount of gory horror films with me instead of watching her Gerard Butler movies but shares with me a love of true crime, and who discovered a gift for proofreading during my PhD. My brother, Antony, who helped me more than he will realise with his seemingly limitless knowledge of mid-2000s viral marketing campaigns. My two dogs, Hemingway and Juno, the best PhD pals and the most critical of conference paper practice audiences. And finally, my husband, Colin, who I bullied into watching all horror all the time, and has the wisdom to tell me when I'm being 'pretentious' (rude). You're the Dan to my Herbert, the Richie to my Eddie, the Will to my Hannibal, and I love you very much.

I dedicate this book to my dear, spartan-esque Dad, Mac. Who would have read this book, looked me in the eye, and said 'That's great, kid. When are you going to get a proper job?'

Parts of Chapter 9 have been previously published in: The (Blum)House Found Footage Horror Built, in Platts, T. K., McCollum, V., and Clasen, M. (eds.) *Blumhouse Productions: The New House of Horror*, and are reproduced here with kind permission of University of Wales Press.

# 1

# Found footage horror: a cinema of absences

> I mean, this genre has had two halfway decent films, one of which was fifteen fucking years ago. Every other found footage film since then has been complete bullshit. I mean, why people waste their money on this vomit inducing amateur hour bullshit is fucking beyond me[1]
>
> It's perfect, it's wonderful, it's found footage[2]

When many people think of the term 'found footage horror', the first film that comes to mind is *The Blair Witch Project* (1999): amateur filmmakers, running around in the woods, ensnared by something they cannot quite comprehend or capture on film. Audiences for *The Blair Witch Project* in 1999 reported feelings of dizziness and motion sickness while watching the film (Wax, 1999), citing the then unusual use of disorientating hand-held cinematography as the cause. This was something fresh, new and as far away from its genre contemporaries of that year – the slickly produced *House on Haunted Hill* (1999) and *The Sixth Sense* (1999) – as well as the concurrent trend towards postmodern slashers such as *Scream* (1996) and *Urban Legend* (1998) as possible. *The Blair Witch Project* felt unedited, it felt raw and crucially, it felt real. It was something of a watershed moment for the horror genre, achieving an unprecedented level of financial success, and was duly praised for being 'ingenious in its simplicity' (Baumgarten, 1999), 'the most inventive and genuinely frightening horror movie to appear in years' (Williams, 1999) and as an 'extraordinarily effective horror film' (Ebert, 1999). Many noted the 'simple, exquisite conceit' (Rose, 1999) of the found footage format: a style that scholar Peg Aloi went as far as to call 'the new horror aesthetic' (2005: 188). If we fast forward seventeen years to the release of the film's direct sequel,[3] simply titled *Blair Witch* (2016), we find a very different critical reception. While some found issue with the film's attempt to recreate the original's sense of realism and tension (Smith, 2016; Watson, 2016) or dismissed it as an unnecessary retread (Travers, 2016; Felperin, 2016), others critiqued the found footage horror format itself, proposing that the release of *Blair Witch* signified 'the loud death rattle of a once exciting sub-genre' (Lee, 2016). Found footage horror has, partially because of the success of *The Blair Witch Project* and the immensely popular *Paranormal Activity* franchise (2007–), become one of the most instantly visually recognisable subgenres in post-millennial North American horror cinema. It has endured – if we take *The Blair Witch Project* or *The Last Broadcast* (1998) as the first examples of the format as we came to know it – for decades. But, as the two quotes that open this chapter and the critical reception of *Blair Witch* demonstrate, it is also a divisive subgenre. Although (or perhaps because) found footage horror is still a popular horror format some decades after its inception, the consensus seems to be that it has become 'tiresome' (Phipps and Tobias, 2014), 'derivative' (Berkshire, 2015), 'unimaginative' (Fontana, 2016) and 'intentionally hard to comprehend' (Ebert, 2012). Moreover, journalistic commentary has suggested that the term 'found footage horror' now functions as 'shorthand for something generic and undercooked, the refuge of uncreative filmmakers' (Darer, 2016) or alternatively posited that, to many, '"found footage" now equals "bad horror movie"' (Barone, 2014).

Despite its prominence in the first and second decades of the new millennium, the subgenre has been widely occluded from a great deal of scholarship working to provide overviews of the horror genre. For example (although, given the time of their publication, appraisal of the subgenre as a whole is understandably absent), the success of *The Blair Witch Project* is not engaged with in any meaningful way within *Nightmares in Red, White, and Blue: The Evolution of the American Horror Film* (Maddrey, 2004), *The Horror Film* (Hutchings, 2004) or *A History of Horror* (Dixon, 2010) beyond cursory mentions. As these works are situated as introductory texts to horror cinema or accounts of the genre's cultural impact, the lack of attention paid to *The Blair Witch Project* within them is significant. This is particularly notable when we consider how often horror cinema has historically been positioned as a way of mediating trauma and anxieties. Collections such as the superb *Make America Hate Again: Trump Era Horror and the Politics of Fear* (McCollum, 2019), for instance, deftly demonstrate the continued resonance of horror cinema within the society it emerges from, but again found footage horror is missing from their consideration. Given that the found footage format is one that ties itself so completely to how viewers are currently experiencing reality and society through its emulation of emerging reality 'looks', this is a notable omission.

It is this imbalance, and the lack of attention paid to how the found footage horror subgenre can function as a vehicle for representations of cultural trauma and societal anxieties, that *Blood on the Lens: Trauma and Anxiety in American Found Footage Horror Cinema* seeks to address.

## Why found footage horror?

This book represents the first long form scholarly invention to specifically make use of a trauma studies-influenced perspective as a framework through which to engage with North American found footage horror. I should note that although I have thus far demonstrated the relative lack of scholarship on the found footage horror subgenre, I am in no way suggesting that there is literally no work available at all. There have been several key interventions before *Blood on the Lens* that have shaped the aims and objectives of this book. Much previous scholarship on the found footage horror subgenre is characterised by a focus on *The Blair Witch Project* and the *Paranormal Activity* series of films. *The Blair Witch Project*, for example, has been the subject of monographs (Turner, 2014) and edited collections (Higley and Weinstock, 2004), in addition to a wealth of scholarly articles (Harris, 2001; Morgan, 2001; Telotte, 2001; Rhodes, 2002; Schreier, 2004; Lavender-Smith, 2009 to note only a few), whereas the *Paranormal Activity* franchise has become a more recent preoccupation (for example in Hahner, Varda and Wilson, 2013; Leyda, 2014; Swanson, 2015 and Jones, 2017). These films are also proposed by Matthew Raimondo (2014) to be the 'pioneer' and 'variation' points of the subgenre respectively. The dominance of these films in previous scholarship has been a causal factor in my decision to largely exclude them from close analysis within this book, as explorations of their themes, formal qualities and context has been so thoroughly (and excellently) excavated elsewhere.

*The Blair Witch Project* and *Paranormal Activity* (2007) also feature as key texts in Alexandra Heller-Nicholas's (2014) monograph on found footage horror, one of the two long form studies that currently exist on the subgenre. Heller-Nicholas's study examines found footage horror's genealogy, tracing its themes and style with an eye towards its prehistory and a timeline of its development and the solidification of its aesthetics between 1998 and 2009. Latter sections of Heller-Nicholas's study explore further thematic developments within the subgenre from 2007 to 2013, where she presents exorcism narratives, family-centred films and concerns around nationhood as the prevailing themes emerging from the subgenre in this time. The last of these themes is of particular relevance to my own research, and Heller-Nicholas's engagement with nationhood encompasses films from the United States, the United Kingdom, Australia, Spain, Norway and Japan. However, there have been several shifts in the subgenre more recently that – due to the publication date of her monograph – Heller-Nicholas was not able to examine. The other monograph currently available on found footage horror cinema is Peter Turner's *Found Footage Horror Films: A Cognitive Approach* (2019), which provides a more overtly psychoanalytical account of the subgenre, with a focus on the mental processes that are elicited by the format's camerawork. Turner examines how found footage horror films create a sense of immediacy through their diegetic cameras and investigates how a viewer's cognition of narrative events is primed through identification. Turner's study is divided into specific examination of three categories of found footage horror: documentary and reality television, home videos and the serial killer film. There are very few parallels between these full-length studies of the found footage horror subgenre and the aims and objectives of *Blood on the Lens*. For although we all analyse the same subgenre, we do so from different theoretical standpoints and with differing primary objectives. Heller-Nicholas's focus is on the prehistory of the subgenre, its emerging themes and the formation of its style, while Turner's is on the priming of the spectator and their cognition. Other accounts exist too that consider found footage horror within a wider examination of horror media, such as Adam Charles Hart's (2019) *Monstrous Forms: Moving Image Horror Across Media* and Adam Daniel's (2020) *Affective Intensities and Evolving Horror Forms: From Found Footage to Virtual Reality*. These publications focus on the subgenre's sensational form of address and affect and embodiment respectively. My own focus is on the multitudinous ways in which cultural trauma and societal anxieties are understood and assimilated by the subgenre and how they are then projected back to its audiences. Therefore, although there may be case study films in common, this book represents an alternative understanding of the subgenre which sits alongside these previous accounts. On this note, I present Duncan Hubber's (2017) study of found footage horror as one that is closely linked to my own. Hubber discerns that the element that ties a great deal of found footage horror together as a subgenre is an engagement with cultural trauma and covers three countries of origin in his work: Australia, Japan and the United States. Hubber argues that the found footage horror films emerging from these contexts specifically reference historical national anxieties: *The Tunnel* (2011) connects to Australia's sense of identity, *Occult* (2009) engages with concerns in Japan following World

War II and *Willow Creek* (2013) is situated as 'an allegory for the apprehensions of contemporary America when confronted with their nation's vast and mythic wilderness' (2017). Although Hubber uses a similar theoretical framework to my own, I would suggest that the relatively short length of his study, which is a scholarly article, and its split focus across three countries, result in it being a key, but not sustained, piece of research on North American found footage horror as a vehicle for trauma and anxieties.

Several other articles and chapters such as Hubber's have within them the seedlings that this book seeks to cultivate. Examples of this include Neil McRobert's (2015) analysis of how the subgenre engages with codes of nonfiction media. McRobert suggests that found footage horror cinema's mimicking of the formal and aesthetic qualities of mainstream news and amateur recordings is crucial to its construction of fear, as it is through these qualities that the subgenre evokes real life spectatorship of world crises. Building on this, a central argument of this book is that the found footage horror subgenre constantly evolves and adapts to new representations of reality (not only mainstream news but more recent developments such as social media aesthetics) in order to maintain a connection with the audience members in their current cultural moment. Despite McRobert's highlighting of the connection between trauma and the subgenre, the edited collection that his essay is part of (Blake and Reyes, 2015) – which currently stands as the only academic edited collection to focus at least partially on the subgenre – largely does not revisit the idea of found footage horror as a site for traumatic representation.

Taking my cue from Andrew Tudor's discussion surrounding the appeal of horror cinema, I will argue throughout this book that found footage horror's engagement with trauma and various societal anxieties can be discerned through the film's aesthetic and narrative correlation with 'our distinctive experience of fear, risk, and instability' (Tudor, 1997: 459). I propose that it is this specific quality of the subgenre that is central to its popularity. *Blood on the Lens* presents the found footage horror subgenre as one that is constantly shifting and changing, a feature that has enabled it to directly and explicitly engage with the conventions of (and anxieties around): documentary filmmaking (and its recent renaissance), video journalism, reality television, the mediated experience of 9/11 and various forms of internet-based communication. Found footage horror has consistently embraced the different ways we experience the world, whether that be through user-generated content websites, the inclusion of bystander footage on mainstream news, or through documentaries, and each of these have sparked regenerations in the formal aesthetics and narrative themes of the subgenre. I present the subgenre therefore as a vital and ever evolving one, which readily incorporates new forms of media and emergent representations of reality in order to retain a connection with its audience members and their changing relationships to technology, media and reality. Overarchingly, I seek to reframe contemporary debates around the horror genre which have largely neglected the rich and ever shifting landscape of found footage horror, as although several questions have been answered by previous work on the subgenre, many still remain.

## Defining found footage horror

As many have noted before me, pinning down the exact definitions of genres is a slippery task, and these debates are replicated when attempting to define the exact characteristics of subgenres. It is a formidable job I have ahead of me then, in outlining the characteristics of what my research has taken the term 'found footage horror' to mean, and to then position this in relation to other definitions of the subgenre. In exploring the various definitions to emerge since the subgenre's inception and rise to popularity, however, I will present a further examination of what the aesthetics, themes and narratives of found footage horror films typically consist of (or at least are assumed to consist of in broader criticism and scholarship) before putting forward my own definition, which I have applied throughout this book.

Early work on the subgenre did indeed seem preoccupied with subcategorising its films, citing its origin point or delineating an umbrella term for the subgenre's output. It has been variously placed within the mockumentary tradition[4] (Roscoe, 2000; Rhodes, 2002), labelled as 'parodic-doc' (Lavender-Smith, 2009) and described variously as 'observational horror' (Raimondo, 2014) or 'verité horror' (Grant, 2013) among other terms. More recently, Xavier Aldana Reyes has argued that found footage horror is not actually a subgenre at all, but a framing device (2015a). The first issue that arises in defining found footage horror cinema, then, is in terms of nomenclature, as the term 'found footage' does not have its origin within horror cinema, but was initially used to refer to a type of filmmaking that appropriates 'found' footage in its construction, in a process alternatively known as collage, montage or archival filmmaking. This kind of filmmaking utilises 'footage shot for one use but [which is] then "found" and repurposed, and thus directed towards new uses' (Anderson, 2011: 65). The footage is, as Catherine Russell outlines, 'already filmed, already screened, decontexutalised and recontextualised' (1999: 18), later describing the look of these films as 'an aesthetic of ruins' (1999: 238). The film historian David Bordwell has also noted this original use of the term 'found footage' and admitted to being 'not delighted' that it is now used to describe such films as *The Blair Witch Project*. Indeed, Bordwell refuses to use it in this way, instead selecting the term 'discovered footage' films (Bordwell, 2012).

Bordwell's distinction, that the found footage subgenre is not made up of actual 'found' footage but populated by films in which footage is 'discovered', calls attention to a key issue in defining the subgenre: that of the footage's origin within the films as being of upmost significance. Many definitions will indeed underline the presence of footage that is 'found' in the narrative as an integral feature of the found footage horror style. For example, Barry Keith Grant, while using his preferred moniker of 'verité horror' to categorise the subgenre, puts forward that

> the style of the films is remarkably consistent. In many of them the narrative is framed as if the footage was somehow discovered after the death or disappearance of those who shot it, and has subsequently made its way to the cinema where we are able to see it. (2013: 155)

The 'foundness' of the footage within these films is perceived as such a key convention of the subgenre that the recurrence of this trope is playfully highlighted in the meta found footage horror film *Found Footage 3D* (2016), where the characters are aware of the tropes and conventions of the subgenre and reference them throughout the narrative.[5] While it is true that 'found' footage forms the basis of two of the most famous entries in the subgenre – *Cannibal Holocaust* (1980) and *The Blair Witch Project* – and a large number of narratives coming under found footage horror's banner have placed the in-universe discovery of footage at the forefront of their storylines, it would be inaccurate to state that the defining feature of the subgenre is that the footage has to be 'found'. Perhaps somewhat controversially, I have not focused on the status of the footage in these films – found or otherwise – as part of my definition of the subgenre. To do so would necessitate the discounting of films such as *The Sacrament* (2013) and *The Bay* (2012) from any overview of the found footage format, as the footage in these films is never 'found' as such but presented as a selection of material shot, collected or retained by characters following an event and then edited into a cohesive narrative. Despite these intricacies around the term, I will continue to use 'found footage horror' throughout this book, as it has been used commonly in both scholarship and journalistic accounts to describe the films I am talking about, and I therefore have no requirement (or desire) to invent a new taxonomic term.

In addition to an emphasis on the 'found' element of found footage horror, there is a recurrent presence in definitions of the subgenre on the 'amateur' quality of its camerawork. Neil McRobert, for instance, suggests that one of the 'essential ingredients' of the subgenre is 'amateur filmmakers' (2015: 135), while Cecilia Sayad proposes that found footage horror is characterised by 'grainy, shaky, and precariously framed images that mimic the style of amateur filmmaking' (2016: 43–4). While I broadly agree that the 'amateur' is a key element of a great deal of found footage horror films, to strictly exclude those that do not appear amateur would preclude an engagement with entries that feature operatorless surveillance cameras, or the more recent emergence of social media horror (a subset of the subgenre explored at length in the third part of this book). Also, as the found footage horror subgenre has evolved, there has been a concurrent decline in the strictly handheld and 'amateur' look. For example, *Invasion* (2005) consists of footage presented as being from a police dashboard camera, *A Ride in the Park* (2013) and *Blair Witch* use Go Pro head mounted cameras, and *Phase 1 Clinical Trials* (2013) features an ocular implant camera. *The Bay* includes a wide variety of camera styles (camera phone, handheld, dashboard, Skype, webcam, surveillance) and more recent films such as *Unfriended* (2014) and *Host* (2020) have adopted the specific aesthetics of communication software such as Skype and Zoom respectively. This increase in the use of different styles of footage in the subgenre perhaps reflects the vast number of different consumer grade recording technologies now available to us. In addition, films such as *The Poughkeepsie Tapes* (2007) and *Savageland* (2016) would need to be omitted from a definition based around the amateur, as they are constructed as professionally produced documentaries (albeit with shaky 'amateur' footage contained within).

I contend, then, that the definitions I have thus far highlighted do speak accurately to specific subdivisions or 'types' of found footage horror cinema. However, they do not begin to indicate the subgenre's tendency to appropriate a vast array of footage styles, framing devices and aesthetic conventions. My own understanding of the term 'found footage horror' and the films that can reside within that category is broader than these previous definitions would allow, and this is due in part to the significant volume of films that could be said to 'belong' to the subgenre. Found footage horror, due to the ease and relative lack of expense required to reproduce its aesthetics, is a subgenre with a very high output of films. In addition to cinematic releases, the format has become favoured by the makers of direct-to-video (DVD, Blu-ray, video-on-demand etc.) productions and low/no budget filmmaking. The sheer volume of found footage horror narratives is perhaps best expressed by referring to the website foundfootagecritic.com, insofar that as of March 2022, the website holds details for over 700 found footage horror films and this number is still climbing.[6] This volume of films necessitated the creation of a loose typology of the subgenre, to enable a thorough survey of its output and to discount films that only loosely adhered to the found footage conceit.

For the purposes of this book, useful definitions are those put forward by Scott Meslow and Neil McRobert. Eschewing a focus on the strictly amateur, journalist Meslow argues that the found footage horror subgenre is typified by 'the conceit that the movie was filmed not by a traditional omniscient director, but by a character that exists within the film's world' (2012). Neil McRobert's definition, meanwhile, states that a found footage horror film is one that rests upon 'the suggestion that the images caught on camera have taken place in the audience's reality and that, whilst the viewer may be detached from the threat geographically and temporally, they are ontologically commensurate with the events depicted' (2015: 139). These definitions have influenced my own: the camera must exist diegetically within the narrative and be acknowledged as such, and the events must be presented as being part of, rather than adjacent or similar to, the audience's reality. Incidentally, I should note at this point that by using the term 'audience', I am in no way suggesting that any audience is a homogenised mass, a thought process that is increasingly meaningless in a contemporary society with high levels of migration. Therefore, although I will use terms such as 'Americans', 'American society' and 'American public', this is not intended to describe an ideal or quintessentially 'American' audience, but in respect of a heterogeneous film viewing public in America, which encompasses all genders, races, nationalities and religions.

In terms of my case study selection, my own definition of found footage horror means that I have omitted films that did not sustain the found footage mode throughout their narratives, such as *Vlog* (2008) and *Evidence* (2013), which alternate between diegetic and non-diegetic cameras. Other films were discounted due to sound design or, more specifically, due to their inclusion of non-diegetic music. The exceptions to this were films presented as edited documentaries such as *The Sacrament*, *Diary of the Dead* (2007), *The Bay* and *The Conspiracy* (2012). In these cases, rather than undermining the reality effect of the film, or even working to 'destroy a found footage film', as is ventured by foundfootagecritic.com, it makes logical sense that a finished documentary product may well have incidental music. It should be noted, however, that this would not function in the same way within a film such as *Quarantine* (2008), which is presented as raw footage that has been edited in camera. To have non-diegetic music in a film such as this would have a significant and adverse effect on its reality claims.

In the following pages, my primary aim is to explore how the subgenre offers new thematic and aesthetic ways of confronting national trauma and cultural anxieties through its narratives and forms. I have selected ten main case study films through which to do this – both high profile and lesser known – which also clearly show how found footage horror responds to shifts in its cultural context in clear and definable ways through their adapting to and adoption of emerging reality 'looks'. Of course, a selection of ten films cannot and does not represent the found footage horror subgenre as a whole, but the case studies within this book were chosen due to their ability to illustrate the overarching themes and aesthetics that are present and recurring within it and stand as examples of found footage horror cinema at crucial points in its evolution. All the films closely analysed in this book are North American (the majority from the United States and two from Canada),[7] but this focus is not to suggest that found footage horror is specific or unique to this part of the world. There is an enormous amount of found footage horror cinema emerging transnationally, and I would venture that a great deal of these films resonate specifically with their own national identities, traumas and anxieties. Examples of this include *Trollhunter* (2010) from Norway, the *[Rec]* franchise from Spain (2007–14), *Exhibit A* (2007) from England, *The Devil's Doorway* (2018) from Northern Ireland, *Lake Mungo* (2008) and *The Tunnel* from Australia, *Jeruzalem* (2015) from Israel, *District 9* (2009) from South Africa and *Noroi: The Curse* (2005) from Japan. It is for this reason that I have, where appropriate, brought in examples of films from other countries to support my analysis of found footage horror cinema more generally, or to contextualise the subgenre more broadly. In short, the primary focus of this book is on North American found footage horror and the enduring themes present within it, but that is not to say that these anxieties are not present elsewhere.

## Finding found footage horror

In order to properly examine the found footage horror subgenre and its cultural impact, it is first necessary to investigate the genre context from which it emerged. It is not my intention here to neatly categorise and summarise the output of North American horror cinema since the turn of the millennium, as to do so would be reductive, irrelevant to the aims of my research, and would commit a disservice to the wide variety of horror cinema that has been released over this time period. Instead, my aim here is to place the appearance and subsequent growth of found footage horror firmly within its genre context by highlighting some key trends and movements before and during the rise of found footage horror cinema.

Although I opened this chapter by discussing the unprecedented success of *The Blair Witch Project*, which grossed $248,639,099 despite its relatively miniscule budget of $60,000 [USD] (boxofficemojo.com), there did not immediately follow a raft of found footage horror narratives in its wake. The 'boom' in the production of found footage horror cinema would not happen until after the release of *Paranormal Activity*. This increase in production is especially apparent if we are to compare the number of films adhering to the format in the four years (2003–6) before *Paranormal Activity*'s 2007 release – sixteen – and the four years (2008–11) following, during which fifty-one found footage horror films were unleashed in North America. It is worth noting, of course, that this number may not be precise – there may well be multiple independent productions I have missed or that passed me by – however, it is fair to say there was a discernable and undeniable rise in the number of found footage horror films produced in North America from *Paranormal Activity*'s release onwards.

As the horror genre entered the new millennium, perhaps inspired by the ongoing success of the *Scream* franchise (1996–), there was a continuation of a definable body of films Peter Hutchings termed as postmodern or 'neo-slashers' (2004: 213). Films falling roughly into this cycle include *I Know What You Did Last Summer* (1997), *Final Destination* (2000) or *Cherry Falls* (2000), with genre savvy characters displaying an 'awareness' of the horror genre (Hutchings, 2004: 214) that allows them an advantage over masked killers and supernatural beings. These postmodern slashers did not dominate the horror genre however, and other popular movements included remakes of both East Asian (see Wee, 2013) and domestic horror films (see Mee, 2022). Horror scholarship around this time began to circulate claims that the genre was becoming stale, and as Steffen Hantke (2007) has highlighted in his discussion of this era of academic engagement with the genre, there was a focus on a perceived 'slump' or state of crisis. North American horror cinema of the late 1990s and into the 2000s was situated as 'moribund' (Phillips, 2005: 181) or as a genre that 'seemed stagnant, struggling to find voice and direction' (Hart, 2014: 329). The 'rhetoric of crisis' (Hantke, 2007) present in these accounts can also be found in a proclamation made by Reynold Humphries, who ventured that 'the state of things is not conducive to optimism, let alone enthusiasm' (2002: 189). Other scholars, such as Christopher Sharrett, duly lamented that

> it has been some time since the genre has advanced the radical ambitions of its greatest epochs [...] neither do we see, nor can we much anticipate, the achievements of F.W. Murnau, Tod Browning, James Whale, George Romero, Tobe Hooper, Larry Cohen, or other horror innovators anytime in the near future. (2014: 71)

Emerging from this topography, however, two distinct subgenres came to the fore: found footage horror, and the subgenre with which it shares its closest kinship – torture horror, or as it is more commonly known, 'torture porn'.

Although *Hostel* (2005) was the first film to be termed as such (Edelstein, 2006), the release of *Saw* (2004) can be seen as the origin point for the torture horror subgenre. In the wake of *Saw*, films such as *The Devil's Rejects* (2005), *Turistas* (2006), *Hostel: Part II* (2007), *The Ruins* (2008), *The Strangers* (2008), *Captivity* (2007), *Horsemen* (2009) and *The Human Centipede: First Sequence* (2009) have been situated as belonging to the subgenre, which was initially widely dismissed as being 'sadistically nihilistic' (McCartney, 2007), with some going so far as to term it 'possibly the worst movement in the history of cinema' (Aftab, 2009: 12). The legacy of 'torture porn' is largely its use as a pejorative term, as can be seen in the criticism surrounding the Season 7 premiere of popular television zombie drama *The Walking Dead* (2010–22), during which the character of Glenn was beaten to death with a baseball bat, prompting critic Erik Kain to ask if the episode was 'just torture porn' (Kain, 2016).

Torture horror is a particularly interesting movement in post-millennium horror cinema, emerging as it did at a similar time to the New French Extremity. Both movements focus on scenes of extended suffering, gore and torture, but are generally framed very differently. For example, an overview of French extremity films takes care to note 'that this is not torture porn [...] although it may be tempting to *reduce* it to that' (Joubert, 2016, emphasis added). It may seem odd to link torture horror, with its excessive displays of violence and gore, with the found footage horror subgenre, more known for its obstructed framing, suggestiveness in place of explicitness and resistance to resolution. Alexandra Heller-Nicholas, for example, seems unwilling to examine any similarities between the two subgenres, asserting that found footage horror ascended in popularity as torture horror fell (2014: 92). However, in addition to the clear cross-pollination between the two subgenres, as seen in films such as *The Poughkeespie Tapes*,

*Penance* (2009) and *Hate Crime* (2012), I argue that one of the strongest commonalities between the two is their move towards realism. In the case of found footage horror, this can be seen in the presentation of the footage as authentic, whereas in torture horror, this is discernible in the drive towards more graphic and anatomically realistic gore. So, what was it about North American culture and society that meant these two ostensibly disparate subgenres found traction? This is another of the questions this book endeavours to answer.

## Found footage horror and trauma

In many ways, my research into the found footage horror subgenre takes its cue from two questions. These are Adam Lowenstein's 'What does cinematic horror have to tell us about the horrors of history' (2005: 2), and Linnie Blake's longer query of 'Why, within a specific national context, at a particular point in time, particular people produce particular horror film texts for the enthusiastic consumption of both their fellow countrymen and those who live beyond the nation's borders?' (2008: 6).[8] Throughout *Blood on the Lens*, then, I will be asking 'Why found footage horror, why now?' My invocation of Lowenstein and Blake points towards their influence on my research, with both having used a trauma studies-inflected perspective previously in relation to the horror genre. A further monograph that highlights representations of trauma in horror cinema is Kendall Phillips's *Projected Fears: Horror Films and American Culture* (2005). Phillips's study is notably different from both Lowenstein and Blake's interventions in that it focuses specifically on North American horror cinema and, as such, is much closer in scope to my own research.

Broadly speaking, trauma studies is the delineation and critique of the various ways in which real-life trauma is echoed or represented in cultural products emerging from that trauma. It is concerned with cultural memory and examines the complex relationship between historical events, the art or cultural products transpiring from those events and the mental processes of that art's audiences, including how cultural 'wounds' are transmitted: particularly to those who may not have experienced the trauma themselves. Looking beyond horror, trauma studies has been employed as a way of understanding cinema more broadly before (see Kaplan, 2005; Sisco King, 2011; Köhne et al, 2014), but it is fair to say that a key tension in this field is the proclivity several trauma theorists have towards separating 'high' from 'low' art. This can be seen in Hayden White's insistence that trauma is best represented through literary modernism, which – in his opinion – reflected the trauma of the Holocaust in a way that 'no other version of realism could do' (1992: 52). A dismissal of popular cinema's ability to represent trauma can also be seen in the dominant focus within trauma studies on literary – rather than cinematic – works emerging from traumatic contexts. This can be seen in Cathy Caruth's (1996) text *Unclaimed Experience: Trauma, Narrative, and History*, in which only one cinematic work – the French arthouse film *Hiroshima Mon Amour* (1959) – is examined, and Kalí Tal's (1996) *Worlds of Hurt: Reading the Literatures of Trauma*, throughout which the idea of trauma expressed through popular cinema is continually undermined.

Although the work of literary theorist Dominick LaCapra marked a movement in trauma studies towards an inclusion of cinematic texts, he is similar to Hayden White in his dismissal of cultural forms considered 'popular'. For example, LaCapra draws a clear contrast between the representations of the Holocaust present in *Schindler's List* (1993) and those within the documentary film *Shoah* (1985), valorising *Shoah* as a distinct masterpiece, while positioning *Schindler's List* as a film 'that seems to provide consolation too facile for the wounds of the past' (1997: 241). Although we cannot be certain that LaCapra's dismissal of *Schindler's List* is due to its mainstream popularity, the favouring of documentary or arthouse over popular forms of cinema – and by extension genre cinema – is characteristic of cinema-orientated trauma studies more widely. As Adam Lowenstein summarises, in trauma studies, dismissive critique is often aimed at 'those representations that rely on "realist" rather than "modernist" modes, "narrative" rather than "nonnarrative" modes' (2005: 4).

This dismissal of popular cinema could also be attributed to trauma studies' apparent mistrust of allegorical representations. For instance, in Carole Cavanaugh's appraisal of *Gojira/Godzilla* (1954), she draws attention to the problematic nature of reading the film as expressing the trauma of Hiroshima, as it has opted to 'engage in fantasy or futuristic monsters, at the cost of confronting the monstrous reality of the past' (2001: 252). Cavanaugh's comments suggest that a film can either be fantasy or be a direct representation of trauma, but not both, and this notion will be revisited in Chapter 3 in reference to *The Sacrament*. Adam Lowenstein has also noted a predisposition within the field of trauma studies towards discounting genre cinema's representations of trauma as inconsequential and as being focused on spectacle. Lowenstein proposes that this disregard is of course problematic and summarises Cavanaugh's above comment as 'a genre film like *Godzilla* has little significance as a representation of Hiroshima, while a film festival-endorsed art film by a "name" director [. . .] attracts much critical attention' (2004: 160). Lowenstein's comment highlights the concern that the perceived frivolous nature of popular cinema (such as horror and exploitation films) would undermine any attempt at 'reality'. By occluding engagement with popular cinematic forms, we ignore a wealth of insight into how trauma is represented by these cultural products, and in response to this critical tendency to ignore allegorical representations, Claire Sisco King has argued that

> Allegory itself might be understood as a post-traumatic form. Characterised by both a repetition (a return to a prior tale) and displacement (a refusal to confront that past openly), allegory performs symptoms characteristic of trauma at the same time that it attempts to enact a sense of mastery. (2011: 128–9)

This is not to suggest, however, that popular cinema is completely absent from trauma studies, and indeed Siegfried Kracauer approached popular cinema thorough a fusion of trauma theory and cultural studies in *From Caligari to Hitler: A Psychological History of the German Film* (2004 [1947]), in which he positions *The Cabinet of Dr. Caligari* (1920), among other early German cinematic works, as allegorical representations of the political and social landscape of Germany following World War I. The theories and connections proposed within Kracauer's influential study were subsequently built upon in *Shell Shock Cinema: Weimar Culture and the Wounds of War* (Kaes, 2011). In this study, Anton Kaes relates films such as *Metropolis* (1927) and *Nosferatu* (1922) to the cultural wounds left behind by the World War I, and proposes that 'despite their manifest differences, all of these films found a way to restage the shock of war and defeat without ever showing military combat. They were post-traumatic films, re-enacting the trauma in their very narratives and images' (2011: 3). More broadly, Elizabeth Bronfen's *Specters of War: Hollywood's Engagement with Military Conflict* (2012) and W. Scott Poole's *Wasteland: The Great War and the Origins of Modern Horror* (2018) have also examined the effect of war on popular cinema from a variety of national contexts. Overarchingly, the theory advanced in the work of Kracauer, Kaes, Bronfen and Poole is that 'the films of a nation reflect its mentality in a more direct way than any other artistic media' (Kracauer, 1947: 5) and as such, these scholarly works stand in opposition to the occlusion of popular cinema characteristic of broader trauma theory.

Adam Lowenstein has previously acknowledged the resistance within trauma studies to engaging with horror cinema and suggests that this may be because of an understandable desire for victims and survivors of trauma to be treated with the utmost respect, and that the traumatic event itself be presented with sensitivity (2005: 4–5). Lowenstein has however recognised the potentially problematic nature of this desire, and argues that 'too often a well intended respect for trauma enables a reductive legislation of representation itself' (2004: 147). The reticence shown towards recognising horror cinema as a traumatic genre is, I propose, due to the fear that horror, often cast in 'the role of provocateur: the genre that will go where no genre has gone before, however taboo' (Frost, 2011: 16), would not tread lightly around representations of trauma and would consequentially risk offending or upsetting viewers. This is in addition to the perception that as an 'exploitation' genre, horror cinema would exploit real trauma for commercial gain. I concur with Lowenstein that although this fear is humane, it can reach an extreme in which trauma and traumatic experience is silenced or marginalised, which I will discuss in more depth in Chapter 3. This book, therefore, aligns with Lowenstein's argument that horror cinema is particularly well suited to the representation of trauma, as it functions in a register of brutality. As such, rather than those cultural products that may attempt to smooth over trauma, horror cinema is by comparison 'very much engaged with, rather than estranged from, traumatic history' (Lowenstein, 2005: 10).

By its broadest definition, my perspective in this book falls also into the wider field of cultural studies, which trauma studies can be seen to function as an arm of. As Linnie Blake summarises in explaining her own use of a trauma theory-influenced cultural studies approach in *Wounds of Nations: Horror Cinema, Historical Trauma, and National Identity*, her – and my – focus is on 'how specific cultural products may be read as manifestations, articulations or repudiations of differentially defined models of national identity or idiolects of historical trauma' (2008: 9). Cultural studies readings have been used specifically in relation to horror cinema multiple times (such as Grixti, 1989; Tudor, 1989; Skal, 1994; Kellner, 1995; Worland, 2006; Lukas and Marmysz, 2010; Bishop, 2010; Zimmer, 2011; Wetmore, 2012; Ndalianis, 2015; Abbott, 2016; Poole, 2018; and Mann, 2020). And, as Victoria McCollum notes, in some quarters there is the distinct feeling that the political, social and cultural resonance of horror cinema has been 'unpacked to death by academics, cinephiles, and critics eager to analyse their latent, and sometimes blatant, implications' (2019: 6). The popularity of these kinds of readings – which are often allegorical in nature – has been the subject of criticism. The idea of a nation's cinema being representative of its sociohistorical context has been critiqued at length by Mark Bernard, who argues that rather than carrying out a 'mere reading of the textual details' of a film (2014: 31), instead film scholars should aim to encompass a filmic product's industrial context and its status as a commercial commodity. Moreover, Bernard asserts that 'overdependence on textual filmic analysis at the expense of film industry analysis is a quandary that affects all of film studies' (2014: 31) and horror studies in particular. Overarchingly, Bernard claims that it is only after a scholar has first considered the 'commodity status' of a film that they may assess its cultural relevance (2014: 31). I would, however, contest Bernard's claims and follow Yannis Tzioumakis in his suggestion that both cultural influences and economic factors play equally significant roles in the themes and narratives of a nation's cinematic output (2006: 169), and propose that horror is far too complex to enable us to rely on a strictly industry-focused, or indeed a strictly textual, reading. Of course, I do not deny that the films analysed in this book are made within a commercial context and so to an extent one of the driving forces behind their production is undoubtedly financial gain, but I refute the idea that the conversation around film production – particularly the production of horror cinema – should stall at this point.

Bernard's argument is also complicated by the existence of films that are both driven by commercial imperative and simultaneously explicitly politically or socially engaged, such as *Get Out* (2017) (see Keetley, 2020) or alternatively the *Purge* franchise (2013–). Stacey Abbott (2021) has positioned *The Purge* series as negotiating its status as commodity with its drive towards political commentary, through it being both overtly political in its themes and narratives, and working within the parameters of an established set of genre conventions within a commercially successful horror film franchise. The films I will examine in the following chapters – in particular those that are the focus of Chapter 7 – stand too as further evidence of this dual financial/sociopolitical drive. Furthermore, I propose that no singular theoretical approach can cover every aspect of a film, and in emphasising one approach, there is a necessary de-emphasis on others. Not only this, but readings of the same film can vary even within the same approach. For example, two dominant cultural readings of *Invasion of the Body Snatchers* (1956) posit that the film can be read as acute conservative paranoia regarding the threat of communism (Newman, 2014), and conversely that the invading force in the film stands in for the conservative majority themselves, with the invasion being an allegory for the pressure to conform (Samuels, 1979). One reading does not negate the other, just as my approach to found footage horror cinema through the lens of trauma and cultural studies does not seek to negate more industry-focused perspectives.

## Structure

Through three distinct sections, *Blood on the Lens: Trauma and Anxiety in American Found Footage Horror Cinema* will address key observations around the subgenre. I will question how these films engage with national trauma and discern what the common themes of this body of films are and how these relate to wider anxieties. I will ask what effect various cultural movements – such as the rise of reality television, the use of bystander footage in mainstream reportage of world events and the popularity of social media – have had on the aesthetics of the subgenre. I will also examine how these films position their spectator and encourage an active viewing mode, and explore how the line between fiction and fact is blurred both paratextually and within the films themselves. Each part of this book will begin with a broader contextual chapter before engaging in close analysis of key case studies.

Part 1 will address the relationship between found footage horror cinema and documentary conventions and engage with three films: *The Sacrament*, *The Poughkeepsie Tapes* and *Grave Encounters* (2011). Each of these films adheres to a distinct type of 'look' related to the documentary tradition: video journalism, true crime documentaries and ghost hunting reality television. Chapter 2 will explore why the found footage horror subgenre has continually returned to documentary conventions throughout its history and will argue that this is in order to take advantage of a type of visuality that audiences intrinsically trust to provide a version of the truth. Chapter 2 will also begin to unravel how the limitations of the camera in found footage horror cinema and the resultant 'artless' look can be read as a form of authenticity.

Chapters 3 and 4 map out how found footage horror recreates specific documentary looks in exacting, meticulous detail. In Chapter 3 I will demonstrate how the subgenre negotiates the needs of traumatic representation by offering a close comparative reading of *The Sacrament*'s relationship to the Jonestown Massacre of 1978, which it reimagines in a contemporary setting. With a particular focus on the position of the Jonestown event in American history and the existence of the Jonestown 'Death Tape', this chapter will ask if there are limits to traumatic representation in popular culture and, more specifically, in the horror genre. Chapter 3 will lay out how the use of allegory is complicated and departed from within *The Sacrament* through its movement towards explicit rather than implicit representation of historical trauma, and how this eschewal of allegory impacted on the critical reception to the film. Chapter 4 will then engage with how found footage horror cinema has deftly responded to evolving documentary forms through analysis of *The Poughkeepsie Tapes* and *Grave Encounters*. I will examine how the aesthetics of true crime programming and ghost hunting shows are adopted in these respective films, before tying these case studies to the traumatic landscape of American history.

Part 2 narrows this research's focus to a sustained examination of how a specific national event and its aftermath has impacted on the subgenre. Chapter 5 picks up on some of the criticisms of allegorical readings noted in this introductory chapter before outlining a palpable culture of anxiety and fear in the United States following the terror attacks of 11 September 2001 (9/11). With reference to different stylistic camerawork that has become popular in horror cinema post-9/11, I discuss the specific aesthetics of 'bystander footage' and build on the connections made in Chapter 2 regarding the link that can be made between perceived 'artlessness' and a status as truthful documentation. Fears relevant to the aftermath of 9/11 and the War on Terror then become the main concerns of Chapters 6 and 7, in which I will detail how these anxieties found a home in the found footage horror subgenre. In Chapter 6, I will position *Quarantine* as a particularly significant film within found footage horror cinema. This is not only due to it being the first (and to date only) American found footage horror remake, but because of its close visual ties to the significant historical media artefact that is the documentary film *9/11* (2002). Approaching the film as a text that re-culturalises the Spanish specificity of its original incarnation, *[Rec]* (2007), to an American setting, I argue that *Quarantine* uses images and themes clearly reminiscent of 9/11 and the War on Terror to present a narrative that resonates with the anxieties engendered by those events within America. This chapter will also further examine the concept of 'inadvertent witnessing', where the camera operator captures extraordinary events by accident or chance rather than by design. Chapter 6 closes on a discussion of the roles of editing, censorship and of the camera as a tool both pragmatic and literal in found footage horror. Chapter 7 will then examine three films: *Diary of the Dead*, *The Bay* and *The Conspiracy*. These films present themselves as edited collections of footage and forefront a mistrust of governmental institutions, engage with a fear of becoming collateral damage to governmental objectives and problematise the role of truth in an increasingly mediated world. Whereas Chapter 6 examined how the found footage horror subgenre featured images reminiscent of 9/11 to work through that trauma, Chapter 7 is more concerned with the paranoid and fearful cultural landscape that followed that event. Here I will engage with the role that editorial control plays within these narratives, uncover the tensions that have emerged around North American self-image and actuality and underline the anxieties these films demonstrate in terms of trust and truth in governmental agencies and media institutions, before investigating the lasting resonance of those themes contemporaneously with the rise of 'post-truth'.

The third and final part of this book will explore more recent trends in found footage horror cinema and how it is evolving within a post-cinematic world, with a particular focus on a subset of the subgenre that I term as 'social media horror' and its engagement with anxieties around internet-based communication. As horror is a genre that historically deals with contemporary anxieties – and found footage horror is a subgenre aware of and respondent to technological advances – it is no surprise that horror cinema in the last decade has turned to the way in which we live in an increasingly mediated society. Chapter 8 outlines the tradition of haunted media I propose these films are part of, indicating that social media horror is an example of both a genre and a subgenre in transition. A particular focus of Chapter 8 is the way in which the internet has increasingly become a mediator of death and dying, and I will propose there are three main ways this is taking place: through real death 'shock' websites, through death memorialisation in social media spaces and, most recently, through the ability to livestream murder and death on various platforms. Within this chapter I address the long standing connection between found footage horror and the internet that has been apparent since the unprecedented viral marketing campaign of *The Blair Witch Project* in 1999. This chapter will examine how the subgenre has been assimilating new media and the internet not only in marketing, but within the aesthetics and narratives of the films themselves. Within this chapter I will propose that although different marketing methods have been used as the internet has matured, the central aim remains the same, to infiltrate the audience's reality. Chapter 9 will then delve further into the subset of social media horror, a distinctive and growing part of the wider found footage horror subgenre. Using three case studies: *The Den* (2013), *Unfriended* and *Spree* (2020), I will trace a connection between the representations of death online outlined in Chapter 8 and these films. In respect to *The Den*, I will connect this film to the proliferation of real death footage that can be found with ease on the internet and present the film as underlining concerns around the commerce/commodity of death online. In *Unfriended*, the internet is presented as a haunted and haunting space, which engages with contemporary concerns regarding digital anonymity and cyberbullying. In *Spree*, the found footage horror subgenre turns to anxieties over selfhood and celebrity in the digital world. The final chapter of Part 3, Chapter 10, will address how found footage horror is adapting to a post-cinematic world, and document its movement into various other media, such as podcasts, user generated content websites and video gaming. This chapter will discern and evaluate how the overarching themes of found footage horror over the last twenty years are represented in these new forms of the subgenre and include discussion around new entries that have reached beyond the strictly cinematic. This final chapter will both look back to the subgenre's history and forward to the future of the subgenre in its adoption of recent cultural phenomena, while bringing together the central arguments of the book as set out in the preceding chapters.

Throughout the pages that follow, then, I seek to answer a series of questions this introductory chapter has begun to uncover. How do these films engage with national trauma? Are there common identifiable themes in these films and how do these relate to wider anxieties? What effect have various cultural movements, such as a rise in the use of bystander footage on mainstream news networks and the popularity of social media, had on the aesthetics and concerns of the subgenre? How do these films position their spectator and encourage an active viewing mode? How is the line between fiction and fact blurred both paratextually and within the films themselves? And, crucially, what is it about found footage horror that has allowed it to endure?

## Notes

1 This quote is taken from *Found Footage 3D*, a meta-horror narrative about a film crew who are making the first 3D found footage horror film (the first actual 3D found footage horror film was *Paranormal Activity: The Ghost Dimension* (2015)). After having his creative decisions consistently overruled by the producer, the film's director Andrew has an explosive rant regarding the pointlessness of the found footage horror subgenre.
2 This statement was made by Sam Zimmerman, the curator of horror streaming service Shudder, regarding the film *[Rec]*, during the episode 'Leigh Whannell' of Shudder's own horror-themed talk show, *The Core* (2017–18)
3 I am, of course, neatly skipping over *Book of Shadows: Blair Witch 2* (2000) here. However, as that film eschewed the found footage conceit and the 2016 sequel directly follows the events of the first film, I would advance that the later film is the true spiritual successor to *The Blair Witch Project*.
4 A categorisation I disagree with and ask: what exactly are these films mocking?
5 For example, the film opens on a black screen with white text that reads 'In May of 2004, Derek James and his wife Amy Mitchel disappeared while vacationing at a

remote cabin near Gonzales, Texas. Their bodies were never recovered. Six months later, their footage was found.' Voices begin to discuss the text before there is a cut to a wider scene, where the titles are shown on a computer screen. One character, Derek, asks another, Andrew, what he thinks of the opening titles, to which Andrew responds 'It's good, it's a little cliché don't you think?' Derek, comically missing the point, retorts 'No, that's not cliché, that's how every found footage movie starts.' The titles themselves closely resemble those at the beginning of *The Blair Witch Project*, which read: 'In October of 1994, three student filmmakers disappeared in the woods near Burkitsville, Maryland while shooting a documentary. A year later their footage was found.'

6  This information was correct on foundfootagecritic.com on 14 March 2022.
7  Two of the films closely analysed in this book are also from the same director/writer team, Jon Erick Dowdle and Drew Dowdle. The Dowdle brothers seem to have a certain affinity for the found footage horror subgenre, having helmed *The Poughkeepsie Tapes*, *Quarantine* and *As Above, So Below* (2014).
8  It would be fair to say that all three of our questions owe something to a query posed earlier by Andrew Tudor, who asked 'Why do these people like this horror in this place at this particular time' (Tudor, 1997: 461).

# Part I

# 2
# Found footage horror and documentary conventions

Various films and programmes have been proposed to be the starting point of found footage horror. Alexandra Heller-Nicholas, for instance, locates the subgenre's origin in the Highway Safety Films of the 1950s (2014: 42), whereas Matthew Raimondo – although he notes there are flashes of the subgenre in earlier films – positions *The Blair Witch Project* as the real 'pioneer' of the subgenre (2014: 68). Meanwhile, others have tracked found footage horror's history transmedially, and back to epistolary novels such as *Dracula* (Stoker, 1897) (Sawczuk, 2020). The large majority of horror scholars, however, consider that the genesis of found footage horror can be found in the 1980 film *Cannibal Holocaust* (see Rhodes, 2002; Petley, 2005; Grant, 2013; Benson-Allott, 2013; Hart, 2014).[1] The narrative of *Cannibal Holocaust* follows Professor Harold Monroe's quest to determine what has happened to a documentary crew last seen entering the Amazon rainforest. Monroe finds their remains and camera equipment erected as a grisly totem by the cannibalistic Yanomamo tribe and returns to New York to review cans of film found at the tribe's camp, which studio executives are eager to include in a planned memorial documentary.

The central plot of *Cannibal Holocaust* – a documentary project during which the documentarians die and their footage lives on – has since become a central narrative premise of a great deal of found footage horror cinema. Gary D. Rhodes, for instance, has noted of the subgenre's output, that 'these narratives must overcome the fallacy (as well as the repetition) inherent in simply having onscreen filmmakers shoot stories that become their own funerals' (2002: 59). Similarly, Caitlin Benson-Allott – while presenting an alternative term for found footage horror – states that 'One of the few conventions all faux footage horror movies follow is that everyone dies, including and especially the diegetic cinematographer' (2013:

168). Although not true of all found footage horror films, this convention of the failed documentary project – which I will discuss further below – is one that the subgenre has repeatedly returned to. However, it is not only this aspect of *Cannibal Holocaust* that has endured in found footage horror, but also a specific kind of aesthetic and form.

Much of *Cannibal Holocaust* is devoted to the 'found footage' shot by documentarian Alan Yates and his crew before and during their excursion into the rainforest. The footage looks raw and authentic – a feeling assisted by its imperfect appearance. Neil Jackson summarises the footage as comprising

> Location shooting, genuine native extras, handheld cameras, imperfect or improvised compositions, camera settings, negative or print quality, lens phenomena, interview footage, use of telephoto and zoom lenses, direct camera address by the cast, print scratches, laboratory markings and sound irregularities. (2002: 36)

These features, which suggest the footage we are watching is unpolished and unedited material, have then reappeared throughout the found footage horror subgenre's history as markers of authenticity. *Cannibal Holocaust*, then, regardless of whether it is the true origin point of the subgenre or not, will always remain a significant film in the history of found footage horror, with its replication of what audiences recognised as documentary aesthetics, leading some viewers to become confused over its fictional status. The result of this was allegations of murder being levelled at director Ruggero Deodato (as stated in both *In the Jungle: The Making of Cannibal Holocaust* (2003) and *The Long Road Back from Hell: Reclaiming Cannibal Holocaust* (2011)).

Just as we can situate a narrative that mixed the authentic and the fake as the beginning of found footage horror, a film often cited to be the origin point of the documentary genre similarly troubled this line between reality and fiction. Within *Nanook of the North* (1922), the audience is presented with a contradiction between what the film purports to capture and what it actually portrays. Patricia Aufderheide explains in reference to *Nanook of the North* that 'Its subjects, the Inuit, assumed roles at filmmaker Robert Flaherty's direction, much like actors in a fiction film. Flaherty asked them to do things they no longer did [. . .] and he showed them as ignorant' (2007: 2). The presentation of reality that documentary filmmaking is thought to be a champion of is, therefore, founded on a form of fakery, meaning that documentary and found footage horror may have more in common than might be initially assumed. Just as documentary filmmaking has historically muddied the line between reality and fiction, its conventions and aesthetics are used by found footage horror cinema to further blur that line, trading on documentary's perceived connection to authenticity to reinforce its own claims to verisimilitude.

The following two chapters in this part of the book will detail the exacting ways in which found footage horror has adapted to and adopted more modern forms of documentary, often on a micro stylistic level. This chapter presents the necessary background for that analysis, by tracing the varied ways in which found footage horror has returned to the documentary format and kept pace with that format's evolution over the last few decades. This chapter will argue that found footage horror hinges on the historic indexical relationship that the camera lens has enjoyed with 'the real', which is traceable back to the earliest use of photography in the sciences. This historical relationship – and the positioning of the camera as a tool for veracity – is key to both documentary and found footage horror's truth claims. I will also highlight here a key proposal of this book more broadly, that found footage horror cinema endeavours to position its narratives as within the audience's reality – as opposed to being what I term as 'reality adjacent' – and how one of the ways in which this is achieved is through the physicality of the camera in these films. The camera in found footage horror is often positioned as a technological witness and framed as being more reliable than its human – and therefore fallible – operator, but also conversely – and contradictorily – as distinctly unreliable too, due to the limitations of its frame. Within the second half of this chapter therefore, I will address how the limitations of the camera in the found footage horror subgenre, and the imperfections of its footage – an often criticised aspect of the subgenre's presentation of horror – can be read as a form of authenticity that has a precedent in the audience's reality.

## 'You must admit, it's exceptional footage!': documentary modes and styles within found footage horror

A framing device and aesthetic we might recognise as 'documentary style' has been used in found footage horror cinema since its inception to explore an incredibly varied array of narratives. Examples of this include films focused on serial killers (*The Last Broadcast*; *Murder in The Heartland: The Search for Video X* (2003); *The Last Horror Movie* (2003); *Murder Box* (2018)), demonic possession or extrasensory perception (*The Last Exorcism* (2010); *The Atticus Institute* (2015)), hauntings (*Muirhouse*

(2012); *Hell House LLC* (2015); *Out of the Shadows* (2017)), myths, legends and conspiracy theories (*Lunapolis* (2010); *Butterfly Kisses* (2018)), the existence of extraterrestrials (*Apollo 18* (2011); *The Phoenix Incident* (2015)), cryptid sightings (*Bigfoot: The Lost Coast Tapes* (2012); *Willow Creek*) and outbreak narratives (*The Bay*), along with stories featuring vampires, werewolves (*Afflicted* (2013); *The Monster Project* (2017)) and other monsters (*Savageland*). Even this brief list of titles demonstrates through their release dates – from 1998 to 2018 – that found footage horror's return to documentary form is long standing and continuous.

It is difficult to discuss documentary discourse and not engage with the documentary modes conceptualised by Bill Nichols (1991), and most of these have appeared within the found footage horror subgenre at some point. The expository mode, for example, which Nichols ventures is the mode that 'most people associate with documentary in general' (2017: 22), can be seen as a clear influence on the presentation of *The Poughkeepsie Tapes* and also that of *The Bay*, which both feature voiceovers and evidentiary editing (Nichols, 2017: 22). The participatory mode, which focuses on the relationship between the filmmaker and their subject, can be discerned in *The Taking of Deborah Logan* (2014) and the case study of the next chapter, *The Sacrament*, both of which feature more involvement on behalf of the filmmakers, 'such as conversations or provocations' (Nichols, 2017: 22). The reflexive mode, which 'increases our awareness of the constructedness of the film's representation of reality' (Nichols, 2017: 22), can then be seen in *The Last Exorcism* and *Digging Up the Marrow* (2014), which feature scenes where the construction of the documentary project is discussed. The performative mode, which is often used for deeply personal projects and positioned as a rough diametric opposite of the more objective observational mode, can then be detected in such films as *Afflicted* and to a lesser extent in *As Above, So Below* (2014). These films emphasise 'the subjective or expressive aspect of the filmmaker's own involvement with a subject [rejecting] notions of objectivity in favor of evocation and affect' (Nichols, 2017: 22). I have, in the above overview of Nichols's documentary modes, neglected to mention both the observational and poetic modes. Previously, Matthew Raimondo has selected the term 'observational horror' as opposed to 'found footage horror' for the films he examines, stating that they 'appropriate the aesthetics of observational documentary cinema's handheld camerawork' (2014: 66). In one respect, Raimondo is correct, as handheld camerawork is common to the subgenre, but this approximation between the observational mode and found footage horror is problematised when we review Nichols's definition of that mode. Although, as Nichols states, the observational mode is limited by 'What occurs in front of the camera' (2017: 108) and these limitations form a key element of found footage horror – as explored below – he also states that the observational mode is defined by its presentation of 'subjects as observed by an unobtrusive camera' and furthermore that 'The filmmaker does not interact with subjects but only observes them' (2017: 22). In contrast, a central aspect of many found footage horror narratives is the growing inability of the filmmaker character to simply observe, often with their crisis of objectivity becoming a main narrative drive of the film.[2] The cameras of found footage horror too are anything but 'unobtrusive', often impacting on and being impacted by their surroundings. Although there is one film, *Invasion*, which stayed within the observational mode for the majority of its narrative, this mode of presentation is definitely unusual within the subgenre. Therefore, it is perhaps more accurate to view found footage horror films as occasionally beginning in the observational mode, before quickly switching to another more emotionally affective mode, or alternatively using the observational mode for sections of the film but not the whole narrative. For example, within the *Paranormal Activity* franchise, in which much of the footage is from operatorless cameras, the observational style is always interspersed with more kinetic handheld camera movement. Finally, to my knowledge, the poetic mode, characterised by a forsaking of traditional narrative content, has not yet been utilised within a feature length found footage horror film. This may be because, as Nichols states, the poetic mode 'seldom advances an argument or tells a story primarily' (2017: 56), having more 'common terrain with the modernist avant garde' (2017: 116). As such, the poetic mode would not be a satisfactory fit within a fictional film genre – the foremost intention of which is to tell a story – much less the horror genre, which is built around affective audience response. The purpose of this overview of Nichols's modes is not to suggest that the found footage horror films mentioned stay consistently within the mode I have placed them in throughout their run time. Just as Nichols cautions when applying these modes to documentary filmmaking, I concur that they are imperfect categories which 'give structure to a film, but they do not dictate or determine every aspect of its organization' (2001: 114). However, this overview serves to give the reader an impression of how found footage horror cinema has previously used, and continues to use, varied documentary modes in its presentation.

Like the found footage horror subgenre, documentary filmmaking has evolved in various directions during its history, leading documentary scholar John Corner to caution that 'the term "documentary" is always much safer when used as an adjective rather than as a noun' (2000: 47). As Richard Wallace argues, over the past few decades, 'the documentary form has been subjected to a series of epistemological and existential challenges that it has yet to adequately navigate' and the wider 'post-truth cultural turn' has somewhat destabilised documentary's claims to veracity (2021: 519). For example, television is now 'by far' the primary domain of documentary (Dovey, 2000) and the emergence of reality television – with tensions around its reality claims due to its utilisation of 'fictional techniques applied to factual formats' (Dovey, 2000: 78) – has been a source of debate for scholars and critics alike. Although some have noted that reality television has its 'roots in the documentary tradition' (Van Bauwel, 2010: 24) or have situated reality television as a revised form of documentary (Corner, 2000) and part of the 'postdocumentary' media landscape (Corner, 2002), others have discussed the troubling way that reality television blurs the line between traditional factual programming and entertainment (Nichols, 1994; Bondebjerg, 1996). John Corner is one theorist who suggests that the radical changes documentary has undergone were 'in order to reconfigure itself within new economic and cultural contexts' (2002: 263), while Brian Winston has ventured that the popularity of reality television can be seen as the 'price of survival' paid by documentary to stay relevant in our modern, hypermediated age (2000: 55). Although this chapter has thus far primarily cited found footage horror films that use the framework of what could be called a 'traditional' documentary, both Chapter 3 and Chapter 4 will examine the ways in which found footage horror has adapted to emerging reality aesthetics that have grown out of documentary realism: the video journalism of *The Sacrament*, the true crime programme aesthetic of *The Poughkeepsie Tapes* and the ghost hunting reality television of *Grave Encounters*. As such, Part 1 of this book will indeed cover traditional documentary's influence on found footage horror, but will also encompass what I will call 'televisual actualities' and other popular offshoots of documentary as key presentations of reality that have impacted the subgenre too. No matter the style of documentary these films ape, however, a constant throughout the entries within this part of the book and those from the broader found footage horror subgenre is their reliance on the idea that a camera can capture the truth.

## 'The camera can see, and what the camera sees the audience sees': documentary truth and the camera as a tool of veracity

Patricia Aufderheide has argued that as an audience, 'we expect that a documentary will be a fair and honest representation of somebody's experience of reality' (2007: 25). This assumed relationship that documentary enjoys with the representation of reality is central to found footage horror cinema's appeal, and essential to understanding the ways in which the subgenre presents itself to audiences as 'real'. The widely accepted connection between documentary filmmaking and 'the real' could be due to the perceived indexical relationship that the camera lens has historically retained with reality or realism. Filmmaker Maya Deren explained that 'since a specific reality is the prior condition of the existence of a photograph, the photograph not only testifies to the existence of that reality [. . .] but is, to all intents and purposes, its equivalent' (1960: 154). This of course connects with Roland Barthes's later definition of the photographic referent, which is 'not the *optionally* real thing to which an image or sign refers but the *necessarily* real thing which has been placed before the lens without which there would be no photograph' (Barthes, 1981 [1980]: 76, emphasis in original). This relationship has been complicated by the introduction of digital filmmaking, and how this type of filmmaking breaks the bond between the object being photographed and the photograph itself, with a different effect being created through the filmmaking process (Binkley, 1988: 10–11). This changing relationship of photography to the real has been discussed by several scholars (such as Wolf, 2000; Niessen, 2011). Arild Fetveit has noted that the paradox between the real and the digitally manipulated is resolved somewhat by the discursive context that photographic images are presented within. To this end, Fetveit explains that the rise of digital manipulation in photography happened simultaneously with the rise of reality television, a form heavily reliant on the truth claims of photographical evidence. Fetveit then argues that there has been 'an increased *compartmentalization of credibility*', which is reliant on the viewer accounting for the 'varying practices and conventions' of the context in which photographic content is presented (1999: 797, emphasis in original). For example, a viewer accepts and even expects a degree of digital manipulation in a field such as advertising or a big budget superhero film, but would not expect it in a televisual news broadcast. Although a large number of found footage horror films are no doubt created through the use of digital cameras and technology, and their effects often produced digitally, the subgenre tends towards an emulation of forms such as documentary, reality television and other factual discourses and as such, essentially borrows their credibility in this respect.

As Carolina Gabriela Jauregui explains, humankind 'has forever been obsessed with the need to understand the world through the eyes, with the need for visual evidence' (2004). The relationship between the real/realism and the camera can be traced back to the symbiotic relationship that developed between early photography and science in the 1800s, 'where scientific naturalism and photographic naturalism became conflated in the presentation of observable fact' (Tucker, 2005: 7). Early applications of photography were overarchingly for scientific purposes, such as the first book to be illustrated with photographs, *Photographs of British Algae: Cyanotype Impressions* (Atkins, 1843), and this was a time that, as Kelly E. Wilder notes, 'Science acted upon photography, only to be in turn acted upon by photography, until the idea of photography and the idea of science were so intertwined as to be inseparable' (2009: 164). Indeed, as Jennifer Tucker argues in her study of photography's relationship to Victorian-era science, 'ever since its invention in the 1830s, many have seen photography as a medium of truth and unassailable accuracy' (2005: 1). This positioning of the camera lens as an instrument of veracity is discernable too in reports of the use of photography in the sciences from the time period itself. Professor Percival Lowell, for instance, was clearly excited at the possibilities that photography could afford astronomers, 'to make the canals of Mars write their own record on a photographic plate, so that astronomers might have at first objective proof of their reality' (Lowell, 1906: 132).

This connection, between scientific fact and photography, was later exploited by creators of spirit photography, the intention of which was to present 'evidence' of the supernatural, an objective that is also often featured in found footage horror films. In terms of the reception of this use of photography, Jennifer Tucker cautions against a tendency for modern scholars to view photography as something that was wholeheartedly accepted as irrefutable proof in scientific circles in the 1800s, noting that 'Although nineteenth-century faith in photography was powerful, the idea that people over a hundred years ago accepted photographs at face value is exaggerated and misleading' (2005: 4). Despite this – and in spite of the increasing use of digital technology in the production of images, as explored above – the perception that the photographic image is a reliable method to capture the truth has remained strong in wider culture. The culmination of this belief can be seen in the admission of video evidence in courtrooms and an implicit trust being placed in the ability of the camera lens to capture events as they actually happened.³ John Durham Peters has stated that in this way, the camera has followed in the tradition of the microscope, in that 'its indifference to human interests' underlines its credibility (2001: 715), with the camera coming to be thought of as an objective tool. The camera's status is underlined by this long held belief in 'the objectivity or neutrality of the lens in capturing actuality' (Flynn, 2005: 136). It is this positioning of the camera as an impartial object and as 'a tool of facticity that collects data considered legitimate' (Moss, 2004: 205) that is highlighted in much found footage horror, where characters rely on the camera to provide them with the evidential proof they need to support their own eyewitness testimony. However, the camera cannot capture all things all the time, and much of found footage horror's construction of fear is based around what the camera did not, or cannot, see.

## 'Tape everything, you hear me? Tape everything!': the limitations of the camera, absence as authenticity and the failed documentary project

A recurrent complaint that is levelled against found footage horror cinema is its supposed lazy artlessness (see Tharpe, 2012; Fowle, 2014; Lodge, 2016; Murray, 2017 among many others), with a great many reviews of the films within the subgenre being littered with references to 'handheld horror induced headaches' (Lee, 2016), accusations of a 'specific, alienating style' (Colburn, 2015) or a noting that the format has become a 'grabby artless gimmick' (Gleiberman, 2016) or a 'one-trick pony' (Kubai, 2016). However, this presumed artlessness of the subgenre, where horrors are often only glimpsed or not seen at all, is not only an essential element of these films' recognisability as part of a specific subgeneric style, but is also central to their affective scares.

Found footage horror is a subgenre that strives to maintain the conceit that the camera exists within the diegesis. In order to do this, the camera must appear to act as such, and it is logical that a dizzying whip pan will accompany the camera operator turning suddenly to capture the unexpected on film, that other bodies in the frame will sometimes obscure the camera's view or that if the operator falls then the camera will fall too. Even in found footage horror films where cameras remain mostly static, such as *Paranormal Activity 2* (2010) – which is primarily made up of footage from security cameras – effort is made to present these cameras as existing diegetically. Found footage horror is a style that, as Douglas Kellner advances

> Lacks the polish of cinematic realism but signifies the authenticity of the events depicted. The muted colours, grainy and unedited imagery, and poor lighting imply the immediacy of actual events in which the filmmakers did not have the opportunity to construct and plan their scene adequately or to make the expected alterations in the footage that would constitute an imposition of artistic order. (2004: 57)

Rather than being artless due to budgetary constraints or unimaginative vision, creators of found footage horror films put effort into the appearance of artlessness, and it is the construction of this artlessness that is partially key to their films' appeal. Even in terms of found footage horror films where severe budgetary constraints or a lack of creative imagination is a concern – and perhaps the format is chosen purely because it provides a good return on investment – a consideration of how to adhere to found footage horror's specific and distinctive style is necessary. Effort must be expended in order for the film to meet audience expectations of the subgenre effectively, and this is significant. The creators of these films have actively chosen a presentation style that is unpolished and sometimes appears crudely assembled in order to convey their narratives. In found footage horror and, as I will shortly move on to examine, in documentary filmmaking, the amateur – or artless – is often read as a form of authenticity. It is vital to note that I am using the term 'amateur' both here and throughout this book to refer to a look or style that appears to be unplanned and steeped in immediacy, rather than using it as a pejorative term for footage that is unskilled, clumsy or inept. In choosing this aesthetic, found footage horror creators are tapping into a longstanding tradition within documentary filmmaking that uses what could be termed as a 'spontaneous' style to portray a sense of immediacy and an authenticity of action. I suggest that this could be traced back to the French cinéma vérité – which I position as a strong influence on found footage horror – a movement that focused on truthful representation of reality and a desire to bring the audience into the moment that the filmmaker is trying to capture. Although sometimes conflated, cinéma vérité stands in stark contrast to the contemporaneous development of American direct cinema, with the former encouraging provocation of its documentary subjects and the latter instead focusing on the purely observational style. I am certainly not the first to note this convergence of cinéma vérité style and found footage horror cinema, as shown by Barry Keith Grant's merging of the two terms in his own conceptualisation of 'vérité horror' (2013). Like Grant, I argue that found footage horror cinema consciously mobilises the conventions of cinéma vérité through its focus on filmmaker provocation or the filmmaker as participant. A further aspect that ties cinéma vérité and found footage horror together is the inclusion of the bodily movements of the camera operator, which function within the frame as a form of cinematic embodiment wrought through the often unsteady and markedly human movements of the camera. My use of the word 'amateur' therefore alludes to these distinct aesthetics, historical referents and narrative premises, rather than from a place of contempt or disparagement in regards to quality.

Amy West, in her examination of the connection between the amateur and the authentic, has suggested that

> the co-incidence of unpredictable content and unprocessed medium adds up to a powerful and pervasive sense of the real [. . .] Compromises in audio and visual pleasure which this mode of production may entail are traded off against a heightened feeling of the real – a trade that audiences are more than willing to make. (2005: 86)

In documentary filmmaking, this sense of the amateur can be present in even the most flawless productions. For example, the inclusion of footage in which a cameraperson – trying to capture a fleeting moment – does not have ample time to adjust their framing composition, change to a more appropriate lens or fix any lighting or sound issues. As Gary D. Rhodes proposes,

> Much modern documentary film output is of a technically imperfect quality, including a great deal of what appears on PBS and A&E Biography, as well as the work of respected documentarians such as Errol Morris. The common assumption remains that lighting, camera, sound, even editing will be different, rougher in various ways, than that of classical Hollywood style. Technical imperfections are understood to be part of the form, and part of what reality looks like on film. (2002: 57)

Although not present in all documentary films, amateur footage is common enough for audiences to recognise it as an element one could reasonably expect to find in a documentary product. As Peter Lee-Wright has stated, 'Documentary has provided the visual grammar that is read as authenticity' (2010: 115) and if we are to understand documentary filmmaking as retaining a close relationship to reality, then it follows that the aesthetics of documentary filmmaking are understood as close to the 'real'. It is perhaps because of this presence of the amateur look in documentary film, and its recent and growing presence in news broadcasts and on social media, that we have come to recognise imperfection as a signifier of reality. As Jane Roscoe notes,

> Such notions of documentary as pure and unmediated hold much cultural sway, and they are reinforced [...] through the action's spontaneity and the visual styles being constructed through the use of the video camera [...] the style looks rather amateurish, which for us viewers tends to signify authenticity and heightens the feeling that we are seeing the world as it really is. (2000: 4)

The arguments of West, Rhodes and Roscoe go some way towards explaining why audiences tend to read the amateur as authentic, and in turn this explains why found footage horror has repeatedly returned to documentary form in its many guises: to appear not as similar to, but as part of the audience's reality.

In found footage horror, danger will often lurk in the offscreen space, with the limits of the camera's frame creating an unknowable area beyond the scope of its lens, increasing the affective 'jolt' of the scare when it occurs and underlining the vulnerability of the camera operator. My use of the term 'jolt' here is informed by the work of Linda Williams, who in examining what she terms as 'body genres' – pornography, horror and melodrama – proposes that the success of these films is predicated upon the extent to which the bodily excesses or bodily sensations present in these genres are reflected or replicated by their audience's affective response (1991: 4–6). Williams outlines that a defining feature of body genres is 'the spectacle of a body caught in the grip of intense sensation or emotion', which have 'a quality of uncontrollable convulsion or spasm' (1991: 4). Williams continues that the horror genre's broad aim is to elicit a bodily response of fear in the audience, whether this be a shudder of revulsion or a scream of fright (1991: 5). It could be argued that what I am describing as a 'jolt' is similar to the term 'jump scare', which has been used to describe the sudden intrusion of a loud noise or shocking vision in horror cinema. However, this term is used in an overarchingly negative way, and has been described as a 'cheap' or 'overused' convention of the genre (Palmer, 2018), in addition to being cast as 'a cliché in its own right' (Bishop, 2012). Although it cannot be completely divorced from the convention of jump scares, the jolt that I refer to is less of a sudden shock apropos of nothing, but more a carefully constructed tension based around the limitations of the camera's framing and found footage horror's restricted vision and exploitation of the threat of the offscreen space specifically.

This is aptly demonstrated in *Paranormal Activity 3* (2012), where no less than eleven passes are made of a large, open plan living area. Within the narrative, a camera has been attached to the base of an oscillating fan to enable it to capture the whole room, and it moves side to side continuously from the kitchen area to the lounge and back again. On the majority of the passes of the area, nothing happens – jolts are only delivered on the third (a playful 'Boo!' from a character who suddenly appears in frame) and the ninth (the appearance of a figure covered in a sheet behind that character) passes. This technique was also used to great effect in the Spanish found footage horror film *Apartment 143* (2011), where on the third pass an operatorless camera makes of a room, a ghost appears in the centre of the frame accompanied by a sharp dissonant noise. Of course, a ghost suddenly appearing in the context of a horror film is not unusual: however, as with *Paranormal Activity 3*, it is the previous passes of the room, their inactivity and the camera's limited field of vision that is significant here. In *Apartment 143*, as the camera begins its first pan, the audience's view is restricted to when the intermittent stroboscopic light of the camera illuminates the room, and this limited vision builds tension around the possibility of something suddenly appearing to startle the viewer. On the second scan of the room, the audience is now aware of the room's layout, so this does not cause tension. However, because nothing happened on the first scan of the room, there is a simultaneous capitalisation on the distinct possibility that the jolt is drawing near, and a lulling of the viewer into a form of uneasy complacency. This is paired with the reality aesthetic of the found footage lens to underline the jolt effect. Whereas the affective response of a typical jump scare is achieved through a loud noise or a sudden shocking image, found footage horror uses building anticipation to encourage the audience to engage in a more active way, leaning towards the screen, scanning for activity, or watching it with more intensity for a clue as to where the scare may come from. This mode of viewing increases the affective intensity of the jolt when it then finally appears. Moreover, the camera's relatively slow scanning of the rooms in both *Paranormal Activity 3* and *Apartment 143* exacerbate the limitations of the audience's vision. Within found footage horror, tensions around the edges of the frame and the unknowable area beyond it are often exploited, with scares breaking into the frame suddenly and with little warning. The limitations of the frame are often used against the characters in these films too. For instance, In *Diary of the Dead*, Jason's fixation on capturing footage is instrumental in the fate of his friend Gordo. As the characters leave the hospital in which they are taking refuge, a zombie appears from the off-screen space, and Jason's vision – being impaired by the camera that he continues to hold – means that he is unable to warn Gordo of impending danger. This sequence highlights the paradox of the camera in found footage horror – in that it has an ability to capture evidence and images, but is also restricted in this capacity by the limitations of its frame and by the focus of its operator.

In addition to seemingly inactive shots and withholding of information on the screen to increase the jolt, it is often the faults or perceived imperfections of found footage horror films, discussed above and throughout this book, that make their claims to realism and authenticity stronger. Found footage horror films will often make use of elements such as dead time, include discussion of the filmmaking process by the characters, or incorporate footage that we would assume would have been edited out in a finished filmic product. All of these add to their 'artlessness' but also a sense of truthfulness. Rather than using these elements to alienate the audience or create distance between them and the action unfolding, as can be the intention of dead time in modernist cinema (Tziallas, 2014: 20), found footage horror uses these scenes to underline the authentic nature of what is occurring. This can be seen for instance in *The Lost Footage of Leah Sullivan* (2018), scenes of which show several failed attempts at a 'to camera' introductory sequence – where Leah trips over her words and starts mocking herself – which have been 'left in' the 'finished' documentary and lend the film a more unedited, authentic feel. Moments where characters discuss the construction of their documentary projects are particularly interesting too, as they effectively highlight the constructed nature of documentary's version of truth, as do conversations where events faked for characters' documentary projects are considered. An example of this can be found in *The Last Exorcism*, where an exorcism scene is intercut with explanations of how effects such as demonic noises and a smoking crucifix were achieved. The inclusion of these kinds of discussions can be seen as producing 'a heightened sense of the actual process of recording what was said and done' (Nichols, 1991: 185) and in found footage horror this is yet another alignment to an impression of the 'real', through an engagement with 'the truer reality behind the process' (Higley and Weinstock, 2004: 21) of creating a documentary product.

A central theme that carries through a great deal of found footage horror films is the ultimate failure of documentary projects. In these narratives, characters often 'sally forth to create a film and stumble, lost, into a primal place where no help comes' (Aloi, 2005: 199). In some films, brave but woefully unprepared documentarians find what they were searching for and capture visual evidence of it, only to have their own technology then work against them. This occurs in *Grave Encounters*, where wristwatches, cameras and laptops begin to break down due to supernatural influence. Other narratives show characters who find what they were looking for only to have their camera fail to capture evidence at a crucial moment, such as in *The Blair Witch Project*, where the titular witch remains unseen throughout the narrative as the filmmakers are never able to react to events quickly enough to get a clear shot, or are too terrified to actively try to record steady footage. There are also a significant number of films which follow characters searching for one anomaly or seeking to record a certain event, only to become ensnared by the unexpected, such as *The Visit* (2015). Another example of this can be found in *Followers* (2017), where two men looking to create a cautionary documentary about sharing personal information online stalk an unwitting social media-obsessed couple into the wilderness, only to end up being murdered by a completely unrelated cult who happen to carry out rituals in the same forest. The predominance of these tropes run deeper than horror-based schadenfreude however, and there is a perennial sense that the documentarian character is being punished: whether this be for their need to provide evidence, their need to look, or their quest for knowledge. This can be seen clearly in *Blair Witch*. In this film, a group of students and friends, one of whom is the younger brother of Heather from the original film, venture into the Burkittsville woods equipped with a dazzling array of technology, including mobile telephones, two-way radios, a camera drone, GPS tracking and earpiece Bluetooth cameras. Only then do they find that despite all their technological assistance and desire to see with their own eyes what happened to the characters from the original film, the one thing they cannot do is physically look at the witch, as it is explained within the film that if you do not look directly at her, she cannot hurt you.[4] In the closing scene of the film documentarian Lisa, now the only character left alive, uses a camera's viewfinder to see behind her and circumvent the need to look directly at the witch, which her companion James has just been (presumably) killed for doing. In this scene, Lisa is tricked – both by her own reliance on the camera to bear technological witness and by the limitations of the camera resulting in a failure to capture an image of the witch – into turning around. The final shot of the film is the camera's view as it continues to record from its position on the floor.

This image – of the camera continuing to document horror after the death or incapacitation of its operator – is a common visual in found footage horror. The last sequence of *Cannibal Holocaust*, for example, with Alan's fallen camera capturing his bloodstained face before the footage mercifully cuts out, is a clear spiritual ancestor to the final scene of *The Blair Witch Project*, when Heather's camera clatters to the cellar floor. Heather's hysteric screaming then abruptly stops and the lens continues to document from its sideways position on the ground. In *The Last Exorcism*, the camera falls in the forest as Daniel – its operator – is hit with a scythe and a discarded camera in *Hell House LLC* dispassionately witnesses the death of Sara, another documentarian. More recently still, a fallen camera in *The Empty Wake* (2021) captures a presumably zombified Hailey leaving the funeral home after she is attacked by the corpse she was supervising a wake in honour of.[5] Regardless of how they end, found footage horror films trade on the promise of documentary: that what you are viewing is a close approximation of the truth and that the camera will capture this truth even in the absence of an operator.

## Conclusion

This chapter has begun to outline the central 'look' of found footage horror cinema: an evocation of documentary form that has been present in the subgenre since its earliest entries. This distinctive style has become so pervasive that recent documentary products have begun, in turn, to ape the found footage horror look, bringing the act of emulation that found footage horror began full circle. An example of this is *Cropsey* (2009), which follows two filmmakers as they tie the origin of a localised Staten Island urban legend to a real-life crime. During the documentary, Joshua Zeman and Barbara Brancaccio attend a disused mental health facility at night, and Zeman convinces Brancaccio to go inside with him. The two walk down a corridor, the only illumination being from their torches. There is a sudden loud noise and Brancaccio yelps, before Zeman sheepishly admits the noise was from him accidentally dropping his torch. They debate whether to stay in the building before ghostly disembodied voices are heard coming towards them. Several figures are approaching, but the lack of light does not allow the audience – or the documentarians – to see with any clarity who these figures might be. As the scene concludes, we realise the figures are a group of teenagers who have come to the building in order to hang out and scare each other. However, the construction of this scene, in which Zeman and Brancaccio discuss devil worship and the spookiness of their surroundings, coupled with Brancaccio's clear reluctance to go inside (countered by Zeman teasingly asking 'are you scared?'), along with its documentary aesthetic, could easily be from a multitude of horror films. The limitations of the camera in the dark and the handheld shaky cinematography, however, clearly align the film to the aesthetics of found footage horror cinema.

Found footage horror's consistent and continual return to documentary aesthetics serves to place these narratives within the audience's reality, rather than as adjacent to it, and in doing so these films blur the line between the real and the fictional. The subgenre's use of a kind of visuality we associate with documentary truth encourages us to read these films as having a relationship with the 'real' too. Within documentary-style found footage horror – of which there are varied styles and subjects – we begin to uncover how the subgenre blurs the line between fiction and reality within the films themselves rather than through paratexts such as marketing (which will be examined in Chapter 8). The assumed relationship between the camera lens and evidential proof, which can be traced back to photography's earliest uses, is capitalised upon by these films, which utilise key visual prompts – the amateur as authenticity and the limitations of the camera – to present the audience with a format and aesthetic we intrinsically trust to provide us with a close approximation of reality. Three connected themes that often reoccur in the large majority of found footage horror films are the inability of the camera to capture what is happening, its failure to assist the camera operator in their search for the truth through the limitations of its frame, and the presence of the failed documentary project. The found footage horror camera gives the audience a sense of immediacy, but tempers this with obscured vision. The often nihilistic endings of these films – where more often than not, everyone involved dies – suggests a tension between wanting to see and fearing the consequences of looking.

## Notes

1 Although I would note that documentary and horror have been linked as far back as *Häxan* (1922) and that an important yet often disregarded predecessor to the subgenre exists in *The Legend of Boggy Creek* (1972).
2 Furthermore, the camera in found footage horror cinema is anything but unobtrusive, being used for a variety of purposes in addition to a recording device up to and including a weapon for bludgeoning.
3 *Savageland* is an example of a found footage horror film that directly and explicitly addresses the tension present when debating photographs being irrefutable proof, although this is a theme that runs through many of the subgenre's entries.
4 The explanation given for this theory within *Blair Witch* is the end scene from the original 'found' footage of *The Blair Witch Project*; the characters in *Blair Witch* surmise that the reason Mike is facing the wall in the basement and has not been killed by the witch is because he has figured out that she needs her victims to look directly at her. However, in the first film, Mike's positioning is implied to be in reference to the victims of Rustin Parr, an individual who is part of the Blair Witch legend, who would make his child

victims face the wall while he killed other victims. There is no implication within *The Blair Witch Project* or *Blair Witch* that Mike ultimately survived, and he is framed as still missing along with Josh and Heather.

5   The connection between the camera and its operator is played with in a highly effective way in *The Sacrament*, the case study of the following chapter. Throughout the film we have seen most of the action through the lens of Jake, the crew's primary cameraperson. Towards the end of the film, we watch as members of an armed militia move on Jake's camera from its position behind some fallen branches, and fear for his life as they get closer. The men pick the camera up, and it becomes obvious that Jake has left it there as a distraction while he escapes. As our link between the camera and the character of Jake is so strong, this is a jarring moment.

# 3

# Found footage horror and historical trauma

A *Vice* magazine documentary crew – reporter Sam, cameraman Jake and photographer Patrick – travel to a remote clean living and religious community named Eden Parish. Their intention is to document the reunion of Patrick with his formerly drug-addicted sister, Caroline. Once they arrive, Sam and Jake become apprehensive about what is really going on at the settlement, despite reassurances that it is an idyllic paradise. After Sam interviews the enigmatic leader of Eden Parish – a man everyone there calls Father – he and Jake are approached by several members of the congregation with reports of abuse and manipulation, and asked for their assistance in leaving the Parish. The next morning, as the crew members prepare to travel to their waiting helicopter, chaos breaks out as fractures appear between those wishing to leave Eden Parish and those wanting to stay. A shooting occurs at a nearby airstrip, while Father hurriedly assembles his congregation and urges them to drink a 'potion' that will end their lives. The majority of the parishioners obey Father's wishes and – overcome by the potion's poisonous contents – lay down to die with their families, while members of the community who refuse the drink or try to escape are executed by armed guards. While Patrick does not survive, Sam and Jake, who were separated in the earlier commotion, reunite in time to witness Father's suicide, and then manage to escape in the helicopter. Their camera captures sweeping aerial shots of the Eden Parish compound as it burns to the ground.

If this description of *The Sacrament*'s narrative sounds familiar, it is because it bears more than a vague resemblance to the events of 18 November 1978 in Guyana, which have become known as the Jonestown Massacre. Jonestown was a settlement created by the American religious group Peoples Temple in 1974. While Temple members had been relocating to Guyana and aiding in the construction of the compound since its establishment, there was a mass exodus to the settlement in 1977 after growing media attention was focused on the Church's leader, Reverend Jim Jones. This media interest was initiated by reports of Jones's abuse of his congregation by former members, some of whom founded the Concerned Relatives Group (Gunn, 2017: 369). After mounting pressure from the group, Congressman Leo Ryan agreed to travel to Jonestown with a small entourage in order to investigate accusations of human rights violations within the community. During Ryan's visit, several Peoples Temple members expressed a desire to leave Jonestown and evidence of this was captured on video by the accompanying NBC news team.[1] On the day of Leo Ryan's departure from the settlement, a number of his entourage, as well as Ryan himself, were shot and killed by Temple militia while they waited to board their plane at Port Kaituma airstrip, some six miles from Jonestown. Meanwhile, back at the compound, Jim Jones urged his congregation to gather under the pavilion and drink a mixture of grape Flavor Aid[2] and a lethal cocktail of drugs in order to commit what he termed as 'revolutionary suicide'. A total of 914 people died at Jonestown – including Jones himself – in the largest mass murder-suicide in recorded history.[3]

Throughout this chapter, I will demonstrate the role found footage horror plays in mediating the needs of traumatic representation and will offer a close comparative study of *The Sacrament*'s relationship to the Jonestown Massacre. Although all of the case studies in this book will be connected to trauma and various anxieties in some way, in this chapter I will ask if there are any limits to traumatic representation, particularly within the horror genre. Drawing on Adam Lowenstein's concept of the allegorical moment, I will illustrate how this term is complicated and negotiated within *The Sacrament* through its movement towards explicit rather than implicit representation of historical trauma, and how this eschewal of allegory impacted on the critical reception of the film. I argue that *The Sacrament* provides a fictional visual accompaniment to a marginalised traumatic historical event in American history that is bereft of images, and in asking 'Why Jonestown, why now?', I will explore the resonance of the event in modern America. *The Sacrament* presents the Jonestown Massacre to the audience in a brutal and unflinching way. However, despite the accusations of exploitation that were levelled at the film, I propose that *The Sacrament*'s evocation of immersionist documentary filmmaking, the aesthetics of video journalism and the style of the *Vice* brand in particular – although criticised as a form of 'trauma tourism' – lend the narrative a sense of endangerment and urgency.

## 'Whatever happens, this story needs to be told': are there limits to traumatic representation?

Despite the obvious parallels between the narrative of *The Sacrament* and the timeline of events in Jonestown, the massacre itself is never mentioned in the film's dialogue or exposition. This may be because the film is a contemporary reimagining of the real event – set in the 2010s rather than the 1970s – and as such, the real Jonestown may not exist in *The Sacrament*'s fictional world. This would certainly explain why characters do not discuss Jonestown with each other once the similarities become clear. The omission of Jonestown within *The Sacrament*, however, was a source of contention for the film's detractors, who argued that using the story of a real-life tragedy but failing to name the event was exploitative. Manohla Dargis of *The New York Times*, for example, called the film a 'pointless, abjectly impersonal recreation of mass death' (2014), while Katherine Hill noted on the Jonestown.edu website that *The Sacrament* was 'grotesque and inappropriate' (2014). Meanwhile, journalist Sam Costello joined this chorus by proposing that 'using real-life horror as a basis for fictional horror is offensive' (2014). These selected criticisms of the film are characteristic of much of the critical response to *The Sacrament*.

Costello's comment is an especially strange critique when viewed in conjunction with the fact that real-life horror has been used as a basis for fictional horror in countless films over many decades. Not only in terms of films that claim to be based on a vague, unspecified 'true story', such as *The Last House on the Left* (1972) or *The Strangers*, but also films that have explicitly referenced real-life crimes, such as *The Town That Dreaded Sundown* (1976/2014), which was based on a series of murders in Texarkana in 1946. Other films have tied themselves to real-life alleged paranormal events, for instance *The Amityville Horror* (1979/2005), which is a dramatisation of the experiences of the Lutz family at the site of the DeFeo murders in the mid-1970s. Real-life serial killers have also provided the horror genre with a wealth of material, resulting in horror-tinged serial killer biopics such as *Dahmer* (2002) and *Gacy* (2003) as well as *Ed Gein: The Butcher of Plainfield* (2007), among others.

The claims of exploitation or bad taste that were levelled at *The Sacrament* suggest that it has a specific quality which positions it as improper and offensive even within horror, still widely perceived as the 'most disreputable of Hollywood genres' (Wood, 1985: 2020). It must be asked, therefore, particularly in terms of horror cinema, given its 'bad' reputation,[4] if there are limits to representations of trauma, and if there are, how do we begin to traverse the tensions between 'those who feel that a certain traumatic event *cannot* be represented and those who feel the same event *must* be represented' (Lowenstein, 2005: 1, emphasis in original). Converse to the critical disdain the film received for not mentioning the Jonestown Massacre by name within its diegesis – which Sam Costello goes on to note is a 'mindboggling omission' (2014) – director Ti West was consistently open in discussing his decision to base the narrative of *The Sacrament* on the real-life horror of Jonestown in various interviews (Lambie, 2014; Dickson, 2014, Foutch, 2014). West noted that,

> What the movie is about was always more important to me, and scarier to me [. . .] that was the goal from the beginning, was to make a movie that was about something that was really scary, and that's manipulation of desperate people and using people's beliefs against them, and I think that's totally relevant, whether its relevant to the 60s and 70s or relevant today. (Atwwalloway, 2014)

West's continual direct references to the Jonestown Massacre in interviews about the film are also vital in reviewing *The Sacrament* against the perspective of such trauma theorists as Cathy Caruth, who insist that a trauma must be directly referenced or acknowledged in order for a piece of art to function as a traumatic work (1996). Although at no point in *The Sacrament* is the Jonestown Massacre specifically named as the trauma the film is working through, West has made it clear in interviews that Eden Parish represents the Jonestown settlement, and the mass murder-suicide that serves as the horrific focal point of the film represents the massacre at the compound in 1978 in every way apart from in name. I propose, therefore, that a need for a trauma to be directly referenced within a traumatic work stalls trauma theorist's engagement with wider cinema.

Essentially, if we are to adhere to an immovable necessity for a representation to specifically name its trauma, *The Sacrament* becomes stuck in a no man's land. It sits between direct representation (but lacking an explicit reference or acknowledgement within the text to the trauma it is representing) and an allegorical representation that moves one step beyond the allegorical; clearly being about a historical trauma, but simultaneously being unable to be read as a traumatic work because of a set of limitations that insist on the trauma being explicitly acknowledged. Placing limitations on what can and cannot be read as a traumatic work essentially reduces the conversation between trauma theory and film, and impedes explorations of how trauma is represented in popular cinema. As Linnie Blake suggests, there is a critical need to shift 'the emphasis of trauma critique away from high modernist cultural artefacts and onto the popular cultural forms as they are daily consumed by millions across the globe: either as victims, perpetrators or witnesses to historical trauma' (2008: 4). In delimiting the debate to include only those works that directly or explicitly name their trauma, we discount a great many films.

If we do read *The Sacrament* as a trauma film, however, the fact remains that there is an element within it that caused particular upset, and I suggest that this is quite possibly the scene that renders a mass murder suicide in detail. *The Sacrament* presents this scene in such an unflinching and unambiguous way that it complicates, closely engages with, and goes one step further than what Lowenstein has termed as 'the allegorical moment'. Lowenstein conceptualises the allegorical moment as

> A shocking collision of film, spectator, and history where registers of bodily space and historical time are disrupted, confronted, and intertwined. These registers of space and time are distributed unevenly across the cinematic text, the film's audience, and the historical context. (2005: 2)

Furthermore, Lowenstein argues that horror films evoke historical trauma through 'horrific images, sounds, and narrative [which] combine with visceral spectator effect (terror, disgust, sympathy, sadness) to embody issues that characterise [...] historical trauma' (2005: 2). To demonstrate this concept, Lowenstein uses the example of the climatic scenes of *Deathdream* (1974), where Andy, a soldier, has returned home as a form of zombie or revenant after being killed in the Vietnam War. Andy takes his mother Christine to a self-dug shallow grave, crawling into it and beginning to pull the grave dirt over himself as his mother tries in vain to lift him out of the ground. When the police arrive, Christine begins to help her son bury himself, holding his hand as he dies once more. As Lowenstein explains, 'it may seem puzzling or even disturbing to juxtapose a horror film with the weighty issues of Vietnam trauma, but it is here, in a film like *Deathdream*, that we catch a glimpse of [...] an allegorical moment' (2005: 2). The last scenes of *Deathdream* do not explicitly reference the Vietnam conflict, but the images of a young man dying, and his mother's grief, with her telling the police 'some boys never come home', embody some of the traumatic themes of the war. Additionally, the fact that Andy returns 'changed' from his time in Vietnam, addicted to blood and displaying previously absent violent impulses, alludes to the psychological changes in veterans returning home from that war, which have been well documented (Byrne and Riggs, 1996; Scurfield, 2004: 202). In order to unpack *The Sacrament*'s relationship to Lowenstein's concept – and how it utilises a specific documentary aesthetic to negotiate the trauma of Jonestown – it is necessary to recount the scene in detail. As it is in the details that it becomes clear how precise *The Sacrament*'s reimagining of the Jonestown Massacre is, and how it moves beyond the allegorical moment to an altogether more direct and explicit form of representation.

## 'I don't want to get any more involved': the (post) allegorical moment and the Jonestown Death Tape

The murder-suicide scene in *The Sacrament* consists of four sequences. These are interspersed with footage from Jake's camera as he evades capture by Father's armed guards. The murder-suicide sequences are filmed in an unwavering and steady manner, which is especially apparent when compared to the intercut footage, which is frantic and moving erratically as Jake runs. The scene begins with a series of shots showing a white powder and different liquids being poured into large metal vats; this is followed by footage of Parish members beginning to drink from prepared cups, and screaming infants receiving injections containing the poison. The editing of the sequence then slows to longer cuts showing Eden Parish members suffering convulsions and vomiting, with some screaming and crying. A member of the community is shown struggling on the floor as the drink is forced on them, and we witness parishioners trying to flee before being gunned down. The film then shows scenes of families holding hands in death, rows of bodies collapsed on the ground near the pavilion and dying mothers embracing their deceased children on the grass. All the while, Father continues to sermonise. The scene closes with both Father and Wendy, Eden Parish's nurse, walking among the bodies.

At the heart of the majority of allegorical readings of horror films, and as Lowenstein advanced, there is a focus on a film's images, sounds or themes implying a link to historical trauma. Lowenstein highlights, for instance, the 'spectre' of Vietnam present in *The Last House on the Left*, filmed 'with the same gritty, unadorned newsreel style' (2005: 118) of the 'unprecedentedly shocking television coverage' of Vietnam (2005: 129) and presenting its horror in a similar 'unflinchingly cruel and graphically extreme' (2005: 127) way. However, Vietnam is never explicitly mentioned in *The Last House on the Left* and images of warfare or soldiers are not present. Although Jonestown is similarly not mentioned in *The Sacrament*, and despite the fact that there is no record of exactly what occurred in the Guyana jungle in 1978 during the Jonestown Massacre other than eyewitness testimony, these sequences in *The Sacrament* bridge a gap between popular memory and the event. They assist the audience to 'fill in the pictures that are missing from the story of Jonestown that is in our heads' (Colesky, 2013). Whether an audience member has in-depth knowledge of the very real tragedy at Jonestown or not, the mass murder-suicide sequences make for an uncomfortable viewing experience, and one that is amplified by a documentary aesthetic. By using the immersionist documentary style of *Vice*, the film directly represents the trauma of Jonestown, albeit under the name of Eden Parish. During the massacre sequence in *The Sacrament*, the film does not simply recount the Jonestown event but becomes synchronous with it. Rather than rendering a connection to the real massacre through allegory, *The Sacrament* presents itself as a visual interpretation of what is known as the Jonestown Death Tape – explained in more detail below – and through this process provides a confrontational filmic space for the trauma of Jonestown, a real horror largely bereft of images. In this way, *The Sacrament* eschews allegory, but represents the event through a documentary lens, which – as I outlined in the previous chapter – is implicitly trusted by audiences to provide truthful representation. In doing so, *The Sacrament* works to uncover a form of 'truth' about the events at Jonestown.

Although photographic evidence was captured of the aftermath of the Jonestown Massacre by reporters attending the site in the weeks after the event, and there are a multitude of photographs available that were taken of the Peoples Temple in the years leading up to it, there is no existing photographic record of the massacre as it occurred. Similarly, although there is video footage of the Peoples Temple while still based in America, in addition to footage recorded at the time of the settlement's construction and even of the moments just before the massacre – captured by Congressman Leo Ryan's entourage – the closest we have to video evidence of the event itself is a few seconds of material shot by NBC cameraman Bob Brown, shortly before his death. This footage, recorded on Port Kaituma airstrip, is grainy, unclear and ends abruptly – much like several found footage horror films – an ending that Niels Colesky suggests signifies that 'Bob Brown has just given his life for the last bit of footage' (2013). No video record exists of the preparation of the poisoned metal vats, of Jim Jones's sermon, or of the deaths of 914 people under the pavilion. There is, however, an audio tape that was recovered from the Jonestown site along with hundreds of other tapes, most of which feature religious music or Jim Jones's sermonising.

This tape, officially named Q042 by the FBI, but more commonly known as the Jonestown Death Tape, runs for a little over forty-four minutes. The content of the tape features Jim Jones urging his followers to commit suicide, and several Temple members are heard on the tape expressing their desire to follow Jim Jones into death. One lone dissenting voice, thought to be that of Christine Miller, is heard before being swiftly silenced (Krause, 1978), and the rest of the tape includes further sermonising and children's screams and cries before it lapses into silence.

It is possible to find the audio of the Jonestown Death Tape, which was released by the FBI under the Freedom of Information Act, on multiple internet shock websites. Various versions can be found on YouTube.com, and the full audio and an accompanying transcript are available on the Jonestown.edu website. The tape stands as a form of auditory horror, and in more emotive terms, has been described as 'what a nightmare sounds like' (Munger, 2013). Its horror is presented without visual referent and it is here, in its replication of the Jonestown Death Tape, that *The Sacrament* finds a function as the visual interpretation of the time leading immediately up to and including the Jonestown Massacre. Essentially then, *The Sacrament* is a horror film that does not 'represent the unrepresentable' (Elsaesser, 2001: 195), but rather, represents the never represented in a multi-layered way, with its creation of a fake documentary-style visual accompaniment to a very real audio horror. This sequence in the film, then, does not adhere to the allegorical – or by extension, the allegorical moment – but is directly confronting the Jonestown event with all allegory

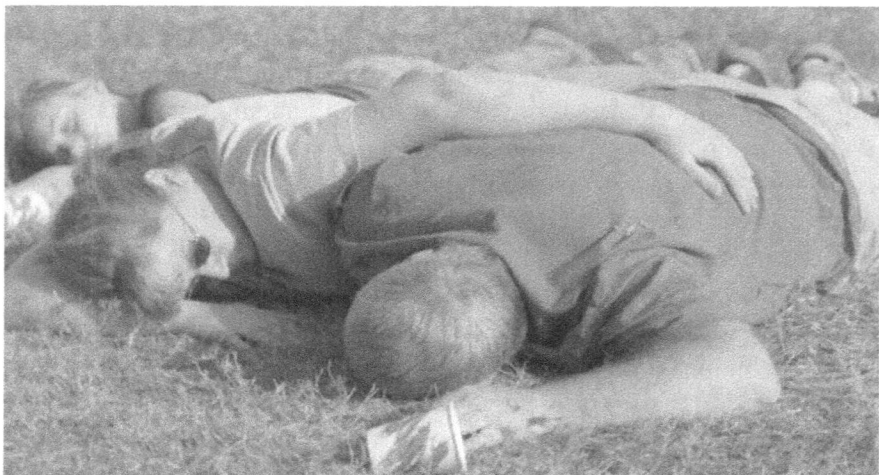

**Figure 3.1** Images of marginalised death in *The Sacrament*.

removed. This is shown not only in the visual lexicon of the sequence, with the large metal vats, wooden pavilion and grassy surroundings covered in bodies, but also in the language used.

In comparing the massacre scene in *The Sacrament* to the content of the Jonestown Death Tape, I have found multiple similarities. The lone voice of dissent is included, although in *The Sacrament* it is a lone male voice that challenges the idea of mass suicide rather than a female one. There are constant reassurances made by both Jim Jones and Father, and the sounds of children's screams and cries are duplicated. In a direct comparison of the two sermons, that of Jim Jones and of Father, it is clear that there is not only a similar syntax here – such as repeated references to the poison as 'medication', of death being 'going to sleep' or a denial that what will occur is suicide (compare for example Father's 'This is not suicide' to Jones's 'We are not committing suicide') – but some lines are repeated in *The Sacrament* practically verbatim. These lines include an illusion of choice given by the two leaders (Father's 'I want us to be able to choose our own death' and Jones's 'I'd like to choose my own death'), encouragements (Father's 'Lay down your life with your family' and Jones's 'Lay down your life with your child') and their responses to dissent (Father's 'Keep your dignity' and Jones's 'Die with a degree of dignity'). Finally, Father and Jim Jones both argue that their followers' suicides will be seen as an 'act of revolution'. It could be argued that this scene, the visual interpretation of the Jonestown Death Tape, is what Sam Costello had in mind when he termed *The Sacrament* as offensive: an inclusion of an almost word-for-word recreation of a mass poisoning for seemingly exploitative purposes. The rendering of this scene without allegory is perhaps a contributory factor in the overarchingly negative critical reception of *The Sacrament*.

## 'We go there so you don't have to': the *Vice* aesthetic and the importance of witnessing

In an interview with the popular horror website Dreadcentral.com, Ti West noted the importance he placed on achieving a sense of authenticity in *The Sacrament*, and that the inclusion of a real-life media brand was a strategy to enable this (Dread Central, 2014a). The brand that features in *The Sacrament* is *Vice*, and part of the immediacy of the film is evoked by this particular brand and its specific documentary style. From *Vice*'s origins in the mid-1990s as a print magazine, it has subsequently refocused on video journalism and documentary filmmaking, becoming in the process a brand that has positioned itself as consistently engaging with new media and new forms of reportage. For example, *Vice* was the first media brand to utilise Google Glass – eyeglasses that display information in the same way as a smartphone and allow the user to record hands-free – in their coverage of protests in Istanbul in 2013. The footage captured by the head-mounted Google Glass camera was described as 'captivating and panic inducing in equal measures' (Dredge, 2013). However, despite *Vice* situating itself at the forefront of alternative documentary journalism, Lizzie Widdicombe of *The New Yorker* has noted that the brand 'has never been celebrated for good taste' due to its 'reputation for provocation' (2013). Meanwhile, other commentators have critiqued the way it walks the 'thin line between entertainment and journalism' (Ip, 2015). *Vice* has also been accused of sensationalism. Aimen Khaled Butt, for instance, notes that the brand is 'hurting journalism by compromising the quality and content of their reporting for increased entertainment value' (2013), while CNN reporter Dan Rather has remarked that the *Vice* brand is 'More "Jackass" than journalism' (Swaine, 2014). It is fair to say, however, that despite these criticisms, *Vice* has earned a 'grudging respect as the unlikely champions of proper, on-the-ground foreign reporting and gritty domestic stories' (Swaine, 2014) and David Carr has proposed that the company's documentaries are 'remarkable journalism' (2014). Similarly, articles on the brand will often note that although *Vice* reportage tends towards gratuitous clips of carnage, 'It feels rough, but also honest' (Ip, 2015).

Building on both the concept of New Journalism from the 1960s and the writings of Hunter S. Thompson, *Vice* advocates 'immersionism', with correspondents attending 'places most other journalists ignored and [becoming] involved with the people they [are] covering in a more hands-on way' (Singular and Singular, 2015: 146). In doing so, *Vice* operates 'with an attitude [. . .] certain to disturb, if not offend, some other journalists and parts of the mainstream media' (Singular and Singular, 2015: 146). *Vice*'s particular brand of immersionism has been criticised for being 'raw and tasteless' (Goldner, 2014), presenting 'a collision of tragedy, hedonism, and world shaping events' (Widdicombe, 2013) and 'favoring shock and outrage over context and depth' (Stuever, 2013). Despite this, the selection of *Vice* for the brand featured in *The Sacrament* allows the possibility of an audience member familiar with the visual qualities of the brand, and *Vice*'s ethics, to take that knowledge into the viewing with them.

Immersionist journalism is not a new phenomenon,[5] but *Vice* documentaries are primarily known for their focus on 'immersion and danger' (Grant, 2013), as well as a tendency to feature reports from correspondents in dangerous areas, crafted into 'highly provocative, award-winning documentaries' (Singular and Singular, 2015: 146). *The Sacrament*'s evocation of the *Vice* brand and its specific documentary aesthetic is established early in the film, during the introductory intertitles that open the narrative. These intertitles work to situate both the film as a documentary, and the narrative as part of the real world in which the *Vice* brand exists. This intention was stated by Ti West, who insisted that the inclusion of *Vice* was to 'add to the realism of the movie. When you leave the theatre and you see that brand out in the world it brings you back to the film' (Sélavy, 2014). The intertitles read

> Vice is a New York City based multimedia company focused on international news, arts & culture. Available in over 34 countries, the company is known for covering provocative & controversial stories usually overlooked by the mainstream media. This new-age type of journalism has produced some of today's most compelling & original content in a style often referred to as 'immersionism'.

The world 'immersionism' remains on screen as the other words fade to black. There is a brief flash of static, followed by a shot of a large *Vice*-branded backdrop. The man seated in front of the backdrop adheres to descriptions of *Vice* staff as 'haute hobo chic: mossy beards, skinny jeans, and thrift store T-shirts' (Tanz, 2007). Text at the bottom of the screen informs the audience that this is 'Sam Turner – Vice Correspondent', and he addresses the viewer directly to explain that Patrick, the team's photographer, has received a letter from his estranged sister Caroline, who has invited him to the clean-living commune she is now part of. After asking Patrick to read the letter aloud, Sam notes that the team have decided, since they have been to 'some of the most fucked up, war torn places', yet have 'never covered something so personal and bizarre' as this, that it would make for a good story, and that they intend to accompany Patrick to the commune.

Clear and sustained effort has been made in this opening sequence to align the aesthetics and language of *The Sacrament* to the *Vice* brand, and this continues throughout the film, such as the team wearing 'VICE'-branded rings. Sam's positioning on the screen, his appearance and his cadence, are in keeping with many *Vice* documentaries that begin the same way. In addition to these similarities, it has been noted that the film captures 'the mixture of reckless bravery, irreverent tone, and self-conscious "craziness" that typifies the magazine' (Sélavy, 2014). Real-life *Vice* correspondents have indeed attended 'fucked up, war torn places', with previous *The Vice Guide to: Travel* documentaries including *The Radioactive Beasts of Chernobyl* (2007), *Illegal Border Crossing Park* (2010) and *North Korean Labor Camps* (2011), all of which are available through Vice.com.

**Figure 3.2** 'Haute hobo chic' Sam Turner in *The Sacrament*...

**Figure 3.3** ... and Shane Smith of *Vice*.

*The Sacrament* also picks up on the *Vice* documentary naming tradition, when Sam suggests that they could call their finished project 'The Vice Guide to: The Carter Family Reunion'.

*The Sacrament* neatly avoids a common criticism of found footage horror – the unbelievability of someone continuing to tape while they are in danger – through its use of the *Vice* brand, representing a body of reporters who regularly attend dangerous locations and manage to capture footage within them. In short, *Vice* is precisely the kind of media brand that would attempt to infiltrate and capture footage of a cult-like commune. In fact, *Vice* already has, in its coverage of The Church of the Last Testament and the church's leader Vissarion in 2011.[6] The *Vice* brand places an importance on the act of witnessing, which is echoed in statements from the brand such as that made by Andy Capper, the editor of *Vice* UK, in that 'we report it as we see it. We are just trying to show people what is happening, to report the news' (quoted in Bowie, 2010). This statement resonates within *The Sacrament* during Sam's retort to Father's accusations of media sensationalism, when he says 'We try to be honestly subjective, we don't have an agenda. We're just trying to document things that are meaningful.' This importance placed on witnessing and documenting the meaningful is underlined in a tagline for *The Sacrament*, which continues the conceit that the film is an actual documentary, reading 'Documented for the first time, witness the untold story of the tragedy at Eden Parish.' An intriguing feature of this tagline is the positioning of the fictional Eden Parish tragedy as a hereto 'untold' story, given its similarity to the Jonestown Massacre and how this real event was marginalised and remained largely 'untold' for years. There is perhaps a hint of exploitation in this, in that the viewers are presented with a promise that part of the film's spectacle will be their witnessing of a narrative with which they may be familiar but which has no real visual legacy. In this way, witnessing the story of Eden Parish, and by extension the story of Jonestown transposed into the setting of a horror film, can be understood as potentially voyeuristic.

Throughout the film itself, the importance of witnessing is consistently highlighted. For example, when Father, during his interview with Sam, advises him to 'Remember what you are seeing tonight, Sam. You have a great responsibility, I hope you're aware of it.' Similarly, later in the film, Father urges Caroline to pick up Patrick's fallen camera in order to document the impending mass suicide, noting 'I want you to film this, it's important.' Father, who displays a mistrust of the media explicitly throughout the narrative, is shown to recognise, then, the power a camera lens has as a technological witness. Tellingly, it is not only Father who values the camera's lens as being an instrument of witnessing and of truth, and these themes resonate in Jake's direct address to the camera towards the end of the film. In this scene, having been pursued through the surrounding jungle by Father's armed guards, Jake finally reaches the entrance of Eden Parish and turns the camera on himself. Jake then states that

> If anyone ever sees this, something terrible happened here. I don't know why but they're trying to kill us. I'm just going to keep rolling, and hope that I get as much as possible. I hope that this footage makes it out of here. Whatever happens, this story needs to be told.

Not only does this scene illuminate Jake's recognition of the importance of his footage, and his willingness to do as Bob Brown did in reality and give his life for it, but it also uncovers a noble intention of the film itself. This underlining of the importance of the fictional footage of Eden Parish, and the story it tells being retold through its technological witnessing, implies that the story of Jonestown also needs to be retold. Whether 'using real-life horror as a basis for fictional horror is offensive' (Costello, 2014) or not.

## 'You have a great responsibility': accidental and endangered – failing objectivity, crisis reporting and trauma tourism in *The Sacrament*

Even if an audience member is unfamiliar with *Vice*'s specific documentary style, the film would still appear to be a documentary product due to its evocation of the participatory mode, as conceptualised by Bill Nichols. Nichols states this mode focuses on a 'direct involvement' between the filmmaker and their subject (2017: 22), but stresses that a limitation of the participatory mode can be that the filmmaker may 'cede control and points of view to others, [and] lose independence of judgement' (2017: 109). Both of these limitations occur in *The Sacrament*, with the documentarians ceding control both in the interview scene, where Sam – a professional reporter – flails under what he calls the commune's 'weird energy', and also towards the end of the film where Caroline takes over control of her brother Patrick's camera to film the massacre at Eden Parish.

Although the objectivity of the camera lens is not questioned in *The Sacrament*, there is a highlighting of the ethical position of documentarians or journalists in crisis situations, and whether they should become active participants in events they are documenting. This brings Susan Sontag's assertion that 'the person who intervenes cannot record; the person who is recording cannot intervene' (1977: 12) to the forefront, which underlines this crisis of objectivity that may occur for journalists in dangerous situations. In an interview, A. J. Bowen, who portrays Sam in the film, notes that the characters in *The Sacrament* start 'with the worst of intentions, just hoping to find some good exploitative material [. . .] it sort of devolves into integrity from there pretty quickly' (Dread Central, 2014b). In this quote Bowen highlights the assumption that *Vice* magazine is known for leaning towards 'stunt journalism' and that it is 'brash, lacking nuance, ultimately fake, and monetized for consumption' (Finnegan, 2016), rather than impartial reporting with an ideal of pure objectivity. An inversion of this assumption occurs within *The Sacrament* too, where Sam and Jake both become active participants during the crisis at Eden Parish, moving towards intervening rather than simply recording. Sam and Jake increasingly find themselves trying to assist the people of Eden Parish instead of becoming journalistic tourists in the trauma that is unfolding. In terms of the ceding of control and loss of independence of judgement that Nichols underlines as a danger of the participatory mode, it is Sam's crisis of objectivity that serves as one of the narrative turning points of the film.

After it becomes clear that something is dangerously amiss within Eden Parish, Jake repeatedly tells Sam to 'drop it', and that 'This is too fucked up, I don't want to get any more involved.' As Sam retorts that they have to do something – although he is unclear what that something is – Jake then argues 'Sam, that's not why we're here. It's not our problem. It's not why we make these films; you're losing sight of things [. . .] we're not the Red Cross.' Despite Jake's attempts to defuse Sam's increasing drive to intervene, he is unable to stop his involvement with the ongoing arguments after Sam sees Savannah, a young child who cannot speak, being manhandled by armed guards on the morning they are due to leave. Sam runs to Savannah's aid while Jake insists he should not become further embroiled. At this point, the style of the camerawork within *The Sacrament* becomes more frantic, and begins to evoke what Vivian Sobchack terms as the 'endangered' gaze. Sobchack's (2004) framework of the ethical gazes of documentary film when capturing danger and death are a useful framework through which to view the majority of found footage horror cinema. Given that these films sit within the horror genre, it is fair to say that at some point they will feature danger and death, with the camera operator's close proximity to these being central to the narrative's development. The use of the endangered gaze also brings the film closer to the aesthetic and narrative conventions of *Vice* documentaries. As Al Brown, a producer at *Vice* notes, a key aspect of *Vice* documentaries is the affective responses of the reporter, in that 'if our journalists are scared, that makes it into the film. What our journalists are feeling is a huge part of our vernacular' (quoted in Martinson, 2015).

In found footage horror, the camera will usually fall into the accidental and/or endangered gaze at some point during the narrative. Although not present in *The Sacrament*, the accidental gaze can be seen in found footage horror films where characters capture horror inadvertently. Examples of this can be seen in *Skew* (2011) *Quarantine*, *The Bay*, *Devil's Due* (2014) and *RWD* (2015) to name only a few. Sobchack has explained that the accidental gaze is 'cinematically coded in markers of technical and physical *unpreparedness* [. . .] such lack of preparation for the encounter is signified by the camera's *unselective vision*' with the camera's focus during the encounter with death or danger being elsewhere (Sobchack, 2004: 249, emphasis in original). Sobchack then explains the endangered gaze as being visually coded by both its proximity to danger, and as being 'marked by the relative instability of its framing', which – as Sobchack argues – points 'to the body that holds it, to a vulnerable human operator' (2004: 251). I propose that the immediacy and sense of endangerment within the found footage format (and its removal of a layer of distance between the viewer and the action unfolding on screen through the use of a diegetic camera) enhances both the verisimilitude of what is happening on screen, and the audience's fear for the safety of the cameraperson, who functions as our on-screen avatar. Through the found footage horror frame, the character's perspective is our perspective and conversely, their danger is our own too.

*The Sacrament*'s use of the endangered gaze bolsters its framing as a participatory documentary, which relies on 'the viewer sens[ing] that the image is not just an indexical record of some part of the historical world but also an indexical record of the actual encounter' (Nichols, 2017: 111–12). Although *The Sacrament* is of course fictional, the presence of the camera in the film works similarly to the presence of the camera in participatory documentary, which 'affirms a sense of commitment or engagement with the immediate, intimate, and personal as it occurs' (Nichols, 2017: 136). This is central to how *The Sacrament* functions as a fake documentary about a real event. And, in its deployment of the accidental/endangered gaze and participatory mode, how it renders the story of Jonestown intimate, personal and immediate.

## Why Jonestown, why now? The Othering of the Jonestown dead and *The Sacrament* as traumatic space

David Chidester, in his extended analysis of the aftermath of the Jonestown Massacre, discusses the way in which the event was perceived by the American public and its place in American cultural history. Chidester outlines that the Jonestown event 'registered as something so obviously outside the mainstream of American cultural life that it stood as a boundary against which America's central values could be defined' (2003: vii). Chidester's focus in his analysis is the treatment of the recovered bodies from Jonestown, which he identifies as being characterised by 'the vocabulary of defilement, impurity, and contagion' (2003: 16). Chidester goes on to conclude that the bodies of the Jonestown dead were essentially Othered by the American media and government because to accept them as being American would be to accept them as part of the cultural fabric and history of America. Instead, they were positioned as 'not "ours", they were not part of "us", they were classified as "them", as "other", and as fundamentally "subhuman"' (2003: 20). The media treatment of the Jonestown Massacre, which Jonathan Z. Smith calls the 'pornography of Jonestown' (1982: 109), is also noted by Danny L. Jorgensen (1980), who proposes that the event was given a large degree of attention by the media because of a combination of factors. These included a slow news period, the commercial value of gory stories, and the topicality of cults at the time, all of which contributed to turning the Jonestown Massacre into a media event. Jonestown therefore stands not only as one of the largest losses of American life in a single event since Pearl Harbor, during which 2,403 people died, but also as the first media event revolving around a self-destructive cult.[7] The cultural relevance of Jonestown is still strong today, with the term 'Jonestown' having become linguistic shorthand for describing cult-like behaviour, and the phrase 'don't drink the Kool-Aid' becoming firmly entrenched in popular culture as a warning against the dangers of brainwashing. Ariana Huffington, for example, used the phrase in reference to George W. Bush supporters (2002); it has also – aptly, given my focus here – been used to describe the popularity of *Vice* magazine (Carr, 2014). While several articles have questioned the appropriateness of using this term (including Richardson (2014); Waldman (2015) and Weinstein (2018)), it has also been utilised more recently by President Donald Trump, who referenced Kool-Aid (and its connection to Jonestown) to dismiss the idea that individuals can benefit from white privilege (CBS News, 2020). In terms of claims of exploitation that could be levelled at *The Sacrament*, Ti West has argued that the reduction of the Jonestown event to a pop culture reference is perhaps 'more exploitative' than

> making a movie that shows how people were actually affected by the thing, how the people who drank the Kool-Aid were actually real talking people who came here to try to help better their lives and they didn't want to die, but they didn't feel like they had a choice, and then you're seeing them die in horrific ways and people dying around them [. . .] it's more in service to that tragedy and reminding people that these terrible things can happen than like, a TV movie. (Quoted in Houtch, 2014)

In the years since the Jonestown Massacre, the event – and the settlement itself – has served as the subject for a variety of books, including survivors' accounts (Layton, 1999; Johnston Kohl, 2010), reconstructive narratives of the lead up to the massacre (Nugent, 1979; Reiterman, 2008; Scheeres, 2012; Gunn, 2017), novels that fictionalise what happened (Roy, 2014), reports of the carnage by first responders (Brailey, 1998) and academic scholarship on its lasting impact (Hall, 1987; Weightman, 1984). Rebecca Moore has noted that in the wake of the 9/11 attacks, Osama Bin Laden was compared to Jim Jones both by the public and by the media, with Al-Qaeda being compared to Jonestown. Moore suggests that this was because 'religious fanaticism, suicide, and murder played a role in both' (2003: 92). Indeed, the lasting trauma of Jonestown has meant that the event has become a cultural reference point for more recent events such as the Waco siege of 1993, and the Heaven's Gate mass suicide of 1997. Jonestown's cultural legacy is as a symbol of the taboo, with this leading to a 'repression of and dissociation from the tragedy' (Moore, 2003: 92).

Linnie Blake, in her assessment of how a nation's horror cinema can be a product of that nation's 'cultural wounds', has proposed that there is a danger of silencing trauma through respect, and that horror cinema fulfils a function here in its provision of 'a visceral and frequently non-linguistic lexicon [. . .] in which the dominant will to repudiate post-traumatic self-examination through culturally sanctioned silence may be audibly challenged' (2008: 189). Blake then goes on to argue that 'horror may offer an insight into our current predicament that is every bit as immediate and considerably more affective than conventional polemical forms such as the documentary' (2008: 190). It is interesting therefore that found footage horror essentially brings these two forms, horror and documentary, together. Similarly, Adam Lowenstein has proposed that there is a need in trauma studies generally to wish for 'representations of trauma to honor the awful pain and complexity of victim/survivor experience, so those experiences and memories can be protected from further harm' but that this respect can transform 'paradoxically, into a silencing of both experience and representation' (2005: 4–5). The trauma of Jonestown and the experience of its survivors has indeed effectively been silenced over the intervening years, with the deaths in Guyana being seen as scandalous and the grief of those left behind retaining a stigma. This has led to what Kenneth J. Doka calls 'disenfranchised grief', in which 'a person experiences a sense of loss but does not have a socially recognized right, role, or capacity to grieve'. This then results in a situation where, 'the person suffers a loss but has little or no opportunity to mourn publicly' (1989: 3). Although Doka is referring in his work to deaths that may be considered 'shameful' from a religious/moralistic perspective such as overdoses or suicides, we can see here how the relatives and friends of those who died in Jonestown would not have been able to publicly mourn their losses. This positioning of Jonestown as a fringe event in American history was encouraged by the media coverage of Jonestown immediately after the event, which Moore proposes worked to create distance between the living and the dead (2011: 46). Survivors of Jonestown, on returning to the United States, were given little support, and 'Some members, unable to find jobs [were] turned away by welfare agencies that refused to deal with "baby killers"' (Hatcher, 1989: 135).

After the bodies of the dead were returned to America, in addition to a vocabulary of defilement being used to describe them, many bodies were left unclaimed or unidentified, and as a result of this more than 400 deceased individuals were buried in a mass grave at Evergreen Cemetery in Oakland, California (Moore, 2011: 48). If we are to compare the mourning of the Jonestown dead to its two closest cultural events (in terms of magnitude of American lives lost), Pearl Harbor (2,403 deaths) and 9/11 (2,753 deaths), we can discern a distinct difference in terms of memorialisation. The Pearl Harbor memorial, which straddles the site of the sunken USS Arizona, was built in 1962 and attracts around 1.8 million visitors annually (Associated Press, 2014). It is also the site of yearly memorials which have been attended by every US President since Franklin D. Roosevelt (CNN Wire Staff, 2011). The 9/11 memorial is located on the former World Trade Center site and the planning of its construction began soon after the event itself. The memorial museum opened to the public in 2014, and in its first sixteen weeks of opening, it attracted over one million visitors (CNN Wire Staff, 2011). In comparison, the grave for the Jonestown dead went un-memorialised until 2011, when four plaques displaying the names of identified deceased were placed above the mass grave. Before the erection of this memorial, there was indeed a yearly service by the grave, but as Rebecca Moore argues, this service was used as a platform to extoll the dangers of cults rather than to memorialise the dead, and as such was not an appropriate place to mourn (2011: 48–9).

In terms of the wider cultural impact of Jonestown, the stereotype of 'suicide cults' is one that is still entrenched in American culture (Laycock, 2013: 81). There has been a steady increase in the number of media products that focus on religious extremism and cults in recent years, perhaps rivalling their popularity in the late 1970s, when they were a 'pervasive presence in popular culture' (Jenkins, 2000: 201). Since the turn of the millennium alone, cults and extremism have been the subject of horror films such as *Red State* (2011) and *The Invitation* (2015), have appeared in episodes of long running series like *Criminal Minds* (within the episode 'The Tribe'), and have been the subject of their own television series, such as *The Path* (2016–18). Cults have also formed a narrative focus of various video games, such as *Outlast 2* (2017), and *Far Cry 5* (2018). This overview does not begin to touch upon the multiple dramatic re-enactments of the stories of real-life cults in popular media and documentaries on the subject since 2000, such as *Waco* (2018), a six-part miniseries starring twice Academy Award-nominated actor Michael Shannon, which covers the days in the lead up to the deaths of seventy-six Branch Davidians at the Mount Carmel compound in 1993.

This rise of interest in cults has been noted by various news outlets (Allio, 2018; Bond, 2018, among others), with journalist Amy Zimmerman suggesting that 'at a time when our nation's most vile ideological seeds are in full, undeniable bloom, it makes sense that we are returning to some of the ugliest moments in our collective history' (2017). Indeed, media portrayals of cults have repeatedly underlined the connection that can be made between religious movements and the threat of potential violence (Bromley and Melton, 2002). Joseph Laycock, a scholar of new religious movements, has proposed that fictional narratives have a unique ability to portray cults and challenge hegemonic narratives of them (2013: 102), and this is key to *The Sacrament*'s use of the story of Jonestown, the popular understanding of which is 'unalterable in its persistence' (Moore, 2000: 7). *The Sacrament* skillfully negotiates the accepted canon of cultists as 'glassy-eyed zombies' (Saliba, 1995: 77), and of Jim Jones's followers as mindless dupes, by calling into question the idea of blind faith rather than individual belief. West's decision to use the story of Jonestown as a framework for his film is centred around his recurrent sentiment in interviews that Jonestown as a cultural event has been, over the intervening years, 'weirdly glossed over' (quoted in Bibbiani, 2014). This sentiment is echoed by journalist Jennie Rothenberg Gritz in an interview with Jonestown survivor Teri Buford O'Shea, in which Rothenberg Gritz describes the Jonestown Massacre as occupying a 'grotesque but fringy place' in American history, with Buford O'Shea being quick to agree that 'Jonestown was an important part of American history, and it's been marginalized' (quoted in Rothenberg Gritz, 2011). We can clearly see this marginalisation at work in the lack of public memorialisation of Jonestown in the subsequent decades.

A possible reason for the lack of memorialisation of Jonestown, however, may be due to the comparative ease with which 9/11 and Pearl Harbor could be narrativised. Kamikaze pilots and terrorists intent on destroying symbols of American culture can be easily geographically, or racially, Othered, as they are the threat of the Other made real. The threat in both of these events was external to America, whereas the anxiety caused by Jonestown may stem from the status of the Peoples Temple parishioners as Americans (albeit living in Guyana at the time). Therefore they can be perceived as an internal threat, yet a threat that the wider populace still desired to be Othered from American values and culture. The statuses of victims and perpetrators of tragedy are also blurred in Jonestown, whereas the individuals who died during Pearl Harbor and 9/11 can be heroised, or at least empathised with. The Jonestown dead, however, those who fed their children poison and lay down to die, could not be situated as completely external to America or America's core values despite geographical distance, and their status as American is an element that the media furore surrounding Jonestown sought to overturn. This can be seen also in the way that ownership of the Jonestown dead was debated by America and Guyana's governmental agencies, where 'The U.S. pressured Guyana to bulldoze the dead into a mass grave – but Guyana refused to clean up what it saw as an American mess' (Scheeres, 2018). Despite this overarchingly negative view of the Jonestown dead, *The Sacrament*'s representation of the community in Eden Parish is overarchingly sympathetic, an attribute that the film's detractors have seemingly overlooked.

## Conclusion

Although *The Sacrament* was the first to use the horror genre to engage with the Jonestown Massacre, it would not be the last. In an episode of *American Horror Story: Cult* (FX, 2017) entitled 'Drink the Kool-Aid', for example, Kai Anderson discusses several cult leaders such as Marshall Applewhite, David Koresh and Jim Jones – who he terms as 'the Kayne of leaders'. All the cult leaders – as seen in 'footage' that plays while Kai speaks – along with Kai himself, are portrayed by Evan Peters with his appearance altered by a bald cap, a mullet and a padded body suit and prosthetics respectively. Later in the episode, we return to Jonestown, where Jones has just imbibed the poison with his followers, who – like him – violently vomited before dying. In keeping with the campy tone of the series, as Jones lays dead on the floor, Jesus Christ (also played by Peters) descends on wires, kisses Jones's head and resurrects him. Jones then revives his congregation by blessing them. More recently, *The Jonestown Haunting* (2020) follows the story of a surviving member of Jonestown who returns to the site after ten years. Her dreams of Jonestown reimagine events in lurid, Giallo-esque set pieces, which include bleeding loaves of bread, hefty doses of dry ice in suspicious looking drinks, and a Jim Jones that cries blood. Arguably, the tone of these two representations of Jonestown, particularly the inclusion of real footage from Jonestown within them, are far more exploitative and offensive that that contained in *The Sacrament*. However, I have found little scathing criticism of them. This chapter suggested that it may have been the murder suicide scene in *The Sacrament* that caused the critical opprobrium directed at it, and this scene was specifically noted by journalist Bilge Ebiri, who argued that 'as the scene goes on and on, it becomes exploitative and cheap, an empty attempt to create emotional resonance in a film that mostly lacks it' (Ebiri, 2014). Given that the texts above have presented the Jonestown Massacre in far more graphic (and it must be said, bizarre) ways and not met with the same level of criticism, I would suggest that perhaps it is *The Sacrament*'s use of a found footage format that may have contributed to the ill feeling directed at the film. *The Sacrament* apes documentary, which – as explored in Chapter 2 – we trust to present us with an approximation of the truth, and although it does provide a visual accompaniment to the very real audio horror of the Jonestown Death Tape in exacting detail, *The Sacrament* sits in an awkward position that perhaps other found footage horror films do not. It is too real to be taken as entirely fictional, and too fictional to be seen as an accurate or respectful representation of the facts.

Ti West certainly achieved his goal of making a film that was 'confrontational and provocative' (The Skinny, 2014), and one which 'should make the audience feel uncomfortable' (Olsen, 2014). When watching the massacre scene in *The Sacrament*, the viewer is suddenly and shockingly reminded that in addition to these images being part of an entertaining horror film, the events they depict really did happen several decades before. This affecting quality of the film stems not only from its treatment of the Jonestown Massacre, but also the way in which Patrick dies at the hands of his sister, which is filmed with an unmoving wideshot in a way that gives the audience no reprieve from his death throes. Also, from its nods towards other mediated images of suicide and death, with Caroline's self-immolation, for example, recalling the suicide of Thich Quang Duc, while Father's self-inflicted gunshot to the head is striking in its visual similarity to the death of Budd Dwyer, whose suicide was broadcast on American television. The found footage framing of the film – its unnerving immediacy – adds to the unflinching quality of *The Sacrament*'s confrontation of these historical visual records of death. In closing this chapter, I wish to situate *The Sacrament* as oppositional to the comments of Carole

Cavanaugh that I highlighted in the first chapter of this book, and her implication that a film can either be fantasy or direct representation, but never both. *The Sacrament*, through its re-enactment of history within an otherwise fictional narrative, and positioning of this through a documentary lens, is both fantasy and direct representation, and it would appear to be this dual status, and the fact that *The Sacrament* is operating within the horror genre, that contemporary critics have found troubling. The critical reception of the film suggests, too, that *The Sacrament* perhaps achieves this dual representation too well, and in doing so the film possibly becomes too close to reality for a 'bad' genre such as horror, hence it was subsequently read as being exploitative.

Although it is unlikely that *The Sacrament* will spark a reconsideration of the position Jonestown holds in American cultural history, it does provide a space for that trauma. The film brings the story of Jonestown to an audience through an emulation of a participatory documentary gone horribly wrong, where the endangered gaze of the camera operator functions as an extension of the viewer's own gaze, and as such creates a fictional embodied experience of the Jonestown Massacre. *The Sacrament* presents itself as part of the media landscape of modern 'immersionist' documentary filmmaking, and as such is also emblematic of found footage horror cinema's ability to deftly adopt new representations of reality to convey its narratives. This is a quality of found footage horror cinema that continues into the next chapter's case studies too, in their emulation of televisual actualities.

## Notes

1 Footage from these conversations can be seen in *Jonestown: The Life and Death of Peoples Temple* (2006).
2 Often erroneously reported as being Kool-Aid, a different brand of drink.
3 A further four Peoples Temple members died in nearby Georgetown on hearing of the massacre. Sharon Amos slit the throats of her three children before taking her own life (Treaster, 1978). The Jonestown Massacre was the largest loss of American civilian life in modern history until 9/11.
4 Although now seen as a legitimate field of study, the horror genre has historically retained its reputation of being a 'bad' or 'low' genre and horror films as 'bad' objects (see Hunt, 1992: 67 and Cherry, 2009: 12).
5 With the first documented example being Nellie Bly's account of being undercover in an asylum, *Ten Days in a Mad-House* (1887).
6 The *Vice* documentary *Jesus of Siberia* (2012) follows Vice correspondent Rocco Castoro and his experiences with the cult. During the documentary, Vissarion grants

his first media interview in three years.
7 Although it could be argued that the media attention given to Charles Manson and his followers in the wake of the Tate LaBianca murders was the first, I would suggest that although the followers of Manson acted in a cult-like way, the Manson family were not self-destructive, focusing instead on causing harm to others rather than themselves.

# 4

# Found footage horror and televisual actualities

Over the past few decades, the documentary mode has undergone seismic changes. As John Corner suggests, 'a new fluidity of representation boundaries in documentary [have] appeared [...] in response to the market need to hybridize across genres in the search for competitively attractive new recipes' (1999: 183). This cross-fertilisation of genres has led to the emergence of several new reality formats. Some of these formats – which include reality television and semi-scripted docudramas – have caused scholarly debate, due to their location, as Annette Hill explains, 'in border territories, between information and entertainment, documentary and drama' (2005: 2). For a subgenre that readily adapts to new reality 'looks', it is perhaps not surprising that the specific aesthetics of various forms of televisual reality formats have been adopted by found footage horror, which has a keen eye towards new developments in representations of reality. For example, survivalist reality programming is a clear influence on *The Hunted* (2013), *I Am Alone* (2015), *Devil's Trail* (2017) and *Survive the Hollow Shoals* (2018). Meanwhile, competition-based reality game shows are evoked in *Tontine Massacre: The Fiji Tapes* (2010), and reality television stars such as Duane 'Dog' Chapman and his show, *Dog the Bounty Hunter* (2004–12) are aped in *Bounty* (2009). The life-affirming family entertainment of such programmes as *Little People, Big World* (2006–) have then influenced the aesthetic of *Delivery: The Beast Within* (2013), which is replete with a TV-G rating icon in the film's opening, while home improvement shows such as *Extreme Makeover* (2002–7) inform the presentation of *They're Watching* (2016).

This chapter, however, will concern itself with two specific strands of televisual reality formats: the true crime television documentary and the ghost hunting reality show. Of particular interest here is how both of these strands have been critiqued for blurring the line between the real and the fake in their mixing of reality, fiction and history. Both true crime documentaries and ghost hunting shows base their content around real events and places, but will often include fictionalised elements such as dramatised reconstructions. These formats sit at an odd juncture, as although they have clear ties to the documentary tradition, they are not all the way 'real', yet also contain too much of the real to be dismissed as purely fictionalised. Perhaps because of these characteristics, both the true crime documentary and the ghost hunting reality show have provided fertile ground for the found footage horror subgenre. Along with this chapter's first case study, *The Poughkeepsie Tapes*, the true crime documentary format is also the basis, for instance, of *Savageland, Head Cases: Serial Killers in the Delaware Valley* (2013) and *Horror in the High Desert* (2021). The specific aesthetic of ghost hunting reality shows that is emulated by this chapter's second case study, *Grave Encounters*, is even more popular in the subgenre, and can be found in *The Mitchell Tapes* (2010), *The Speak* (2011), *Hollows Grove* (2014) and *Night Stalkers: Paranormal Investigators* (2017) to name only a few examples.

The films that have been selected for this chapter not only recreate – in exacting detail – the aesthetics of their chosen reality 'looks', but engage with anxieties common within and around them. This chapter, therefore, will address each case study in turn, first examining *The Poughkeepsie Tapes*, which uses the structure and look of a true crime documentary – along with a degraded VHS aesthetic – to convey its narrative. *Grave Encounters* will then be explored, in order to examine how it emulates the performative reality present in ghost hunting reality programming while also functioning as a critique of it. I will then move on to discuss more broadly the wider traumas and anxieties these films, and their real-life counterparts, engage with. This chapter, therefore, will demonstrate how deftly found footage horror adapts its format to assimilate varied and distinct reality aesthetics even within the same overarching televisual 'reality' genre.

## 'I don't think either of us are going to want you alive for the things I'm going to do to you': making a murder documentary with *The Poughkeepsie Tapes*

*The Poughkeepsie Tapes* was originally scheduled for release by Metro Goldwyn Mayer in 2007. Had the film been released in that year it is reasonable to assume that it could have rode the wave of popularity that found footage horror cinema was enjoying at that point. Even though *The Poughkeepsie Tapes* may well have reached a good level of financial or critical success had it been released when it was initially created, it is equally as likely that the film would have been overlooked due to the influx of found footage horror releases in this time period. However, we will never be able to know how the film would have been received with any degree of certainty, as it was not officially released in the United States until 2017, through a Blu-ray release from Scream Factory. As of the time of writing, *The Poughkeepsie Tapes* has yet to receive an official home media release in Europe. This is not to say that *The Poughkeepsie Tapes* disappeared entirely in the intervening decade. It did, for example, appear briefly through an online video streaming service, DirecTV, in 2014. However, the film was only available on DirecTV for a week (Barton, 2014) before it was again removed from official circulation (Lee, 2015). Despite this, *The Poughkeepsie Tapes* maintained a visual presence on the internet during this ten-year period between creation and release: on file sharing websites and through GIFs on social media. Copies of the film would also regularly appear on user-generated content websites such as Vimeo and YouTube, only to be routinely deleted due to copyright infringement. Following the rise in production of found footage horror films in North America in the years following the release of *Paranormal Activity*, the volume of high-profile entries into the subgenre began to plateau.[1] It was not long after the boom in found footage horror production that commentators professed their boredom with the subgenre or complained about the saturation of the horror genre with the format (Lyne, 2015; Blyth, 2016). Characteristic of this malaise around found footage horror, a review of *The Poughkeepsie Tapes* in 2012 suggested that a possible reason for the non-release of the film may have been due to the fact that the surge of found footage horror releases was over, and that *The Poughkeepsie Tapes* was 'possibly no longer culturally relevant' (Somma, 2012). Contrary to this, however, I argue that the film possesses, by virtue of being released in 2017, a prescient resonance with the period in which it was finally made available. *The Poughkeepsie Tapes* achieves this specifically – and it must be noted, unintentionally – in two ways. Firstly, through the adoption of a true crime documentary aesthetic, which brings the film into a dialogue with the renaissance of interest in that genre of programming since 2015, and secondly through its use of faux snuff sequences, which align the film with online death videos, the likes of which have featured as the subject of true crime documentaries such as *Don't F\*\*k With Cats: Hunting an Internet Killer* (2019).

*The Poughkeepsie Tapes* is not the first found footage horror narrative to focus on the exploits of a serial killer. In fact, there is a distinctive strand of serial killer-centred films within the subgenre, including both North American and international releases. These films vary in style; for example some feature documentary crews following serial killers, such as *Man Bites Dog* (1992), *Long Pigs* (2007) and *Behind the Mask: The Rise of Lesley Vernon* (2006), whereas some present themselves as self-made films by the serial killer themselves, as is the case with the *August Underground* series (2001–7) or *Be My Cat: A Film for Anne* (2015). Meanwhile, others consist of footage collected by amateur sleuths investigating suspicious disappearances, such as *Megan is Missing* (2011). Conversely, the true crime documentary framing of *The Poughkeepsie Tapes* is, for the most part, presented in a way we have become accustomed to through our exposure to the content of outlets such as Investigation Discovery (1996–), The Crime and Investigation Network (2006–) and The Sony Crime Channel (2018–20). There is a sense of aesthetic and narrative commonality between true crime shows that *The Poughkeepsie Tapes* adheres to, such as 'wide ranging talking-head interviews' (VanArendonk, 2018), 'sweeping drone-filmed shots of bleak, barren landscapes [and] inserts of newspaper headlines' (Evangelista, 2018) and 'mapped layouts of crime scene locations' (Berros, 2017). Along with these elements, *The Poughkeepsie Tapes* includes expert testimony from FBI officials and forensic specialists, 'authentic' 911 calls, clips from contemporaneous news reports, archival footage and crime scene photography: all components we could reasonably expect to find in a true crime documentary. In using the conventions common to true crime programming, *The Poughkeepsie Tapes* works to engender the audience's documentary engagement with the film as if it were real, and the content of the film could be read as – or confused for – a particularly sensationalistic retelling of crime fact. Where *The Poughkeepsie Tapes* differs from real-life true crime documentaries, however, is in its inclusion of footage from the eponymous tapes.

The tapes within *The Poughkeepsie Tapes* are introduced as a collection of over 2,400 hours of VHS recordings found in the killer's home after he evades capture by the police. These tapes are mentioned several times by various characters before we are shown their content, and they are described as 'something of a homemade porn film' by FBI profiler Felton Lewis, presumably kept by the killer 'as a reminder' of his crimes. The first time we actually see the physical tapes themselves is after they are introduced by Simon Alray, an FBI-employed audio visual specialist. They are set up on a long series of tables, and as Alray explains, while showing the

Televisual actualities   71

Figure 4.1  The physical presence of *The Poughkeepsie Tapes*.

audience the sheer number of tapes recovered, they consist of footage from the abductions, torture, murder and dismemberments of the killer's victims. Whereas the majority of the film adheres – in terms of professional image quality – to what we have perhaps come to expect of true crime shows, the aesthetics of these tapes are distinctly amateur. They are characterised by unsteady framing, unclear sound and almost ruined in places by audio visual decay due to the nature of their VHS format.

Early in the film we are shown one segment that is particularly marred by this degradation, introduced by a title card reading 'Part 2: First Blood'. This clip begins with someone inside a vehicle filming a young girl playing in her front garden. This person, while continuing to film, approaches the child. She is reluctant to speak to him but he is undeterred, asking if she would like to see the view through the camera and crouches next to her. We then hear the girl being hit several times before the footage becomes unsteady and frantic as the man carries the now unconscious child to his car. When compared to the rest of the footage shown from the tapes, this sequence is not graphic or gory. There is no blood visible on screen, the child doesn't scream and the audience is never shown any footage of the girl – Jennifer Gorman – after she is abducted. However, we gather from interview footage with her parents and FBI agents after the tape is shown that she was subsequently raped and died due to blunt force trauma to her head. The violent act of the girl being struck is implied both through sound – the noises of impact and the grunts of effort from the killer – and emphasised through the odd, decayed quality of the footage. It is grainy, our vision is impaired by the amount of static and tracking marks which deform the image, and the colour saturation swings wildly from bright and unnatural to black and white. These qualities are common to VHS tapes that have suffered generational loss or that have been excessively used over time. This aesthetic was clearly a stylistic choice created in post-production, and although the other clips from the various tapes shown in the film do not reach the level of distortion and degradation shown in this particular clip, this aesthetic of VHS decay is a constant presence within the killer's tapes.

Other than being a novel means of disguising or 'hiding the seams' of special make up effects, the VHS decay of the tapes has another function within the narrative, which is to align the tapes with reality.[2] *The Poughkeepsie Tapes* does this in three primary ways. Firstly, as we know that VHS degrades over time and through use – and we are told that the killer uses these tapes as a form of memory repository – it stands to reason that they would be in poor condition. In another tape sequence later in the film, for example, the killer reattends the site of Cheryl Dempsey's abduction – her parents' home – and speaks with her mother. As he converses with her, Cheryl's mother realises she is talking to her daughter's kidnapper and he runs laughing from the scene. Cheryl's mother then recounts this experience in an interview and notes that she replays that moment in her head often. Judging by the quality of the recording the killer captured of this encounter, it is clearly a moment he replayed often too. Secondly, the authentic quality of the tapes – underlined by this VHS decay – is emphasised by the fact that the audience – or at least an audience familiar with true crime – may be aware that several real-life serial killers have committed their atrocities to videotape. Examples of this include Paul Bernardo and Karla Homolka, who recorded the rape and torture of their victims in the early 1990s (Makin, 2000), as well as Maury Travis, who likewise videotaped several of his murders (ABC News, 2014). Finally, the look of the murder tapes emulates, perhaps, what we might expect – or know – real death footage to look like. Early examples of internet-distributed beheading videos, for instance – such as those showing the execution of Nick Berg – were characterised by crude editing and 'a grainy, chaotic aesthetic' (Astley, 2016: 153), and videos such as *1 Lunatic 1 Icepick* and *3 Guys 1 Hammer* – explored in more detail in Chapter 8 – are similarly filmed on low quality cameras. However, despite the eponymous tapes containing a fair level of gore and bloodshed, a significant amount of their violence happens off camera. For example, although the aftermath is shown in fuzzy, barely visible footage, the violent acts visited on two early victims, Frank and Jeanette Anderson – which include the removal of Frank's head and it being placed in Jeanette's torso while she is still

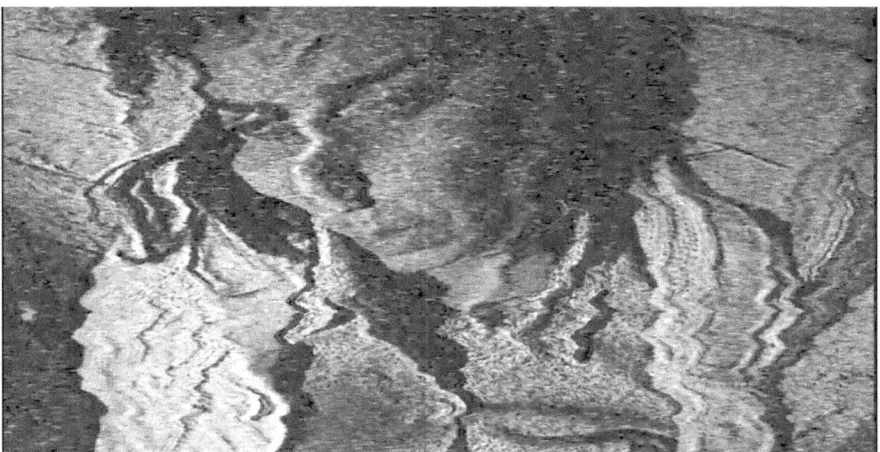

**Figure 4.2** VHS decay underlines the illicit nature of the tapes . . . and their overuse.

alive – occur offscreen. Additionally, before Cheryl is abducted, the killer beats her savagely, but this is seen through the visuals of their shadows on the wall, captured by the killer's fallen camera, and several of Cheryl's subsequent 'punishments' happen just outside of the limits of the frame. As Geoff King argues, 'One of the markers of real, genuine authenticity in audio-visual media generally is a reduction often in the plentitude of images [and] Absences or reduced quality [that] signify that events have not been staged for the convenience of the production of images' (2005: 50). *The Poughkeepsie Tapes* is not only a violent film because of what we do see, but also because of what happens just out of shot and that which is obscured by VHS decay.

The imperfect, decayed nature of the eponymous tapes also connects them to other forms of 'illicit' real-life recordings. Following a moral panic in the UK in the 1980s around the easy availability and possible behavioural impact of violent horror films, for example, a list was constructed by the Director of Public Prosecutions of 'potentially prosecutable horror videos available, at that time, in British video shops' (Egan, 2007: 1). This inventory of 'video nasties' did not mean that the market for these films disappeared; on the contrary, 'the moral panic had ensured that there was a demand for these films so the market moved underground and the films circulated illegally for many years' (McKenna, 2020: 128). The quality of the copies distributed through informal channels such as fanzines was often 'verging on indecipherable [. . .] as copies-of-copies-of-copies circulated', with this degradation acting as 'a material marker of both their danger and add[ing] to the impression of authenticity' (Heller-Nicholas, 2014: 11).

The degraded quality of the tapes within *The Poughkeepsie Tapes* similarly adds to their realism. Caitlin Benson-Allott also discerns this air of illicitness to VHS decay, noting that it leaves the viewer with 'the impression that it was unethically obtained, that we are not supposed to be watching these images' (2013: 184). Given that, for a decade, the only way that audiences could see *The Poughkeepsie Tapes* was through illegal downloads or bootleg copies sold over the internet, this forbidden quality may have been emphasised for viewers at that time. Similarly, this authentic look of VHS decay coupled with the film's 'lost' or unreleased status until 2017 may explain why audiences were confused by its truth status.

## 'I wonder what was on those tapes': the mythology of *The Poughkeepsie Tapes*

The ephemeral nature of *The Poughkeepsie Tapes* in the decade between its production and release has only added to the film's mystique. To suggest that Metro Goldwyn Meyer deliberately withheld the release of the film as a marketing ploy is patently absurd, but uncertainties around whether the film was real or fake have been a fortuitous side effect of its previously unreleased nature. The language used in reviews and commentary once the film was released through Scream Factory in 2017 were full of illicit promise, with many mentioning that it was previously 'banned' (Perrie, 2017; Clayton-Lea, 2017; Marchman McNeely, 2017; Vella, 2017 among others): an assertion with no grounding in reality.[3] Whereas the majority of these reviews specifically state that *The Poughkeepsie Tapes* is a fiction film, audience response is characterised by a greater level of confusion over the narrative's fictional status. In my observation of responses to *The Poughkeepsie Tapes* on Twitter, I have found that a number of users have generally noted that *The Poughkeepsie Tapes* is part of a history of cinematic limit experiences, and compare it to other notoriously violent and graphic horror films such as *A Serbian Film* (2010). Meanwhile, however, a significant body of users have debated the truth status of the killer's footage. One user, for instance, notes that they are 'scared to watch poughkeepie [sic] tapes . . . its [sic] real footage of what police found of a serial killer where i [sic] live . . . i [sic] know the house! how creepy! (Lizzlexsizzle, 2010). Of course, there is no way of telling with any degree of confidence if these users actually believe *The Poughkeepsie Tapes* is real, but even if they do not, the fact that they are committing themselves to feigned confusion over its truth status is still significant.

I have found nothing to suggest that *The Poughkeepsie Tapes* went unreleased for a decade for reasons beyond speculated financial problems suffered by Metro Goldwyn Meyer around the time of the film's intended release and since (Clark, 2010). Nor is there any record of the production company being in 'fear' that the film may have become 'lost in the already crowded sea of found footage trash to sift out of Hollywood' (Somma, 2012). However, a lack of evidence for these claims has not halted the rampant myth building around the film on social media. The significance of a ten-year gap between the film's production and release is that it gave time for this kind of myth building and confusion to develop and gain traction with potential audiences. It would seem, too, that the unbelievability of a true crime documentary containing lurid footage from a serial killer's personal video collection did not quell the truth debates around the film either, although there are possible reasons for this. For instance, if we are to review mainstream news broadcasting in recent years, we are able to chart a gradual acceptance – or at least increasing presence – of more extreme and graphic content. The immediate aftermath of the murder of Lee Rigby in 2013, for example, was shown on the early evening news on ITV in the UK, allowing viewers to clearly see the victim's blood on one of the killer's hands as he brandished the murder weapon in front of a bystander's camera. This footage caused Ofcom to caution both ITV and the BBC to use warnings for explicit material before showing similar footage in the future (Sweney, 2014). On user-generated content websites there was similar controversy in 2017 over YouTube 'celebrity' Logan Paul's footage from Japan's Aokigahara forest, which included shots of a real suicide victim (Griffin, 2018). In addition to this, the current saturation of the true crime programming market has created more competition between content creators, who may well be looking for the next big audience draw. More recently, the growing presence of graphic content in true crime products has led to complaints being raised regarding, for example, the use of real crime scene photography and gory reconstructions in the docuseries *Night Stalker: The Hunt for a Serial Killer* (2021) (Kent, 2021).

We can clearly see a trend, then, towards increasingly graphic depictions of death and violence in mainstream media, with death having a visual prominence in our cultural moment unlike at any other time. When *The Poughkeepsie Tapes* was originally scheduled for release, the idea of a documentary featuring actual footage from a serial killer's personal tapes would have been unlikely. Indeed, Xavier Aldana Reyes positions the inclusion of the Water Street Butcher's footage as having a negative effect on *The Poughkeepsie Tapes*'s believability, as

> The strong material in some of these films sometimes goes against the premise that the film should be fit for public consumption. For example, *The Poughkeepsie Tapes* has the look of a finished documentary, but the excerpts extracted from the titular murder tapes show too much violence in too much detail. The purpose and effect of their showing would no doubt be questioned by TV channels and ordinary consumers.
> (2015a: 135)

I argue, however, that these 'ordinary consumers' only have to believe, or play into the idea, that the inclusion of this footage in the film may well have been the reason it was pulled from Metro Goldwyn Mayer's release schedule and then 'banned'. In other words, although I am in no way arguing that in 2017 the inclusion of death footage would have been deemed more acceptable, I propose that an audience member does not necessarily have to play into the idea that *The Poughkeepsie Tapes* is a true crime documentary containing real death footage, but rather that they only have to play into the possibility of it being a documentary that was banned between 2007 and 2017 precisely for including this kind of footage. This 'call to play' (Hight, 2008: 2014) is then strengthened by the flurry of articles about the 'banned' nature of the film, and debates concerning the veracity of its footage on social media which appeared in the ten-year gap between production and release. When read in this way, the fictional premise of *The Poughkeepsie Tapes* could be equated with real-life mondo documentaries such as *Faces of Death* (1978), which was banned temporarily in several countries despite containing more faked footage than authentic. Mark Seltzer has suggested that our cultural appetite for records of bloody destruction and murder can be attributed to what he terms as our 'wound culture', a place where celebrity culture and bodily destruction intermingle. Seltzer describes wound culture as being 'the public fascination with torn and open bodies and torn and opened persons, a collective gathering around shock, trauma, and the wound' (1997: 3). Seltzer later positioned the serial killer as the emergent superstar of this wound culture (1998: 2). *The Poughkeepsie Tapes* takes this concept of wound culture to its most extreme, with its rendering of a documentary which shows moments of death, torture and degradation for our viewing pleasure, housed in a format resembling what we recognise as part of the 'discourses of sobriety' of televisual documentaries (Nichols, 2017: 26).

## 'Edited strictly for time': the look of the real in *Grave Encounters*

*Grave Encounters* eschews the common use of title cards within the found footage horror subgenre, instead opening with an extended verbal explanation of the footage we are about to watch. In doing this, the film explains both the origin of the 'found footage' and places it firmly within the audience's reality. The first scene of the film introduces us to 'Jerry Hartfeld – Executive Producer', who gives the footage the following framing statement:

> I run a video production company here in Anaheim, California. We focus mainly on reality television shows. If you've ever seen the show Tornado Trackers? That's one of ours. A tape arrived in the mail, it was a pilot episode of a new reality series called Grave Encounters, and it was by a young producer named Lance Preston. The idea was him and his group of paranormal investigators would investigate ghost sightings and hauntings, things of this nature, and he was, you know, years before all the other ghost hunting shows that are out there now. I mean, I really felt like he was ahead of this time.

There is a cut to a short promotional advertisement for the 'Grave Encounters' series, explored further below, before the audience are returned to Hartfeld's introduction. He notes that 'Everything was going really smoothly. I mean, the edits that were coming back were great, we were very excited. We really had something, you know? And then, and then of course we got to episode six.' Hartfeld pauses, and his eyes now begin to dart between the offscreen interviewer and directly at the audience. He continues

> I want to be very clear about this. What you are about to see is no movie, ok? This has been assembled from some seventy six plus hours of raw mini DV footage that was shot for Lance's show. Not a frame of this has been doctored, it hasn't been manipulated in any way. This is just raw footage. It's been edited strictly for time.

Although the role and act of editing will recur in the films analysed in Chapters 6 and 7, and it is unusual for found footage horror films to present themselves as one long unedited shot, it is also atypical for the process of editing to be addressed so explicitly and for such length as in this introduction.[4] By confronting the presence of these edits, *Grave Encounters* underlines the authenticity of its footage through its stated untampered nature. This plays into ideas around the truth status of reality television, and how – as discussed below – the real is performed. This introduction also works to place the film within the reality of the audience, where there are indeed 'all the other ghost hunting shows' that Hartfeld mentions. It is fair to state that ghost hunting reality television is one of the most popular subgenres of reality programming. This can be seen in the sheer number of programmes available, such as *Ghost Adventures* (2008–), *Paranormal State* (2007–11), *Paranormal Lockdown* (2016–) and *Extreme Paranormal* (2009) to name only a select few. Although these kinds of shows differ slightly in their 'angle' (for example, *Ghost Brothers* (2016–17) features a team of black men (in what is an overarchingly white-dominated genre); *The Girly Ghosthunters* (2005) are women; *Paranormal State*'s angle is that the team are University students), their aesthetic presentation is remarkably similar.

As mentioned in the introduction of this chapter, the ghost hunting show format has been widely appropriated by the found footage horror subgenre, and this may well be because these shows possess such a distinct appearance. Mike Hale has outlined the typical 'look' of a ghost hunting show as

> On each show a team [. . .] descends on some purportedly haunted location, often a large, decrepit structure, like an abandoned hospital or factory. They venture inside with the tools of their trade: K2 meters to detect electromagnetic field, parabolic dishes to capture the faintest noises, night-vision lenses to penetrate the darkness. Everything is bathed in sickly green light, and people say "Oh my God!" and "Did you hear that?" a lot [. . .] Eventually someone yells that something is touching him, everyone runs like a frightened child and the camera flails about. (Hale, 2009)

As ritualised and, perhaps, predictable as the aesthetics of ghost hunting shows have become, they are – through their use of markers of authenticity – based in what we have come to recognise as reality. At the very least, they utilise a visual aesthetic that we now associate with the real. For example, as the investigations on these programmes largely take place at night and within buildings, it stands to reason that the footage these shows present as authentic would indeed be of lower quality or clarity because of the lack of natural light, and that the distinctive green and black shades of a night vision lens would also be common. As Jon Dovey notes, 'the low-grade video image has become the privileged form of TV "truth telling", signifying authenticity and an indexical reproduction of the real world' (2000: 55). This particular reproduction of reality is distinct from the traditional cinematic image, due to it appearing 'immediate and hypermediated at once' (Shaviro, 2017: 323). Furthermore, the aesthetic presentation of these ghost hunts may be familiar to an audience conversant with found footage horror films. Karen Williams, for instance, suggests that in ghost hunting shows the low quality and amateur framing of shots lends an authenticity to proceedings, in which the camera must 'represent evidence just missed by a panning camera or just offscreen at the other end of a terrified gaze' (2010: 154). These characteristics, of the 'just missed' and the limitations of the camera in capturing all of the things all of the time are – as demonstrated in Chapter 2 – common to found footage horror cinema. As such, I propose, given that this type of ghost hunting show emerged in the wake of the unprecedented success of *The Blair Witch Project* in 1999 and how, conversely, ghost hunting television aesthetics now form a significant part of the found footage horror cinema oeuvre, that this influence is multi-directional. Moreover, this just missed quality, among many other elements I will go on to discuss here, ties *Grave Encounters* to the documentary tradition more broadly.

*Grave Encounters* is intent on emulating the television series *Ghost Adventures* in particular.[5] This can be seen in the thoroughness of similarities between the fictional promotional advertisement we see in the opening of the film – as mentioned above – and the real promotional advertisement for the first season of *Ghost Adventures*. Both advertisements have voiceovers by their respective hosts, and the similitude of these mean it is worth recounting them in full. The advertisement for *Ghost Adventures* has the following voiceover:

> My name is Zak Bagans. I never believed in ghosts until I came face to face with one. So I set out on a quest to capture what I once saw onto video. With no big camera crews following us around, I am joined only by my fellow investigator Nick Roth, and our equipment tech Aaron Goodman. The three of us will travel to some of the most highly active paranormal locations, where we will spend an entire night being locked down from dusk until dawn. Raw. Extreme. These are our Ghost Adventures.

We can then compare this to the 'Grave Encounters' promotional video, where the voiceover explains

> My name is Lance Preston. When I was a boy, my family moved into a house that I soon discovered was haunted. The things I encountered have stayed with me forever. Ever since then I have been obsessed with trying to capture proof that these things were real. Come along with me and my team of skilled paranormal investigators, as we dare to venture into some of the most haunted locations known to man, spending the night and capturing everything on camera. If you're ready, it's time to have some Grave Encounters.

We can discern immediate similarities in the style of language used here. Both voiceovers begin with the host introducing themselves and their reason for ghost hunting, and both close by stating the title of their

**Figure 4.3** A ghost hunting show gone horribly wrong: Sasha's blood on the lens in *Grave Encounters*.

respective shows. Both hint at a past trauma in the host's life related to a ghostly encounter. Both underline the potential danger or risk involved in attending 'the most highly active paranormal locations'/'the most haunted locations known to man' and proceed to emphasise this risk by underlining how the teams will be 'locked down from dusk till dawn'/'spending the night' in these haunted spaces. There is also an underscoring of the intimate nature of their ghost hunts, with Bagans noting the small size of his team and Preston inviting the audience to 'come along' with his, intimating a sense of participation for his viewers. The advertisements themselves are very visually similar too: both show three team members (although the 'Grave Encounters' team numbers five within the film itself), include the prerequisite night vision footage, and shots of gravestones and cemeteries. Both advertisements also highlight the respective team's intention to 'capture what I once saw on video' or promise to be 'capturing everything on camera'. This drive for visual evidence is a central theme of found footage horror cinema and a key element of real-life ghost hunting shows: both genres construct their believability and claims to the truth around this. It is through these similarities that *Grave Encounters* not only positions itself as a horror film that plays on the possibility of a ghost hunting show gone horribly awry in its quest for visual evidence, but also functions as a critique of the constructed nature of this kind of programming.

# 'Be a fucking professional and stay in character': performing the real, participation and privilege in *Grave Encounters*

Reality television – in all its guises – is a genre that relies on its 'reality credentials' for its spectatorial appeal, promising viewers the 'spectacle of, supposedly, the "real" itself' (King, 2005: 13). Ghost hunting reality shows work within the premise that cameras will capture – and the audience will be shown – untampered visual evidence that will allow them to make up their own mind about the existence of the supernatural. Annette Hill, for example, notes that 'reality paranormal TV is based on the centrality of ambiguity' (2010: 66), and that these shows will 'specifically leave issues of evidence and authenticity open to multiple meanings, [and] allow audiences to decide for themselves what may be happening' (2010: 66).

John Corner has highlighted that from the 1930s onwards, there was a move in documentary filmmaking to employ *recorded images and sounds of actuality* to provide the viewer with a distinctive kind of "seeing" and "hearing" experience, a distinctive means of knowledge', before reminding us that documentary has since been 'grounded in an appeal to *sensory evidence*' (Corner, 1995: 208, emphasis in original). Ghost hunting television, with its emphasis on terrified reaction shots and the drive to capture visual evidence, brings itself in line with these specific documentary intentions. Indeed, the physical reactions of the paranormal investigators within these shows are presented as being equally supportive of the veracity of hauntings as their array of ghost hunting technology is. This technology, such as electromagnetic frequency meters, digital sound recorders and electronic voice phenomenon detectors, functions within these programmes to provide supposedly scientific evidence to support the team members' physical responses. This technological evidence is, however, often subordinate to these very reactions, with the camera often trained on the investigators' faces. As Karen Williams states, 'their bodies and their reacting first-person cameras become the main instruments by which unseen phenomena are registered'. Williams moves on to clarify that 'Reacting bodies and performance, then, become central to these experiential ghost shows' (2010: 153). The fear of the ghost hunting teams can be read, then, as a form of performativity, and as a way of constructing the real within these shows.

During *Grave Encounters*, Lance pays a groundskeeper to invent a story for the camera to underline the haunted status of their location – The Collingwood Psychiatric Hospital – and has a constant eye towards the aesthetic of the show. At the beginning of their investigation, for example, the team members discover graffiti on the main entrance doors that reads 'Death Awaits', and briefly discuss whether or not it will make it into the final edit. Sasha – the team's occult specialist – sighs that the graffiti is 'so lame', while Lance insists that in 'slow motion, music behind it, everything is creepy'. At the opening of the film, then, Lance appears to be less interested in actually capturing the supernatural – although he remarks that it would be great if they could – rather, he is more invested in getting, as he explains to Sasha, 'some good scares'. The performative reality of ghost hunting television is further emphasised shortly after this exchange, when Lance asks T. C. if he can get some footage from the various corridors in the building and capture some of 'that floaty hallway stuff', which T. C. confirms as meaning 'arty shit'. However, the privileged position of the ghost hunting team is soon undermined in a subsequent scene, as T. C. dutifully films Lance's requested footage and comes across an old wheelchair. On seeing the wheelchair, which is illuminated only by the camera light, T. C. switches to night vision mode before noting 'that's about as creepy as it gets, how the fuck did we miss this? Lance, you are going to love me.' Up until this point, *Grave Encounters* has presented the crew as being in a position of editorial privilege, who have discussed what footage will and will not eventually make it into the episode. But when T. C. places his camera on the ground to take a phone call, the audience are given visual information that the crew are not exposed to. The audience, from the camera's position on the floor, watch as T. C. paces while talking on the telephone, clearly showing that the camera is not – at this moment – functioning with an operator's gaze. T. C.'s legs halt, his feet facing the camera, and we see the wheelchair slowly move forward behind him. In this moment, the audience are granted a position of privilege over T. C. and the rest of the team. This is unusual in found footage horror films, in which the audience's epistemological status is usually stalled at the same distinctly unprivileged position as the characters, with information often being revealed to both viewers and characters at the same time.

The constructed nature of ghost hunting reality television has been debated previously; for example, when the creators of *Most Haunted* (2002–) claimed to have captured evidence of the supernatural in 2017 (Boult, 2017). The fallibility of ghost hunting technology (Nees, 2015) and the repetitive and formulaic nature of these shows (Hale, 2009) have also been critiqued. Most continually criticised in journalistic accounts, however, is the authenticity of claims made by the psychic mediums who often feature in ghost hunting reality television, for example Derek Acorah on *Most Haunted*, who was accused by the show's own parapsychologist, Ciaran O'Keefe, of deceiving viewers (Roper, 2012). The fictional team within *Grave Encounters* also includes a medium, Houston Gray, who is the most performative personality in the film. Soon after Houston's arrival, he dramatically remarks on the incredible amount of 'energy' the building has, before cautioning that 'there is something else here, it's like a dark spirit, it might even possibly be a demon. We have got to be extremely cautious tonight, Lance. We do not want to be messing with something like this, at all.' Lance and Houston continue into a bathroom, where other members of the team and Lance have already been told a young woman committed suicide. Lance asks Houston if he is sensing anything, and Houston replies 'I'm sensing a deep well of sadness in here. Profound sadness.' Pausing to raise his hands and close his eyes, Houston continues 'I see a patient, a girl. There's water. Red, red water. Blood! Blood! She died right in here, she slit her wrists in the bathtub.' Lance quickly confirms to both Houston and the camera that the caretaker advised them a suicide took place in the room as Houston described. Houston nods sagely, and adds 'Her spirit is still with us.' At this final dramatic intonation, Lance motions for the camera to cut and the crew burst out laughing before Houston asks 'Was that too much?' The construction of an 'authentic' haunted space, aided by Houston's flair for the dramatic, is of utmost importance to Lance, and even after the spirits within Collingwood Psychiatric Hospital make contact with the team – slamming a door on T. C. and manipulating Sasha's hair – Lance insists that a terrified Houston remain with him, as they 'need another face on camera', and that he needs to 'be a fucking professional [. . .] and stay in character'. The presence of exaggerated characters and dramatic performance does not necessarily undermine the reality presented in ghost hunting television – the specific reality that is emulated within *Grave Encounters* – because, as Richard Kilborn has argued, 'in the public mind [. . .] "reality" becomes more and more equated with a phenomenon closely associated with the idea of performance. "Reality" becomes increasingly something that is staged by groups of semi-professionalized lay-performers for the entertainment requirements of consumers' (2003: 184). Reality television consumers are not mindless dupes however, but instead this 'character-driven realism' serves to satisfy the 'sophisticated palette of a new generation of reality television viewers' (West, 2005: 89). *Grave Encounters* engages with the line that ghost hunting reality television treads, of presenting enough interest and action to keep viewers entertained, but situating this within the realm of the real in order to retain its claim to authenticity.

## 'People are going to want to see this': the ever present threat of a haunted landscape

The renaissance of interest in true crime documentaries – a documentary genre *The Poughkeepsie Tapes* emulates thoroughly through its format and aesthetics – can be tied to a growing serial killer fan culture post-2000. Along with offshoots of thanotourism[6] – a visiting of sites associated with tragedy and death – there has also been the emergence of the True Crime Community on microblogging website Tumblr.com.[7] True crime blogging or podcasting has also become so pervasive in fact, that *Halloween* (2018) opens with two true crime bloggers travelling to meet with Michael Myers, the prolific fictional serial killer. Obviously, a public interest in true crime is not a new phenomenon and can be traced back to not only crime pamphlets of the 1600s (Clark, 2003: 145), but the popularity of true crime literature such as *In Cold Blood* (Capote, 1966) and *Helter Skelter* (Bugliosi, 1974). True crime programming can be seen, therefore, as a logical progression of this public fascination with killers. The success of the Netflix series *Making a Murderer* (2015) brought new attention to the true crime genre, particularly on social media. There has also been a subsequent upswing in cinematic releases that focus on real-life murder, such as *My Friend Dahmer* (2017), *Extremely Wicked, Shockingly Evil and Vile* (2019) and *No Man of God* (2021), in addition to well received television series such as *Mindhunter* (2017–19). Deborah Allen, the vice president of Jupiter Entertainment – one of the key producers of true crime content in the United States – has noticed this surge in true crime-focused entertainment, stating that 'It used to be that the networks saw true crime shows as their dirty little secret' but this is no longer the case (quoted in Cooper, 2019a). Clearly, the prevalence of true crime in popular culture shows no sign of abatement, but this growing interest in the genre has given some outlets cause for concern, with debate over whether murder can or should ever be considered entertainment (Maelstrom, 2018; Bogart, 2018). Jeff Pope, for instance, the executive producer of true crime dramatisation *Appropriate Adult* (2011) – which presents the case of British serial killers Fred and Rose West – proposed that true crime content creators have a responsibility 'not to show something grotesque and sick. You leave that to Quentin Tarantino' (quoted in Jeffries, 2017).[8] This is in addition to discussion around the negative or desensitising effects of consuming true crime content (Smith, 2018; Hensley, 2019) and the moral ambiguity of the genre's popularity (Fosco, 2016).

Anita Biressi claims that true crime documentaries present

> the pathology of its subjects (the harm they suffered and the case history of that harm) in a form that lurches between horrific, damaging or intense recollected events and representational strategies that elide such intimate confession with broader cultural myths of trauma – the bogeyman in the woods, the killer under the stairs, the mobile serial killer. (2004: 402)

This connection between serial killing and broader cultural myths perhaps goes some way to explain the popularity of true crime, particularly in the United States. There is a conception that there is always 'a large number of serial murderers active at any given time' in America (Schmid, 2005: 14), and that crime is 'always already happening' (Murley, 2008: 100). This idea, that serial murderers are a constant – and close – presence for residents of the United States is an idea touched upon in *The Poughkeepie Tapes* by FBI agent Leonard Schway. Both in a scene where he narrates over an infographic map and tells us that many active serial killers operate at the same time, and when he notes that his agency will be attending as many public screenings of the film as possible to try and apprehend the killer. The serial murderer is constructed as the ultimate outsider or cultural Other and has, as Julie B. Wiest argues, become a 'perverse icon in the United States, as legendary as other monsters known throughout history in cultural myths' (2011: 91). This connection to monstrosity, Wiest continues, is emphasised by the nicknames given by the media to serial killers (2011: 93). The connection between serial killing and the horror genre is clearly shown in these, with names such as the Butcher of Plainfield (Albert Fish), the Boston Stranger (Albert DeSalvo), the Night Stalker (Richard Ramirez), the Hollywood Slasher (Doug Clark) or the Dallas Ripper (Charles Albright), a tradition that the 'Water Street Butcher' of *The Poughkeepsie Tapes* taps into. The killer within *The Poughkeepsie Tapes* – as we never see his face – also engages with the presence of the 'faceless criminal predator' (Surette, 1994: 135), a figure that haunts the American landscape and its mediated representations of serial murder.

Serial killers are not the only thing to haunt America. Ghost hunting television shows, given their focus on restless spirits, will often feature sites of historical trauma. *Ghost Hunters* – the longest running ghost hunting show in the United States – for example, has previously attended Myrtles Plantation ('Myrtles Plantation'), Alcatraz Island ('Alcatraz') and the Peoria Asylum ('Prescription for Fear'), along with murder sites such as the home of axe murderer Lizzie Borden ('The Lizzie Borden House') and the alleged site of the Black Dahlia Murder ('Hollywood Horror Stories').

The connection between haunting and traumatic memory was also made clear in an episode of *Paranormal State*, where the team members investigate a Vietnam veteran's experience of haunting and conclude by way of a voiceover that 'Whether we're dealing with post-traumatic stress or poltergeist phenomenon, the cure begins with therapy [...] like the fog of war, paranormal cases aren't always clear' ('Smoke and Shadows').

Revisiting a traumatic past is a central feature of ghost hunting reality television, and a further intriguing point is contained within Jeffrey Sconce (2000) and Annette Hill's (2010) respective claims that a popular interest in ghosts and hauntings tends to emerge during periods of political, civil or social unrest. As Steve Pile states, ghost stories function to 'expose the traumas and tragedies of the past in a place' (2005: 174) and in this way the act of watching ghost hunting reality television, attending traumatic sites or engaging in dark tourism may well be 'part of a structure of feeling in the way people respond to human vulnerability and mortality at this historical juncture' (Hill, 2010: 180). Indeed, Anita Biressi and Heather Nunn have noted that trauma, the reliving of trauma or the 'public expression of traumatic memories' [...] can be considered as an important ingredient of the reality TV format' (2005: 108). It is perhaps no surprise that a former mental institution is the setting of *Grave Encounters*, as these are a recurrent presence in ghost hunting shows. They also offer 'a site of representation that is rich in possibilities for cultural and social comment' (Earle, 2017: 259). The decrepit, deserted asylum is a place repeatedly revisited in found footage horror; for instance the narratives of *The Crying Dead* (2011), *Greystone Park* (2012), *Reel Evil* (2012), *Sanatorium* (2013) and the South Korean *Gonjiam: Haunted Asylum* (2018) all take place in abandoned mental institutions, and most of these films follow paranormal investigation teams who dare to enter them. In *Grave Encounters* and the majority of these other narratives, the teams that attend these sites – ghost hunting or otherwise – are terrorised by the spirits of those who died within their walls. It is often explained within these films that these occupants suffered under terrible conditions, power mad staff and insane doctors. Horror cinema's accounts of mad doctors experimenting on patients, gross abuses of power by institution staff or appalling living conditions, however, do have some connection to reality. The growth in the number of asylums within America in the 1900s was rapid (Baker and Benjamin Jr, 2014: 40). The Kirkbride plan – a proposal that mental health institutions should be arranged architecturally as a shallow 'V' – was introduced soon after in an effort to move towards more open plan living, with more personalised treatment aimed towards rehabilitation (Yanni, 2007). However, by the early part of the twentieth century, these newly built institutions too were overcrowded and understaffed, and patients were kept in dirty, inhumane conditions.[9]

Although predated by *The Titticut Follies* (1967) – a documentary about the treatment of patients at Bridgewater State Hospital which was banned for many years in the United States – possibly one of the most famous accounts of American mental hospitals was *Willowbrook: The Last Great Disgrace* (1972). In this exposé, investigative reporter Geraldo Rivera walks among the inmates of Willow Brook State School and shows the institution's deplorable conditions. This film won Rivera a Peabody Award, and as its images entered popular consciousness, they also became the overarching way in which mental health facilities would be portrayed in horror cinema from that point forward. For example, the documentary footage at the beginning of *Grave Encounters*, of the conditions at Collingwood Psychiatric Hospital, is remarkably aesthetically similar to *Willowbook: The Last Great Disgrace*.[10] As mental health care increasingly moved into the community within the 1900s, abandoned asylums such as Trans-Allegheny Lunatic Asylum, Waverley Hills Sanatorium and Danvers Lunatic Asylum – the latter being referenced directly in *Grave Encounters* – stood empty for decades, with some being repurposed later as the sites of various ghost tours. Ghost hunting reality television shows, then, perhaps function to feed the traumatic memory of the United States, as their teams' 'paranormal experiences connect our modern world to one that has faded into history' (Fitch, 2013: 157). Asylums, then, haunt the landscape of the United States and the topography of found footage horror, as a grim reminder of past fears about mental health, 'madness' and what went on behind the closed doors of these institutions.

## Conclusion

As Annette Hill argues, reality genres on television have been 'consistently attacked [. . .] for being voyeuristic, cheap, sensational television' (2007: 7). This is a characterisation that neither *The Poughkeepsie Tapes* nor *Grave Encounters* shy away from, with *Grave Encounters* in particular critiquing the 'reality' of ghost hunting programs quite plainly. Televisual reality genres have been said to be 'united less by aesthetic rules or certainties than by the fusion of popular entertainment with a self-conscious claim to the discourse of the real' (Murray and Oulette, 2009: 3). I have argued here, however, that both the true crime documentary and ghost hunting show strands of reality television do in fact possess their own aesthetic rules, conventions and narrative structures. These are emulated and exploited by the films discussed in this chapter to convey horror, trauma and anxieties. Found footage horror may well have started in simple evocations of documentary style, but just as Miska Kavka has advanced that reality television has a 'stubborn ability to renew itself' (2012: 4), the careful recreations of the format, personalities and 'looks' of these shows within *The Poughkeepsie Tapes* and *Grave Encounters* demonstrates that this ability to regenerate is a commonality the found footage horror subgenre shares.

The mythmaking that has become inextricable from found footage horror cinema – and which is central to the subgenre's willful blurring of reality and fiction – has been explored here as a key element of *The Poughkeepsie Tapes*'s appeal, and found footage horror's blurring of this line paratextually will be returned to in more depth in Chapter 8. The troubled release schedule of *The Poughkeepsie Tapes* contributes to its significance and status within the subgenre. The air of illicitness around the film is emphasised by both the ten-year gap between its creation and release – during which time it could only be seen through illegal means – and by the visual quality of the decayed VHS aesthetic used within it, with a variety of perceived faults such as tracking errors, glitches and distortion underlining its authentic nature. As Chapter 2 made clear, these imperfections are read as what reality on film looks like and have become a mainstay of both real documentaries and the found footage horror subgenre. This can be seen from *Cannibal Holocaust* and *The Blair Witch Project* – where cameras hit the ground with such force that their lenses are knocked out of alignment – to entries such as *Tuesday the 17th* (2012), in which a spectral monster is embodied by onscreen distortion. Having the eponymous tapes couched in the form of a true crime documentary – a format often criticised as blurring the line between fact and fiction for sensationalist ends – only underlines the realism of the violence within *The Poughkeepsie Tapes*, which quite often uses the limitations of the screen to chilling effect.

While eschewing corporeal killers in favour of more spectral terror, *Grave Encounters* is one of a long line of found footage horror films that have chosen the ghost hunting reality show set up and aesthetic to convey a narrative. If *The Poughkeepsie Tapes* used imperfections to highlight its reality claims, then *Grave Encounters* touches on discussions around the process of capturing the real to situate its horror in the audience's reality. It then simultaneously critiques and unpicks the reality claims of ghost hunting shows by underlining their performative aspects. Again, markers of authenticity such as dead time are included to emphasise that this is what unfolding and unplanned reality captured on film looks and sounds like. *Grave Encounters* presents itself as a participatory experience and engages with a sense of immersion that is central to ghost hunting reality television. Alissa Burger has noted that in this kind of show,

> the combination of crew cameras and hand-held video cameras carried by individual team members *simulates* participation by creating a sense that viewers are positioned alongside the [...] team members throughout pivotal moments of the investigation, 'experiencing' the suspense of the hunt and the thrill of witnessing paranormal activity. (2010: 164, emphasis in original)

This simulation of participation is also emphasised by team members directly addressing the camera, and an acknowledgement of the camera as an extension of the camera operator. Mikel Koven, for example, has noted that a recognition of the camera as physically existing within the diegetic space and a converse acknowledgement by the camera of everyone present during the phenomena, work to support the investigative truth claims of ghost hunting television (2007: 188). Meanwhile, Annette Hill has assessed the active viewing mode encouraged by ghost hunting shows, in that 'audiences are not passively sitting at home waiting for the producers to put on a show; they are actively engaged in an emotional, physical and psychological participation' (2010: 78). This sense of immersion is key to the found footage horror subgenre too, where – as Barry Keith Grant explains, monsters, ghosts and other threats

> exist in physical environments that are common public spaces, looking like footage we might take on our cell phones or our own digital cameras and share on the internet. It is in these spaces that characters and cameras alike move, avoiding the monsters, in narratives of survival. (2013: 171)

Through the found footage frame, the spectator is positioned as part of the action, and in one of the last scenes in *Grave Encounters*, this spectator is directly addressed by Lance Preston, who asks 'Anybody watching? Fuck you, fuck you, fuck you guys! This was for you.' Despite the fact that his crew are dead or missing, his camera's battery power is low and he is alone in the labyrinthian tunnels under the asylum, Lance's final sign off demonstrates his hope – and perhaps his disgust – that there is still an audience out there to witness his experience.

Both *The Poughkeepsie Tapes* and *Grave Encounters* – and indeed the televisual actuality genres they are based on – are preoccupied with the landscape and history of America, haunted by both the ever present threat of the serial killer, and the looming, empty asylums that once held American society's 'inconvenient' members. The chapters that make up the first part of this book have, through an engagement with found footage horror's repeated adoption of emerging documentary forms, illuminated some of the recurring themes of the subgenre – its use of the limitations of the frame and the offscreen space, its characters' compulsion to document and its sense of bleakness through the convention of the failed documentary. As a main concern of this book is the ways in which trauma and anxieties 'haunt' found footage horror cinema, it is perhaps fitting that this first part ends on the enduring presence of ghosts within the subgenre.

## Notes

1 I have specified 'high-profile' releases here, as found footage horror continues to be a popular format for low-budget independent filmmaking.
2 In a similar way to *WNUF Halloween Special* (2013), *The Poughkeepsie Tapes* uses the VHS aesthetic to align itself with a specific 'pastness'.
3 Examples of found footage horror films that have actually been banned (at least in the United States and the United Kingdom) only number two: *Cannibal Holocaust* and *Hate Crime*.
4 As we will see in Chapter 7, *Diary of the Dead* is one of the only other found footage horror films I have found to bring the audience's attention to editing so directly.
5 Interestingly, Zak Bagans, the host of *Ghost Adventures*, would go on to write and direct *Demon House* (2018), a horror documentary that at times feels very much like a found footage horror film.
6 The first instance I have found of this term is used in reference to a fascination with the site of President Kennedy's assassination (Foley and Lennon, 1996). Seaton (1996) suggested five types of dark tourism: travel to witness public enactments of death, travel to sites of mass or individual death, or travel to sites of recreation or re-enactment of death.
7 For an explanation and discussion of the true crime community on Tumblr.com please see McMurdo (2019).
8 A comment ironic in hindsight, given that Tarantino would go on to direct *Once Upon a Time in Hollywood* (2019). This film and its rewriting of history were indeed criticised as being in poor taste (Beck, 2019).
9 In *Grave Encounters*, a scene where the team consults a map of Collingwood Psychiatric Hospital shows that it adheres to the Kirkbride plan style of construction.
10 More broadly, Lana Winters's exposé of Briarcliff Manor in *American Horror Story: Asylum* (2012–13) clearly takes Rivera's footage as a reference point.

# Part II

# 5

# Found footage horror, 9/11 and a culture of fear

During the morning of 11 September 2001, audiences around the world witnessed the largest terror attack on American soil in history, after members of the Islamist extremist group Al-Qaeda hijacked four passenger aeroplanes. One of these, American Airlines Flight 77, was flown into the Pentagon in Virginia. Another, United Airlines Flight 93, crashed into a field in Pennsylvania after its occupants fought against and overcame the plane's hijackers. The other two flights, American Airlines Flight 11 and United Airlines Flight 175, collided into the Twin Towers of the World Trade Center in New York City at 8.46am and 9.03am respectively. Live on television, viewers both domestic and international witnessed the collapse of the South Tower at 9.59am. The North Tower remained standing until 10.28am, when it also fell. Only 102 minutes after the first strike into the North Tower, two of the most iconic buildings of the New York City skyline had gone. Scholar Jeff Greenberg, in a testimonial regarding his own experience of watching the attacks, notes that what he saw was

> the World Trade Center, with a burning hole in the tower on the right, as if it were bleeding. Before I could even formulate a thought, a plane came around the burning tower from the right, and made a sharp left turn into the second tower, like a stab wound into the heart of New York. (Quoted in Pyszczynski et al., 2003: 4)

This kind of emotionally charged language, particularly the use of words like 'bleeding', 'stab wound' and 'heart', compares the attacks to an assault on the very flesh and body of America, and begins to demonstrate how these attacks were viewed and experienced by many Americans.

The attacks caused widespread confusion throughout the United States and globally, as airspace over North America was shut down (Donnelly, 2001; Cain, 2016) and first responders from around the country took leaves of absence to help find survivors in the twisted metal remnants of the Twin Towers. In the immediate aftermath of the attacks, many countries remained on high alert, and the media coverage of significant events both during and after was extensive: this included live coverage of United Airlines Flight 175 flying into the South Tower and the fall of the towers as they happened. Looking at the coverage retrospectively, a constant element discernible throughout is repeated variations of news anchors uttering the phrase 'It's just like a movie'. The attacks on the Twin Towers – in addition to the events that were occurring in Pennsylvania and Virginia – were so immense and unprecedented that there was a turn to the language of film in order to comprehend what was being broadcast the world over. In the wake of the tragedy that was unfolding, passing comment that the destruction was 'just like a movie' may give a flippant or insincere impression. However, as Wheeler Winston Dixon proposes, the use of this language by news anchors may have been 'simply because they had no other referent to fall back on in the face of such apocalyptic destruction' (2004: 9). It is imperative therefore to view the attacks in context, and remember that the United States, and indeed audiences and news readers in many other countries, witnessed 9/11 through a collective knowledge and experience of a multitude of films in which the decimation of American buildings, landmarks and monuments is a long standing cinematic tradition. Los Angeles, for instance, was destroyed in *War of the Worlds* (1953) and in the disaster movies of the 1970s – such as *Earthquake* (1974) and *The Towering Inferno* (1974) – we can see urban destruction on an epic scale. If we move into the 1990s, there are some notably spectacular examples of this in films such as *Independence Day* (1996), *Volcano* (1997) and *Fight Club* (1999). New York City specifically has served as the site of fictional devastation several times, with the Twin Towers in particular featuring prominently. For example, in *Deep Impact* (1998) they are the only surviving buildings in Manhattan after an extinction event level tidal wave. Eerily, after a meteor storm early in *Armageddon* (1998), a shot of the New York City skyline shows a dark plume of smoke billowing from one of the damaged towers, in much the same way that we saw in many live images from 9/11. As Geoff King proposes, the filmic language used in the reportage of 9/11 captured 'the extraordinary and "unbelievable" nature of the scenes they were witnessing' and these events were 'experienced – at least in part – through a frame provided by Hollywood spectacle' (2005: 48).

Decades after 9/11, we are still discussing and reappraising the events of that day, as well as their cultural, historical, political and traumatic impact. Books on the subject range from discussion of the effects on psychology, politics and education (Arndt et al., 2002; Morgan, 2009; Morgan and Sternberg, 2010) and explanations of the reasons behind the attacks (Wright, 2007) to minute-by-minute recounts of that morning (Dwyer and Flynn, 2005; Arkin, 2021). We can also find accounts from surviving civilians (Walch and Walch, 2021) and first responders (Picciotto, 2003; Luft, 2011; Pfeifer, 2021) as well as celebrations of their bravery (Merrill Jr, 2011). Although the fall of the Twin Towers is located temporally on a bright Tuesday morning in the past, the echoes of 9/11 can still be felt years later; for instance, President Donald Trump's wielding of 9/11 as a political weapon during his 2016 election campaign.[1] More recently, President Joe Biden's withdrawal of US forces from Afghanistan in 2021 has reinvigorated debate around the legality of President George W. Bush's 'War on Terror': an act many have suggested was driven by vengeance for the 2001 attacks (Critchley, 2011; Brady, 2012; Tanguay, 2013; Connah, 2020). In addition to these lasting political shockwaves, the images of 9/11, too, still haunt the present. Retrospective programming on the event – most notably the slew of documentaries that appear around each anniversary – recirculate photographs and footage of the destruction. Examples of this include *102 Minutes That Changed America* (2008), *9/11: Day That Changed the World* (2011) and to a lesser extent the series *Turning Point: 9/11 and the War on Terror* (2021). The documentary film *9/11* – which will feature prominently in the following chapter – has been updated with new footage and rebroadcast every five years since (Littleton, 2016; Tapp, 2021). The continual refreshing of our cultural memory of 9/11 means that the event can never really leave our consciousness and instead, these documentaries operate in the background as recurring refreshers of trauma.

This second part of *Blood on the Lens* does not seek to comment on the multitude of discourses surrounding the lasting effect of 9/11 on American politics, nor does it strive to deliver the last word on the impact that day had on popular culture more broadly. Instead, it will examine how found footage horror cinema has engaged with 9/11 and its impact both directly and indirectly through its formal aesthetics and its narrative themes. In this chapter, after a brief discussion of some of the criticisms of allegorical readings of post-9/11 horror films, I will explore the new cultural landscape of the United States in the wake of 9/11, by outlining the features of an anxious America that feared a form of violence which is 'always unexpected though constantly awaited' (Liénard Yeterian and Monnet, 2015: 1). Following this, I will broaden the scope of this chapter to examine how 9/11 was being represented by wider cinema before narrowing to explore how the horror genre specifically was engaging with both this event and its traumatic aftermath. With reference to different stylistic camerawork that has become popular in horror cinema post-9/11, I will then move on to examine the concept of 'bystander footage' and its centrality in both real-life coverage of world events and in relation to found footage horror: in particular the much criticised 'unbelievability' of continuing to record in the midst of destruction and death. The aftereffects of 9/11 within the United States, in addition to the horror of 9/11 itself, stand as one of the most resonant national traumas in recent American history. Despite this, in post-9/11 North American found footage horror cinema, the actual event of 9/11 is not always explicitly referenced; it is a more insidious fear and a palpable sense of dread and paranoia that this chapter will begin to uncover, and which the films selected for this part of the book engage with.

## Horror with a message(?)

Within this part of the book, I will offer readings of several films that relate their aesthetics and themes to 9/11 and its aftermath. I do not present my readings as the singular and definitive 'meanings' of these films, but as possible ones. I mentioned in the introduction of this book some criticisms that have been aimed at cultural studies or trauma theory-based readings of horror cinema, and I bring the topic up again as these critiques are particularly rife when it comes to allegorical readings of post-9/11 horror films specifically. In the wake of 9/11, and that event's undeniable psychological, social, political and emotional impact, there was a renewed vigour towards trauma studies perspectives in film scholarship. The impact of 9/11 and the subsequent War on Terror on popular cultural forms has been the subject of several monographs and edited collections. Examples of these include *Film and Television After 9/11* (Dixon, 2004), *Reframing 9/11: Film, Popular Culture and the 'War on Terror'* (Birkenstein, Froula and Randell, 2010), *Post-9/11 Cinema: Through a Lens Darkly* (Markert, 2011), *Parallel Lines: Post-9/11 American Cinema* (Westwell, 2014), *9/11: The Visual Culture of Disaster* (Stubblefield, 2014) and *American Cinema in the Shadow of 9/11* (McSweeney, 2017) among others. Additionally, there has been a wealth of journal articles published on the subject (Rehak, 2011; Walliss and Aston, 2011 and Riegler, 2016 to indicate only a few). Particular attention too has been paid to the impact these events had on the horror genre, with monographs and edited collections such as *Horror After 9/11: World of Fear, Cinema of Terror* (Briefel and Miller, 2011), *Post-9/11 Horror in American Cinema* (Wetmore Jr, 2012), *To See the Saw*

*Movies: Essays on Torture Porn and Post-9/11 Horror* (Aston and Walliss, 2013), *Post-9/11 Heartland Horror: Rural Horror Films in an Age of Urban Terrorism* (McCollum, 2016) and *Troubling Masculinities: Terror, Gender, and Monstrous Others in American Film Post-9/11* (Donnar, 2020) to name a few. However, I would argue that the growth in scholarship that focused on the connection between 9/11 and the horror genre was equalled by academic work that sought to undermine or dismiss these readings.

This is not to say that some of these criticisms were not sound. Aviva Briefel and Sam Miller, for example, note that allegorical readings can be 'overly formulaic' (2011: 5) and that quite often, more nuance is required. I would agree that there is indeed a danger when examining the relationship between 9/11 and horror cinema of falling into a 'direct-ratio approach' (Briefel and Miller, 2011: 5) and making connections that are at best tenuous, and at worst potentially offensive. For instance, Kevin Wetmore Jr's likening of Marlena's death in *Cloverfield* (2008) to a 'monstrous suicide bomber' (2012: 52), and his comparison of the 9/11 hijackers to 'slasher film killers' (2012: 200), strike me as overreaching.[2] Another reasonable concern regarding allegorical readings can be found in Steve Jones's (2013) volume on torture horror, in which he notes that directly relating this subgenre to the War on Terror impedes debate as this 'pins torture horror down to that epoch, thereby invalidating the subgenre's lasting relevance' (2013: 63). Although this part of *Blood on the Lens* is focused on how found footage horror used key visual and narrative markers related to 9/11 and the War on Terror (and as such is essentially tying the films in this and the following two chapters to those events), I would also note that the first part of this book engaged with the subgenre's continual return to documentary conventions and discussed how found footage horror has evolved in tandem with these. Similarly, the next part of this book will discuss how the subgenre has made use of computer-based technology and social media. I am not arguing therefore that found footage horror is pinned to one cultural epoch, but rather to many, which is part of its appeal and key to its longevity.

A key critique of allegorical or cultural studies readings is that this kind of analysis focuses on the connections between a film and the culture in which it was made at the detriment of other factors, such as economic and industrial contexts. Mark Bernard, for example, refutes what he sees as an overreliance on allegorical readings in film studies, noting that these are often carried out 'without due consideration given to the industrial and technological factors that play a role in what types of films are produced, distributed and widely seen by audiences' (2014: 31). An element that

Bernard undermines, however, is directorial intent. This is seen clearly in his claim that Eli Roth's director's commentary track for *Hostel: Part II* (2007) – in which Roth claims the film is politically charged[3] – is 'ideological waffling', particularly when viewed in conjunction with Roth's inconsistent claims regarding his own political stance on various issues such as the death penalty (2014: 105). Bernard also more broadly discusses the work of the so called 'Splat Pack' – a group of directors who emerged in the early 2000s and worked primarily in the torture horror subgenre – and how their films, particularly *Hostel*, were often read as being related to the War on Terror and images of torture from Abu Ghraib. This is a reading Bernard refutes, asserting that 'Horror films are not "political manifestos" but rather, commercial commodities placed on the market with one ultimate goal in mind: to generate profit' (2014: 5).[4] Of course, I doubt anyone enters filmmaking with the intention of living up to the stereotype of the starving artist, but the question must be raised: why can't horror be both?

## Searching the wreckage: the paranoid landscape of post-9/11 America

David L. Altheide proposes that since 9/11, a 'discourse of fear' has dominated the cultural landscape of America. Altheide goes on to explain that this discourse, and the 'safety rhetoric' espoused by government officials in the wake of the terror attacks, has been used to promote 'the politics of fear and numerous surveillance practices and rationales to keep us safe' (2010: 19). Using Altheide's argument, I will, in this section and for the rest of this chapter, explore the psychological and cultural landscape of the United States following 9/11 to elucidate the context that the films featured in this part of the book were responding to. Particular attention is paid here to how cultural anchors of reference involving 9/11 and the War on Terror were distilled both visually and narratively into horror, and other forms of cinema.

In terms of the traumatic impact of 9/11, we cannot ignore the enormous death toll, with almost 3,000 individuals losing their lives during the attacks (Bridge and Stastna, 2011; Shortell, 2015). This number includes those on the four passenger planes involved, people in the World Trade Center and surrounding area, and a great many of the first responders who died when the towers collapsed. Also included are those who perished at the Pentagon when it was attacked on the same morning and the occupants of United Airlines 93. In addition to this staggering number of deaths, thousands more were injured. It would be no exaggeration then, nor a sensationalist claim, to suggest that the sheer amount of lives lost on 9/11 alone would have profoundly affected America. This would, however, be discounting the traumas that followed, and the legacy of trauma that continues today. Several individuals, for instance, have been successful in claiming compensation for respiratory illnesses thought to have been caused by the dust and toxic materials in the air following the collapse of the World Trade Center buildings (Barry, 2006), while a number of people have died as a result of these aftereffects (Stephen, 2007; Walters, 2016). Similar to the lasting impact of the atomic bomb attacks on both Hiroshima and Nagasaki, the death toll for 9/11 continues to rise years after the event. In the immediate aftermath of the attacks, the agitated, fearful and tense atmosphere was then compounded when several letters containing anthrax spores were posted to various media workers and to the offices of Senator Daschle and Senator Leahy a mere week after the devastation in New York. Twenty-two people were subsequently diagnosed with anthrax poisoning as a direct result of these letters, with five of these individuals dying (Cole, 2003: ix). America was a country made fearful of even opening its mail, and the Bush administration-approved War on Terror was set into motion soon after. The War on Terror then in turn reaped thousands of military and civilian deaths through the conflicts in Afghanistan and Iraq, adding to the litany of traumas that befell the United States in the first decade of the twenty-first century.[5]

What followed in the wake of 9/11, the anthrax letters and the beginning of the War on Terror was what Linnie Blake has referred to as 'an effective suspension of many long-prized civil and political rights in the United States' (2008: 130). One example of this was the initiation of the Patriot Act of 2001, which was intended to strengthen the security controls of America. This act resulted in fundamental changes to Americans' civil liberties, made in the name of safety, and to protect against the now allegedly immediate threat of terrorism. This was seen by some as 'the dismantling of the Bill of Rights' (Froula, 2010: 196), with changes made to Americans' right to freedom of information, freedom of speech and the right to liberty (Dixon, 2004: 1–2). The changes made under the Patriot Act included the indefinite detention of any 'alien' believed by the Attorney General to be capable of carrying out a terrorist act, and the allowance of the confiscation of property belonging to any foreign person believed to have been involved in terrorism. It also included permitting the use of National Security Letters (NSLs), which allow the FBI to search telephone, email and financial records without first obtaining a court order.[6] Understandably, due to the recent trauma of 9/11 and the introduction of these new measures, there was a new sense of vulnerability in America. This vulnerability was not only due to the profound loss of life that America had experienced, but also from living under what was presented as the ever present threat of imminent terrorist attack.[7] New York City in particular became 'a place not so much of death as the terror of death' (McGrath, 2005: 1). In the wake of these traumas, and in this climate of death, paranoia, bioterrorism and destruction, America did indeed find itself living in the culture of fear that David L. Altheide speaks of, with terrorism becoming 'the new marker of dread in the twenty-first century' (Thompson, 2007: 17). It is prudent at this point to explore how North American cinema more broadly, and the horror genre specifically, began to respond to these post-9/11 cultural anxieties, in order to – in the following two chapters – examine the specificities of found footage horror's engagement.

## Fear on screen: cinema and horror post-9/11 – a brief overview

In the wake of 9/11 several films were significantly edited or reshot to remove scenes featuring the World Trade Center towers, such as *Men in Black II* (2002), or their presence was digitally removed, such as in the case of *Zoolander* (2001) and *Serendipity* (2001) (Schneider, 2004: 36). *Collateral Damage* (2002) had its release date moved back due to themes of terrorism, while other films such as *Behind Enemy Lines* (2001) and *Black Hawk Down* (2001) were moved forward, perhaps due to the belief that their 'highly militaristic displays of patriotism' (Markovitz, 2004: 201) would appeal to an American public living in a 'bleak landscape of personal loss, paranoia, and political cynicism' (Dixon, 2004: 3). These two films, along with *Windtalkers* (2002), were said to have also received 'considerable assistance from the Pentagon in exchange for script changes to ensure favourable representations of the military' (Westwell, 2014: 9). It would take several years, however, before Hollywood engaged with 9/11 directly, for example through *United 93* (2006) and *World Trade Center* (2006) – and indirectly, such as in the repeated references to terrorism, images of downed planes and posters of missing people in *War of the Worlds* (2005). Debate was had over the 'propriety' of representing 9/11 on screen (Sterritt, 2004: 65) and the delay in featuring 9/11 in films was influenced perhaps by how earlier attempts to engage with the event, such as *11'09"01 September 11* (2002) had been criticised as 'stridently anti-American'

(Godard, 2002). In terms of representations of terror attacks, a particularly intriguing development in American cinema post-9/11 has been the emergence of what has been termed as 'terrorsploitation' (Sherwin, 2016), such as the . . . *Has Fallen* series of films (2013–). These films are action thrillers that explicitly deal with terror attacks on governments, where the lone ex-military protagonist Mike Branning will almost singlehandedly defeat terrorist uprisings. The . . . *Has Fallen* series came under fire for its seemingly xenophobic leanings, demonstrated in *London Has Fallen* (2016), when Mike Branning tells a terrorist to 'head back to fuckheadistan or wherever it is you're from', and which led to the film being condemned as 'jingoistic' (Schager, 2016) and 'approaching flat-out racism' (Heritage, 2016). These films, of course, follow a tradition of action movies with either explicit or implicit right-wing ideologies, such as *Missing in Action* (1984), *Invasion U.S.A.* (1985), *Rules of Engagement* (2000), *We Were Soldiers* (2002) and in particular the cinematic adaptations of the novels of Tom Clancy, such as *Patriot Games* (1992).[8]

The themes present in terrorsploitation cinema, such as the fear of imminent attack or morally compromised government agencies, are however remarkably similar to those found in post-9/11 horror cinema, and this stands as evidence of the prevalence of these anxieties in American culture. Despite this, the two types of films engage with these fears in markedly different ways, primarily through their characterisation of the American Army and government, which although admittedly often in a state of flux in horror cinema, are now presented in an overarchingly negative light. In post-9/11 horror films, the military are cast as mindless dupes committing atrocities by following orders, often enacting scorched earth contingencies at the behest of faceless governmental superiors and at the cost of civilian lives. This portrayal of the American Army in horror cinema sits in a position of contention when compared to the wider portrayal of the War on Terror, the way that those who serve in the American military are seen on the majority of mainstream news channels, and the initial burst of patriotism in the wake of 9/11 (Prividera, 2006). In this immediate aftermath of 9/11, America became a place where at worst 'even raising questions is considered unpatriotic' (Chang, 2002), and where at best the idea of patriotism was problematised by dissenting views on the ethical implications of a War on Terror. Agnieszka Soltysik Monnet suggests that the negative characterisation of the Army in post-9/11 horror cinema might be a result of the discovery of atrocities occurring during the War on Terror, such as the 2006 Al Ishaqi massacre, or the group rape and murder of a 14-year-old girl in Muhmudiyah in the same year (2015: 124). It may also reflect a wider cynicism in relation to the legitimacy and morality of the War on Terror itself. Connected to this characterisation of the Army, there is a distinct fear emerging in post-9/11 horror of not only becoming collateral damage, seen in films such as *Cloverfield*, but more specifically of the military, government and media actively working towards covering up their involvement in your death. These particular fears and anxieties are at the forefront of films analysed in the following two chapters in particular.

Professor Robert J. Thompson, barely over a month after 9/11, stated to *The New York Times* that

> The horror movie is just sitting there waiting to deal with this [. . .] It is one of the most versatile genres out there, a universal solvent of virtually any news issue. And it is now perfectly positioned to cop some serious attitude, to play a role where it's not simply a date movie but [. . .] the horror movie as metaphor. (Quoted in Lyman, 2001)

Although I would argue that the horror movie is rarely 'simply a date movie', it did not take long for the genre to begin to pick at the edges of 9/11, the War on Terror and the culture of paranoia and fear in America. As Kevin Wetmore Jr notes, 'the scope of death on September 11 brought home the reality and possibility of death at the hands of people who did not know you and were not targeting you specifically' (2012: 84). This threat of random death is present in films such as *The Strangers*, where a masked assailant answers the question of why they are attacking a young couple specifically with the reply 'because you were home'. *The Purge* series also deals with the threat of random violence through its construction of an annual 'Purge Night', where all crime is legal and emergency services are suspended. Of course, representations of death, random or otherwise, are not particularly strong evidence to argue that these films are dealing with the aftermath of 9/11 specifically. Agnieszka Soltysik Monnet, however, argues that 'The suspension of civil rights in the US and the outright abuse of the human rights of detainees and civilians abroad have stirred anxieties far more subtle and profound than the fear of terrorist attack' (2015: 131). We can see these more subtle anxieties most clearly in post-9/11 horror through the imagery of torture horror, which has been read as being directly influenced in particular by images showing human rights violations in Abu Ghraib (Prince, 2009; Hallam, 2010; Middleton, 2010; Kattelman, 2010; Zimmer, 2011, Kerner, 2015 among many others). More broadly, Douglas Kellner sees a connection between 'the violence and brutality of the era' and torture horror narratives and aesthetics (2010: 7).

In post-millennial society, images once seen as unusual, then, have taken on a new familiarity. In addition to images of torture, photographs and footage relating to bioterrorism, contagion and viruses have become increasingly common. For example, commuters wearing protective facemasks, trucks bearing the logo of the Center for Disease Control or glimpses of emergency containment tents during viral outbreaks. In the years following 9/11 these images stemmed primarily from the Anthrax panic, and also from the SARS outbreak of 2002–2003.[9] Contemporary horror cinema responded energetically to these new cultural markers of fear. For example, films such as *Dreamcatcher* (2003), *Land of the Dead* (2005), *Mulberry Street* (2006), *28 Weeks Later* (2007), *The Mist* (2007), *World War Z* (2013) and the remake of *The Crazies* (2010) all contain images of armed paramilitary, emergency lighting, sirens, gasmasks, containment protocols and characters wearing hazardous material suits. These films also engage with some of the themes this chapter has mentioned so far, such as bioterrorism, the destruction of towns and cities, paranoia and the fear of living under constant threat.

In the aftermath of 9/11, there seemed to be an immediate need to place the attacks into a frame of understanding, in order to narrativise the event. Laura Frost has connected this desire to make sense of 9/11 to the comparisons made on the day and since between the real images of devastation and filmic images of destruction, proposing that this was part of a 'cognitive effort to integrate 9/11 into the order of things by establishing a collective, public understanding of the events' (2011: 15). Linnie Blake, taking her cue from trauma theory, suggests that following the Vietnam War there was a similar drive towards fitting that war's trauma into a redemptive narrative arc in order to comprehend it fully, and to bind the wounds caused to the nation's psyche (2008: 74). What is especially significant here, in Blake's analysis, is her argument that the attempt to bind the wounds of Vietnam was premature, causing the trauma to spill into 1970s horror cinema. I similarly advance that the rush to bind the metaphorical wounds inflicted by 9/11 has resulted in the trauma caused by the event bleeding into contemporary horror cinema, where the language of horror facilitates the representation of these wounds, both visually and narratively, in a way that other genres cannot. In other words, and to borrow Thomas Elsaesser's phrase, the horror genre is a place to 'represent the unrepresentable' (2001: 195). The drive towards placing 9/11 into a narrative that Frost and Blake discern can be seen in the news coverage of the event (Mandell, 2001), and Jay David Bolter has proposed that this may be because 'an event that has not been narrativised constitutes a source of anxiety' (2005: 12). It was not only in news media where these attempts were made however, and in Lee Jarvis's (2011) analysis of the website Wherewereyou.org he discusses the recurrence of ordinary individuals' attempts to make sense of 9/11 by placing it as part of a longer ongoing story. Jarvis then moves to explain how contributors' interpretations of the events went beyond the limits of dominant discourse. This website is fascinating precisely because it offers an alternative or counter version of 9/11 from the 'official' discourse, and this is a concept that will reappear in my analysis in the following two chapters of *Quarantine, Diary of the Dead, The Bay* and *The Conspiracy*. Another recurrent element from the first entry on Wherewereyou.org on 15 September 2001, to the last entry before the website closed to submissions on 14 September 2002, is a continual theme of fear. Whether this be a fear of further terror attacks, fear of the impact of retributory actions from the United States or fear of bioterrorism. Within America there was a 'general sense of hysteria, fear, and paranoia' (Phillips, 2005: 196). It is this undercurrent of fear and terror which horror cinema engages with, and that I have identified in this part of the book's case studies. Horror cinema emerges here as 'a rare protected space in which to critique the tone and content of public discourse' (Briefel and Miller, 2011: 3). As Stacey Abbott advances, 'The events of 9/11 and their depiction on screen [. . .] have become a prism through which we understand the language of twenty-first-century apocalypse' (Abbott, 2016: 76). The films I will go on to examine in the next two chapters use the frantic and unsteady frames of found footage horror to engage with the overarching feeling in North America post-9/11 that apocalyptic terror was close, and they do so by using a new visual language of fear, which is referent to our mediated experience of 9/11.

## A new visual language of terror: bystander footage and the (un)believability of continuing to tape

Two quite distinct kinds of camera aesthetic came to prominence within the horror genre in the years following 9/11. Firstly, there was a distinct rise in the use of static surveillance-style cameras in the genre. Catherine Zimmer has noted the relationship between surveillance technology and torture horror in the *Saw* series (2004–), proposing that this kind of camera style 'blurs the distinction between who is the subject or object of torture' (2011: 89). Similarly, Steve Jones has also discerned 'surveillance's sinister function' (2013: 106) in his analysis of *Detour* (2009). Within found footage horror cinema, the *Paranormal Activity* series is perhaps the most enamoured with the surveillance look, with *Paranormal Activity 2*, for example, being conveyed almost exclusively through various security cameras. Many subsequent found footage horror films have emulated this franchise's model of combining surveillance-style footage with the paranormal, for example: *21 Days* (2014), *The Unfolding* (2016) and *The Blackwell Ghost* (2017) to name only a small selection. The security camera aesthetic also features heavily in *Apartment 143* and *Closed Circuit Extreme* (2012). David Lyon has suggested that following 9/11, we became far more aware of just how often we are captured on CCTV (2007: 11), but public reception to increased surveillance, however, is complex. Adam Penenberg (2001) argues that the American public generally viewed surveillance as a benign and even reassuring presence in the wake of 9/11, but as Steen Christiansen demonstrates through his analysis of 'uncanny cameras' in found footage horror, this desire for a presumed safety through surveillance is 'exposed as also being an anxiety' (2015: 49). Christiansen concludes his account by noting that our familiarity with seeing surveillance-style footage, 'in a culture where CCTV cameras are omnipresent and the news is filling with surveillance footage of criminal acts' (2015: 48), has meant that we have become accustomed to the look of surveillance feeds. He then goes on to suggest that the strange and unnerving quality that this kind of footage once possessed is no longer present, and that the style is 'slowly receding into the background of our media relations as simply one mode of image presentation' (2015: 48). Unlike surveillance-style footage, which has – if we follow Christiansen's argument – become less effective in a horror context due to audience familiarity, it is precisely audience familiarity with the 'look' of bystander footage – through its inclusion on mainstream news broadcasts from various world events and our recognition of its power as a conveyer of terror – that is key to its effectiveness in horror cinema. The cultural experience of 9/11 was, and continues to be, lived through the lens of other people's cameras, and in many ways the aesthetics of 9/11 bystander footage has taught audiences to accept this kind of amateur filming as authentic and truthful. Our repeated exposure to this type of footage has resulted in its adoption by found footage horror as a mode we recognise as real: whether this be footage filmed from a safe distance of the Twin Towers burning, or the more frantic and handheld footage captured by people caught up in the events on the ground. It is this second kind of bystander footage – characterised by imperfect framing, obstructed vision, hysteric commentary and grainy resolution – that found footage horror emulates most forcefully. Susan Sontag has argued that 'pictures of hellish events seem more authentic when they don't have the look that comes across from being "properly" lighted and composed' (2003: 26–7) and – as I argued in Chapter 2 – these imperfections are certainly utilised by the found footage horror subgenre. The jolting, shaking and sometimes unfocused nature of handheld footage in particular limits how much the audience can see, as a person running while holding a camera is unlikely to be able to keep it steady. This is common in real-life footage from 9/11, where camera operators were often not filming events from a distance, but caught up in crowds fleeing from the dark and portentous cloud of debris rushing through Manhattan after the collapse of the towers, their footage confusing, erratic, jostled and frantic.

However, the continually recording protagonists of found footage horror have invited criticism, as many argue that continuing to tape in a life or death situation is unbelievable (McHargue, 2012; Seitz, 2012; Schedeen, 2012; O'Keefe, 2014). I argue that the sheer amount of amateur footage in existence from 9/11 surely stands as evidence that in a crisis, people do indeed continue to record. Many found footage horror films feature a camera operator who will be repeatedly told to put their cameras down only to answer that they are 'documenting' (Hudd from *Cloverfield*), that it is 'the only proof we have' (Angela in *Quarantine*) or insist that 'this could be evidence' (Nick from *Followers*). This desire to keep on recording is shown as overriding any other instinct. This compulsion, for a camera operator to continue to film even when their life is in danger, is examined by Amy West (2005), who discusses the legacy of 'low-tech' actuality filming by critiquing the popular trope of 'caught on tape' video clip shows. West assesses a piece of footage in which the camera operator persists in their recording of a dangerous mudslide despite being in grave danger. West explains that as the mudslide comes perilously close to the operator, 'it becomes something special, and the impulse to continue recording is predicated on a palpable desire to capture something rare, powerful, and fleeting' (2005: 87). Furthermore, to explain the compulsion to record, we can also examine Andrew Schopp's argument that looking through the lens of a camera may be a type of mediation which provides 'a sense of control, even safety' (2004: 125). This is highlighted too by Thomas Stubblefield, who similarly proposes that

> the camera's presence at the scene of the catastrophe is typically read in terms of a defence mechanism which safely removes the subject from a scene that is too great [. . .] this phenomenon is understood in terms of a failure to fully comprehend let alone experience the reality before the lens. (2014: 27)

This concept, of a reality once removed by way of a camera lens, is touched upon too in the dialogue of *The Blair Witch Project*, where after relieving Heather of her camera and putting a stop to her constant recording, Josh informs her that he can now understand why she likes looking through the camera so much, because – as he puts it – 'it's like filtered reality'. There is also a connection to be found between the compulsion to tape and the idea of the image as fetish. A repeated line in a great deal of real bystander footage, not only from 9/11 but other catastrophes too – and indeed in found footage horror cinema itself – is 'did you get that on film'. As E. Ann Kaplan reveals, when speaking of her own need to document New York City after 9/11, there was a 'desire to make real what I could barely comprehend' (2003: 95). Author David Friend also notes his impulse to film the aftermath of 9/11, stating that he felt 'only rendering this act visually would confirm its reality' (2011: xi). There was a need, then, for clarity and understanding in the wake of the destruction, and a desire to 'slow down and make sense of an event that happened too fast' (Stubblefield, 2014: 30). The use of the camera as a tool that can help document and make sense of what is unfolding around characters often features in found footage horror narratives. Characters will repeatedly ask if their camera operator caught an event, both to check it has been committed to film and perhaps to confirm to themselves that it actually happened. Brigid Cherry relates this need to capture and own the image to *Cloverfield* specifically, which she describes as 'the ultimate movie for people who don't feel a cataclysm has happened until they can videotape it, upload it and stream it live to the rest of the world' (2009: 194). As Cherry notes, we live in an era where 'nothing it seems is "real" until it has been recorded and replayed' (2009: 194).

## Conclusion

Condoleezza Rice, the National Security Advisor to President Bush from 2001–5, has stated that 11 September 2001 'was one of those rare dates that forever divides history into distinct categories of before and after [. . .] We commonly hear the refrain that everything changed on September 11th. In many ways that is true' (Rice, 2001). In some ways, this book is further evidence of that statement, taking as it does – at least in this part of the book – the event of 9/11 as a starting point for a particular kind of found footage horror 'look' and set of prominent narrative themes. There are, of course, several comparative links that can be drawn between found footage horror aesthetics and the bystander footage that emerged from 9/11: both can be characterised as being made up of frantic, panicked and unsteady amateur footage which imperfectly conveys images of terror, and there is – as I began to outline in Chapter 2 – an artlessness to this footage which underlines its horror. This includes poor audio capture, reduced quality of vision or events being out of focus or not even in frame. These imperfections remain key signifiers of authenticity in found footage horror cinema throughout its history, and as Mark Freeman explains, 'the foregrounding of aesthetic imperfection has by its very difference, come to suggest concepts of immediacy, verisimilitude, truth' (2015: 11). The found footage aesthetic has become so prominent as a way to represent real-life horrific events that it has found its way into non-horror films too. The aforementioned *United 93*, for instance, uses a handheld aesthetic throughout, but this is particularly effective (and affective) in the scenes showing the initial takeover of the plane, and in the closing sequence when passengers overcome the hijackers. The bombing sequence in *Patriots Day* (2016), too, not only features real surveillance footage from the Boston Marathon bombing in 2013 (Awan, 2017), but employs a distinctly found footage aesthetic – frantic handheld shots, impaired sound and the lens of a fallen camera continuing to record – to convey the panic and terror of the aftermath.

This chapter opened with a discussion of 9/11 itself and reportage of that event, before moving on to examine the culture of fear and mistrust that grew in its wake and which had a lasting effect on American culture, society and politics. The impact of this is still relevant today, with Kendall Phillips, for example, noting that 'Recent polls of Americans have consistently found levels of trust in government and other institutions in decline' (2021: 2). Stephen Prince has argued, however, that 'The most significant long-term influence of the terrorist attacks of 9/11, and of the Iraq war that followed, is likely to be found in the provision of new templates for genre filmmaking' (2009: 286). This influence can be seen in post-9/11 found footage horror cinema's use of 9/11 bystander footage as a 'template' for its aesthetics. For, although there were shaky handheld scenes in found footage horror before 9/11, they have since taken on much more of a specific bystander footage look. It is difficult to look at the scenes in *Cloverfield*, for example, where characters run through the streets of Manhattan from a huge cloud after an explosion, and not think about images very much like them in the reportage from 9/11. The influence of the terror attacks and their aftermath have also resulted in North American horror cinema's confrontation of the 'mood [. . .] in the nation becoming much more psychological and internal, shifting to the more insidious and subtle dynamics of paranoia and dread' (Frost, 2011: 15).

Whether an allegorical reading of films such as *Quarantine*, *The Bay*, *Diary of the Dead* or *The Conspiracy* was encouraged or intended by the filmmakers or not,[10] I offer an analysis in the following two chapters that presents these films as underlining a fear that we are all secondary to institutional interests, and that 'during a crisis, the military would be permitted exceptional and extraordinary powers, such as killing civilians to protect themselves or a higher imperative' (Monnet, 2015: 131). Overarchingly, the films I will now go on to examine engage with the creeping dread that 'we are all collateral' (Pease, 2007: 71) and highlight anxieties that had been stirred in the wake of the Patriot Act of 2001, the War on Terror and unease around an increasingly surveilled society. In these films, although the main threats are fictional, the real fear is of powerful institutions leaving you to die.

## Notes

1 Trump's campaign rhetoric was steeped in xenophobia, and along with endorsing the murder of terrorists' families (Matharu, 2016), he attempted to paint the Muslim faith as radical, extreme and dangerous, with the only real answer to terror threats being more surveillance and less 'political correctness' (Weigel, 2016).
2 Laura Mee (2022) puts forward an excellent critique of the pitfalls of these kinds of readings.
3 This is an argument that Roth has presented regarding his larger body of work elsewhere too (see Boult, 2013 and Rowat, 2013).
4 It should be noted here that Bernard is making reference in this quote to the work of Peter Hutchings, who noted that horror films are not 'political manifestos bearing a cohesive ideological message; they are horror films designed to provoke emotional responses from audiences, and whatever social-critical elements they might contain tend to get mixed up, often in a very messy way, with the sadistic-masochistic thrills that the films are also offering' (2004: 123). I might be tempted, then, to rephrase my follow up question as 'Why can't horror be all three?' – a political manifesto that works as a commercial commodity and also offers sadistic/masochistic thrills.
5 I am in no way suggesting that America was the only country to suffer trauma at this time, and acknowledge that America was indeed responsible for traumas suffered by many other countries in the wake of 9/11.
6 Although NSLs existed long before 9/11, the Patriot Act imbued them with much more power, enabling them to be used against US citizens and containing a gag order to prevent the target of the NSL ever knowing they were under surveillance. If they did become aware, this also limited their ability to tell anyone else about it, with no probable cause being required to request an NSL.

7 Thomas A. Pyszczynski, Jeff Greenberg and Sheldon Solomon have explored the psychology of terror extensively in their volume, *In the Wake of 9/11: The Psychology of Terror* (2003), which analyses wider reactions to the attacks through an engagement with terror management theory. The book examines post-threat cognition and emotion in depth.
8 The films of S. Craig Zahler, too, which include *Bone Tomahawk* (2015), *Brawl in Cell Block 99* (2017) and *Dragged Across Concrete* (2018), have been criticised as being 'vile, racist right wing fantasy' (Stern, 2018) among other terms (see Sims, 2019).
9 Since then there has been the West African Ebola outbreak (2013–16), and much more recently these kinds of images have become terrifyingly familiar once more due to the Covid-19 pandemic, which provided photographs and footage of mass burials in New York City (Lewis, 2021) and mass cremations in India (Barnes, 2021).
10 In *The Conspiracy*, the connections Christopher MacBride is making to 9/11 are made explicit through dialogue and images, while George A. Romero has stated that *Diary of the Dead* was inspired by a mixture of media over the past decade, and noted that he purposefully referenced 9/11 in the radio reports heard during the hospital scenes in the film (Dawson, 2008). I cannot, however, find any evidence of a specific connection to 9/11 or its aftermath that has been stated by Barry Levinson or John Erick Dowdle in reference to their respective films.

# 6

# 'They're going to let us die': trust in found footage horror

*Quarantine* is both a remake of a Spanish film, *[Rec]*, and simultaneously a film that is a product of distinctly American anxieties, for although it shares similarities with the original film, it is not an unequivocal duplication. For example, an interesting alteration was made concerning the origin of the contagion in the narrative. In *Quarantine*, the infection is a form of accelerated rabies that has been developed by a tenant in the apartment building the characters become trapped within; towards the end of the film, we see newspaper clippings in their home relating to a doomsday cult stealing the virus from a chemical weapons laboratory. This origin stands in contrast to the story of the original film, in which an agent of the Vatican, who has isolated the supposed viral cause of demonic possession, has developed the virus. Jaume Balagueró, the co-writer and co-director of *[Rec]*, was reportedly displeased with this movement from virus of religious origin to one of biochemical threat, and Javier Botet, an actor in *[Rec]*, stated 'I don't understand why they avoided the religious themes in the movie. They lost a very important part of the end' (Turek, 2009). Throughout this chapter I will call attention to several further changes *Quarantine* makes to the narrative of *[Rec]*. I do this not to compare and contrast *Quarantine* to *[Rec]* and ultimately champion *Quarantine* as the more valuable film, or to suggest that it is in any way more clearly engaged with the global impact of 9/11, as *[Rec]* could well be presented as an example of how the event was being processed outside of North America. Instead, I position these changes as being made to perhaps specifically resonate with the anxieties of an American audience, through *Quarantine*'s more explicit construction of fear around the military, governmental agendas and media agencies.

Within this chapter, I will compare *Quarantine* at several points to the documentary film *9/11*, which was released in 2002 and consists mainly of footage filmed by two cameras belonging to French-American brothers Jules and Gédéon Naudet. The Naudet brothers, along with New York firefighter James Hanlon, were shadowing a probationary firefighter named Tony Benetatos, and their original intention was to make a film about his experiences in this new role. On 11 September 2001, the brothers' cameras captured unprecedented footage from inside a disaster. The film includes footage from inside and outside the North Tower of the World Trade Center as the South Tower was hit, and one of only two pieces of footage known to exist showing American Airlines Flight 11 striking the North Tower. The film stands therefore as not only a significant piece of documentary filmmaking, but also as a piece of American history, its place cemented by the inclusion of Jules Naudet's camera in the Smithsonian Museum in Washington, DC. In keeping with this book's commitment to explore how found footage horror cinema is representative of national trauma, a comparison of *Quarantine* and the significant historical document that is *9/11* is an important and valuable addition.

The narrative of *Quarantine* details the containment of an apartment building in Los Angeles, after an accelerated form of rabies is discovered to be infecting its occupants. The audience follows Angela and Scott, a local news reporter and her cameraman, as they film footage originally intended for the late night cable television show they work for, following a team of two firefighters on a night shift. They accompany the fire crew on what appears to be a low risk call out to an apartment block, but once inside they are trapped as the building has been quarantined. Representatives from the Center for Disease Control, as well as emergency services and news vans, are outside the building, but no information is forthcoming to the contained group. Throughout the film, the group's attempts to gather information are quashed, and with a growing military presence assembling around the apartment building, they realise that they will not be allowed to leave there alive.

It is necessary to note that given *Quarantine*'s status as an American remake of a Spanish horror film, my argument that *Quarantine* relates to American anxieties specifically could be argued to be problematic, and readers might well question why I do not simply analyse *[Rec]* as an example of the global resonance of the 9/11 event. I would note however that there has been various scholarly work previously on *[Rec]*, which has focused on its representation of Spanish tabloid television (Rowan-Legg, 2013), its filming techniques (Raimondo, 2014) and style (Reyes, 2015b) and of the film as sociopolitical commentary (Goss, 2017). In addition, it has also been examined in relation to European horror more broadly (Monnet,

2015), and Spanish horror specifically (Pueyo, 2017; Lázaro-Reboll, 2017; Nichols, 2017 and Seguin, 2017 make up a four chapter section on the *[Rec]* franchise in *Tracing the Borders of Spanish Horror Cinema and Television* for example). In contrast, *Quarantine* is a clearly under-researched film which is widely ignored within academic accounts of post-9/11 American horror cinema, or dismissed due to its remake status despite its traumatic resonance with the event and aftermath of 9/11. This chapter will demonstrate how the relocation of the narrative to the United States and a reworking of the original film provides an overt engagement with both the event of 9/11 and *9/11* the documentary. This chapter begins then by examining a convention that has become common to found footage horror, the inadvertent witnessing of events by people who did not actively seek them out. Just like the Naudet brothers, Angela and Scott of *Quarantine* begin the film with one assignment in mind and have their documenting intentions thrown into disarray by the intrusion of the extraordinary.

## 'They're not going to let us out of here alive, are they?': inadvertent witnesses

Within *Quarantine*, Angela and Scott are accidentally caught up in horrific events: they did not actively seek out the possibility of danger. Although there are several found footage horror films, such as *The Tunnel*, *The Dyatlov Pass Incident* (2013), *Crowsnest* (2012), *Mr. Jones* (2013) and *As Above, So Below*, where characters actively seek out risk or ignore warnings regarding potential hazards, the framing of Angela and Scott as inadvertent witnesses to horror is common to the subgenre. This inadvertent witnessing is also one of the first ways in which *Quarantine* is linked to the documentary film *9/11*. We follow Angela and Scott for an extended period of time before they, and the firefighters they are shadowing – Jake and Fletcher – arrive at their first callout. For around fifteen minutes we watch Angela and Scott spend time getting to know the firefighters, much like the initial scenes in *9/11*, which show Jules and Gédéon Naudet spending time with the firefighters at the Manhattan firehouse they are filming at. The Naudet brothers are shown cooking at the firehouse, speaking to its firefighters and joking around as they document how Tony Benetatos – the probationary firefighter whose journey they are following – begins to gain acceptance and respect from his colleagues, all of this occurring before the events of 9/11 take place. There is also an emphasis on waiting; for example, at an early point in *Quarantine*, when Angela and Scott wait for a callout to come into the firehouse. Angela makes it clear that she wants 'not a big one, a little call, so we can see some action'. Tony Benetatos too, early in his probationary period at the beginning of *9/11*, tells the Naudets that he is 'waiting for a fire, you know, just waiting for a fire'. The first few months of Tony's probation – July and August of 2001 – are shown to be very quiet, and his shift receives hardly any callouts.

On the morning of 11 September, Jules Naudet accompanies the fire crew to a gas leak at the corner of Church and Lispenard, while Gédéon Naudet remains at the firehouse with Tony. In a voiceover, the Naudet brothers explain that as Gédéon was the more experienced cameraman, Jules would often go with the firefighters on callouts to practice operating the camera. As the fire crew investigates the leak, there is a loud engine noise. Jules aims the camera towards the sky, and follows the path of American Airlines Flight 11 into the North Tower of the World Trade Center. During one of the many formal interviews that intersperse the footage from 9/11, Jules talks about his inadvertent capturing of the impact, remarking that 'They say there is always a witness for history. I guess that day we were chosen to be the witness.' Other individuals who directly witnessed the events of 9/11 have advanced similar sentiments. William D. Nuñez, for example – who snapped a photograph of United Airlines Flight 175 just before it hit the South Tower – wanted to capture an image of the smoking North Tower 'for history's sake'. Nuñez did not realise what he had caught on camera until the photographs were developed (Friend, 2011: 13). Similarly, Richard Drew – a professional photographer who captured the infamous 'falling man' images from 9/11 – has been specifically described as a 'witness' to the events (Junod, 2021). Although they are still photographs, these images can be – along with the footage from the Naudet documentary – understood within the tradition of 'caught on tape' that Amy West identified, and that I discussed in the previous chapter. These are examples of 'a critical coincidence of rolling camera and spontaneous or aberrant incident' (2005: 84). Just like William D. Nuñez, Richard Drew, the Naudet brothers and anyone else in Lower Manhattan on 11 September 2001, the characters of *Quarantine* are inside a newsworthy event, but no wiser for it. The lack of information and subsequent anxiety that Jules and Gédéon Naudet experience, due to their locations and proximity to unfolding events (for instance, Jules, who has been in the North Tower since shortly after the first plane's impact, goes outside and is shocked to find the South Tower collapsed), is amplified in *Quarantine* to become an intentional embargo of information from outside the apartment block.

Throughout the unfolding initial panic in *Quarantine*, Angela insists that Scott continues to tape what is going on, and keeps relatively calm and collected in the face of extraordinary circumstances. This is to be expected perhaps of a professional reporter. When she witnesses a broadcast from outside the quarantined building however, Angela becomes hysterical, realising that her position as a member of the press has no bearing on her safety or any rescue efforts to retrieve her. In this scene, a resident named Bernard and his roommate Sadie begin to sneak upstairs to their apartment, where they hope that their old analogue television will give them more information. Angela and Scott follow them and the four characters witness a news report from the street outside. The broadcast has heavy interference, the sound and vision are distorted, but this lessens enough for them to see a police chief informing reporters that the building has been evacuated. Angela begins to panic, as the police chief does this with the explicit knowledge – as police have been outside the building since it was locked down and Officer Wilensky has radioed for assistance – that this is far from the truth, and that one of his crew, Officer McCreedy, along with Fletcher, is severely injured inside the building. Angela's panic is personal too, as she has previously used her status, as a reporter inside the story, to threaten the soldiers maintaining the quarantine. For example, she yells through a window, 'Tell your boss, we have a TV crew in here! We are filming this!' This position of relative privilege is made all but redundant after the television broadcast scene, with a report running counter to her experience being seen by outside audiences. Significantly, this scene does not have an equal in *[Rec]*.

Once the residents, the reporters, the firefighters and the attending police officers are contained within the building, their mobile telephones cease to work, and their vision of outside is obscured by plastic sheeting. The only information they receive is from the aforementioned television report and educated guesses regarding the virulent infection from a resident who works as a veterinarian. Jake is seen on his radio shortly after the building is locked down and later advises the quarantined group that the incident has been classified as a 'BNC': a biological, nuclear or chemical threat, but this is the only piece of information given to them from outside.[1] As Kevin Wetmore Jr proposes, post-9/11, 'the only source of information in a horror film is the television and the rumours that other people share. The leadership is not seen or heard from. We suffer horror in a vacuum of information and nothing from the top of the social pyramid' (2012: 43). The most privileged characters in the film in terms of knowledge – the two CDC officials that enter the building two thirds of the way through the narrative – are unhelpful: withholding information and trying to force Scott to stop recording. Wetmore's comments regarding television bring *Quarantine* in line with films such as *Night of the Living Dead* (1968), in which the characters watch television for further information about the zombie outbreak they are in the midst of. However, this neat comparison is problematised, as in *Night of the Living Dead* the broadcasters are, at worst, incompetent and unknowingly giving inaccurate information. In *Quarantine* there is a far more insidious agenda at work, given that characters seen to be in charge – the police chief and the CDC – are shown to be actively lying or downplaying the situation. *Quarantine*, then, effectively speaks to a culture of growing paranoia, where the government had already pushed the boundaries of privacy and liberty under the excuse of increasing national security, and those suspected of being a threat to the country could be detained indefinitely.

After Angela realises that people receiving the television broadcast will believe it to be the truth, her efforts to record her and Scott's experience become more frantic, as does her dwindling hope that her counter version of events will ever reach an audience. After the infected begin to overrun the building, we find one of the most potent scenes in the film, where several residents, as well as Scott, Angela and Jake, lock themselves in one of the apartments. As they argue about what to do, the owner of the building, Yuri, suggests that the best idea is to 'stay here and wait until somebody comes and gets us'. Angela, incensed, shouts in response that

> They're not going to come and get us! They're not going to come and get us! They don't give a shit about us, they're going to let us die here! They don't care about us! Scott, we're going to die!

Shortly after Angela's outburst, they discover one of the CDC agents who has been bitten by an infected resident, and barricade him in a room. Bernard, who has just discovered his friend Sadie has been infected too, slices open the plastic sheeting covering the windows in a panic and leans outside to plead for help. Bernard is shot dead by a sniper on the opposite building. The camera momentarily swings wildly near the window, and we can clearly see fire engines, a CDC truck, and various firefighters and officials below. The audience have been trapped in the building with these characters for the better part of an hour, and seeing the sky is almost like a palpable breath of air. In the aftermath of Bernard's death, Angela turns to Scott's camera and almost whispers: 'They're not going to let us out of here alive, are they?'. The fear engaged with in *Quarantine* therefore is not so much of terrorism, or even of biochemical threat. It is more the unease that the institutions which repeatedly espouse that they are here to protect us would abandon us without a fight to protect their own interests.

## 'I signed up for brave and courageous': the heroic firefighter in *Quarantine* and *9/11*

The similarities between *Quarantine* and *9/11* do not cease at their inclusion of inadvertent witnessing, or at *Quarantine*'s emulation of 9/11 bystander footage. One of the longest surviving characters in the film is a firefighter, Jake, who – as Fletcher tells Angela near the beginning of the narrative – is a 'third generation engineer'. The police officers within *Quarantine* – Officers Wilensky and McCreedy – are shown as being verbally aggressive towards the residents, physically aggressive towards Scott and Angela, and borderline frenzied in a crisis, for instance when Wilensky pulls a gun on Angela. Jake, in contrast, is repeatedly presented as heroic within the narrative. In various scenes he is shown to be concerned with the welfare of other characters, and as intent on receiving answers as to why this situation has happened as Angela and Scott are. Jake is killed assisting Scott, his death brutal and bloody. This stands in opposition to the death of Jake's equal character – Manu – in *[Rec]*, who is infected offscreen. The heroic characterisation of Jake – and indeed of Fletcher, although he is taken out of action early in the film – can be compared to the presentation of the real-life firefighters in *9/11*. Similarly, the characterisation of the police within *Quarantine* – although Officer Wilensky is redeemed in his death scene: holding back the infected child, Brianna, while yelling 'Go! She's got me, go!' – is close to the portrayal of the few police officers we see in *9/11*. Within the documentary, the police are shown as being more hostile towards the Naudet brothers than the fire department, and similarly it is both Wilensky and Officer McCreedy who are the most combative towards Angela and Scott. Despite his initial belligerence however, once Wilensky suspects that a false narrative is emerging outside of the quarantined building, he is the first to defend Scott's 'right to shoot this' when a CDC officer attacks the camera. Whether firefighter or police officer, the overarching sense we receive from *Quarantine* is that Jake, Fletcher, Wilensky and McCreedy are blue collar workers who have found themselves in the middle of a horrific situation with no support from their superiors, or hope of backup.

The trope of the heroic firefighter is what Martin Randall describes as 'one of a number of compelling mythologies that rapidly arose in the aftermath [of 9/11]' (2011: 113). This relates to Susan Faludi's exploration of the 'mythic firefighter', and what she terms as the 'magnification of manly men' (2007: 14). Faludi constructs her argument around what she suggests was the 'collective media inspired retreat to American archetypes' following the terror attacks (2007: 66). Faludi's discussion centres on a belief that the glorification of heroic and traditionally masculine qualities was an attempt to erase women from the immediate memories of 9/11, Ground Zero and their legacy. While I agree with Faludi that in both the firehouses in *Quarantine* and *9/11*, women seem oddly absent,[2] I would contend that it is less the 'magnification of manly men' that is the cause of this, and that, in *9/11* at least, this may have been because at the time of the event, women made up less than 0.3 per cent of firefighters in New York (Reynolds, 2016). As can be seen in the credits of *9/11*, when the firefighters who died on that day are shown on screen; the fatalities suffered by the fire department were overarchingly white and, without exception, male. This evidence suggests that rather than a wilful underrepresentation of female firefighters by the documentary, it may be more the lack of female firefighters working in the city that contributed to their absence.

E. Ann Kaplan, in recounting her first-hand experiences of 9/11, outlines the 'gap' left behind when the Twin Towers collapsed, and explains how that gap 'was filled with other images [. . .] of firemen rushing up to rescue people and being crushed when the building collapsed' (2005: 13). Among the most iconic of these images, which have become part of our collective visual memory and understanding of 9/11, is the Thomas E. Franklin photograph of firefighters raising the American flag at Ground Zero, and Shannon Stapleton's image of firefighters carrying the body of Father Mychal Judge to the altar of St Peter's Catholic Church. In a time of grief and trauma, it is understandable that heroism of almost mythic levels was emphasised in news casting. In *9/11*, there are repeated references to the undoubtable bravery of the firefighters who attended the World Trade Center, including specific references to being a hero. Early in the film, for example, when footage is shown of several different men who were training to become probationary firefighters (and who were also considered by the Naudet brothers and Hanlon when choosing whose journey they would follow), there is a clip of Tony Benetatos considering why he wants to become a firefighter. Benetatos concludes that 'it sounds kind of cheesy, but I always wanted to be a hero, and this is the only thing you can do to do that'. The bravery of firefighters is also referenced explicitly in *Quarantine*. This happens within the opening scenes in particular. Angela, in her first scene, describes firefighters as 'a special breed of hero', and when she jokingly tells Fletcher that she thought, given his job, that he would be more dignified, he replies 'I signed up for brave and courageous, not dignified.' Again, as with the television broadcast scene I highlighted earlier, these lines are absent from [Rec]. We also spend more time in *Quarantine* with the firefighters before horrific events unfold. In comparison to [Rec], there are five more minutes – consisting of several additional scenes – before Angela, Scott and the firefighters arrive at the apartment block they will become trapped in. These extra scenes include a conversation about the firefighting 'tradition', more conversations between the reporters, Jake and Fletcher, and an amusing scene in the firehouse locker room. It is fair to say that – perhaps because we spend more time with them before they arrive at the apartment block – Jake and Fletcher are more rounded out as individual characters than their counterparts in [Rec], Alex and Manu. Fletcher is gregarious and flirtatious, Jake is more shy and reticent and there is a sense of brotherhood in the fire station as Angela and Scott meet or are in the proximity of several different firefighters as they are shown around the building. This is not overtly present in [Rec] as we simply spend far less time with the firefighters before the action begins. The addition of the above lines in *Quarantine*, along with this extra time getting to know the fire station and its occupants, stands among the ways in which *Quarantine* reworks [Rec] to imbue the narrative with an American specificity.

Robert De Niro, in his introduction of *9/11* before its first broadcast on 10 March 2002 on CBS, noted that 'what you're about to see is how brave men work under stress, surrounded by chaos'. Stef Craps wonders if – in much of the reportage of 9/11 – there was a subtle substitution of heroism for terrorism through a de-emphasis of the horror of the events and a

**Figure 6.1** Getting to know Jake and Fletcher in *Quarantine*.

converse emphasis on stories of 'grace under pressure' (2007: 190). James Berger also notices a movement in the language used around 9/11 immediately following the event, and states that the effect was 'the transformation of overwhelming loss into a kind of victory. The media soon spoke more about the heroes of September 11 than of the dead' (2003: 55). It is clear that E. Ann Kaplan is correct: the 'gap' left by the destruction of the Twin Towers was filled with heroic images of firefighters rescuing people, which have become both part of the collective images of 9/11 and anchored themselves to our cultural memory of the event. These collective images of bravery, along with the representation of the fire department on mainstream news channels following 9/11 as brave, courageous and dignified, may account for the characterisation of Jake and Fletcher in *Quarantine*. Whether intentional on behalf of the filmmakers, or merely because the fire department also featured in *[Rec]*, the resonance of a narrative concerning firefighters trapped in a doomed building, heroically trying to save members of the public and with no chance of escape, is given a unique resonance and tonality in a post-9/11 American horror film.

## 'Turn it off!': editing and crisis censorship

Throughout *Quarantine*, Angela urges Scott to 'tape everything', in order to capture evidence of their containment within the building. She and Scott find themselves in multiple arguments with the police officers present, and later with the Center for Disease Control representatives, due to their constant documentation of events. However, when a rabid dog attacks the character of Randy, Angela angrily shouts at Scott to turn the camera off, thus avoiding recording the gory aftermath. In this moment, Angela, the reporter who wants everything that is happening committed to film, is effectively censoring what the camera captures, and is actively engaging in what Laura Frost terms as 'discretionary censorship' (2011: 22). This type of discretion is another link between *Quarantine* and *9/11*, as several times in the latter film, there is a conscious decision made as to what is shown or indeed heard. This happens both in camera, by Jules Naudet, and in editing, post-production. The first occurrence of this self-censorship is when Jules Naudet enters the lobby of the North Tower with Chief Pfeifer and his crew of firefighters. Moving through the lobby's reception area, the camera abruptly swings to the left, avoiding the right-hand side of the lobby. By way of a voiceover, Jules Naudet explains, 'I hear screams, and right to my right there is two people, on fire, burning. I just didn't want to film it. It was like, no one, no one should see this.' During this voiceover, the audience, although they cannot see the people burning, can hear their screams, which continue as Chief Pfeifer and Jules Naudet leave the lobby. Jules Naudet has noted that there was an 'auto censorship' that occurred in his filming of this scene (quoted in O'Carroll, 2002). This is similar to how Angela acts as an in-camera censor in *Quarantine*, making a decision to avoid capturing Randy's bloody demise on film, and altering what the camera can visually capture, although still capturing sound. A sequence in *9/11* where it is the sound that is censored, through editing in post-production, occurs forty minutes into the film, during the time when individuals trapped on the upper floors of the World Trade Center buildings began to fall to their deaths. James Hanlon, both co-director of the film and New York City firefighter, explains in a voiceover that 'most of the people in Tower One came out on the mezzanine above the lobby. The chiefs didn't want anyone going through the lobby doors. First, it was because debris was falling outside. Then, it was people falling.' A second or two after this voiceover concludes we hear a huge crash, the noise of a high velocity impact from outside. The camera, held by Jules Naudet, spins around wildly, as if trying to place where the noise is coming from, and a muffled voice is heard saying 'Jumpers'. As Jules explains his thoughts during this time by way of another voiceover, the camera tracks over the faces of several firefighters in the lobby, who have been shocked into silence. Jules explains

> You don't see it, but you know what it is, and you know that every time you hear that crashing sound, it's a life which is extinguished. It's not something you can get used to, and the sound was so loud.

Only two impacts are heard during this sequence, with another heard later in the film. It was reported that more crashes were captured, but subsequently edited out. The producer of the film, Susan Zirinsky, specifically addressed the editing of the impact noises during a press conference, arguing that 'to have that incredible crush of sound every 20 or 30 seconds would have been very tough for the audience' (cited in de Moraes, 2002). Television critic Ken Tucker (2002) discusses this suppression of the impact noises, and notes

> I was startled to read various reports that the CBS producers who helped shape the Naudet's work actually edited out the sound of some of the bodies that fell with loud crashes as the filmmakers recorded the firefighters' rescue missions. To presume what might be in good taste – in this case, to decide that we could hear a few bodies falling to their death, but not the 'rain' of them, as one firefighter told us – is the umpteenth

example of the way network news condescends to and insults both the victims and the viewers. Why must TV always act like a national grief counsellor? Why do we always need to be lulled into comfort, rather than left deeply shaken, enlivened, or furious, when a tragedy occurs?

This element of 9/11 is still a contentious one, not least due to debates around the nature of these individual's intent, and whether the falling people made a decision to jump to their deaths of their own volition, or if they fell due to being jostled in the crowded spaces of the windows. Footage showing people falling from the towers was broadcast very briefly, before being swiftly removed from mainstream news channels; it continues to be strangely absent from a great deal of the retrospective programming about 9/11. Images and footage of falling people were subsequently pushed to internet fringe websites – which will be discussed at length in Chapter 8 – namely Rotten.com and Bestgore.com. Tom Junod has discussed how

> in a nation of voyeurs, the desire to face the most disturbing aspects of our most disturbing day was somehow ascribed to voyeurism, as though the jumpers' experience instead of being central to the horror, was tangential to it, a sideshow best forgotten. (2021)

Laura Frost connects the view that a desire to see images of the falling people is pathological or shameful directly to the role of horror cinema, as such a perceived deviant desire 'can only be addressed by low forms, such as horror' (2011: 19).

In *Quarantine*, it is Fletcher who falls, or jumps, from an upper level of the apartment block. He lands with a sickening thud in the middle of the lobby, shocking the characters who have assembled downstairs into momentary silence. This can be seen as an attempt to, as Stacey Abbott argues, 'reinsert into the narrative a factor that has been removed from the 9/11 story and its representation' (2016: 73), namely, the bodily trauma absent from the reportage of the day's events. It is definitely true that the bystander footage used in retrospectives of 9/11 is, more often than not, a curiously bloodless affair. Some scholars have noted this strange lack of blood in images of 9/11, with Laura Frost noting the suppression of gory or graphic images was possibly intended to protect viewers from trauma. Frost states that with *9/11*, 'the omission of damaged bodies is not presented as a deliberate, stylized effect; rather, it operates according to the same kind of discretionary censorship that characterized mainstream news reportage' (Frost, 2011: 22). In its own representation of the trauma of 9/11 however, *Quarantine* does not shy away from graphic gore. As this chapter has shown so far, the camera is used in *Quarantine* as a metaphorical tool for the truth. We move now to an examination of the camera as a

**Figure 6.2** The fallen firefighter takes on a new resonance in post-9/11 found footage horror.

literal tool in the narratives of found footage horror cinema, as I explore how its physical presence impacts upon its surroundings, and conversely, how the surroundings impact on the diegetic camera.

## 'Hit her again': the camera as a tool in found footage horror

In Chapter 2, I addressed how the camera is used in found footage horror as a tool of veracity, and the camera is foregrounded in *Quarantine* in terms of its ability to record a counter version of events to that shown in the media reports from outside the building. It is also used here, and in other found footage horror films, as a more pragmatic tool: to assist the characters in seeing what they usually could not, for instance, through their use of the night vision function. During parts of *9/11*, the camera is also constructed as a tool, not only metaphorically as a witnessing tool, but also literally, such as when Jules Naudet uses the floodlight on his camera to help the firefighting crew find each other after the South Tower is hit. In *Quarantine*, Scott utilises the camera in a similar way, as a tool to illuminate areas before he and Angela enter them, but also as a literal weapon, such as when he bludgeons Elise, an infected resident, to death. As Elise runs towards the camera, Scott beats her with it repeatedly, the camera swinging into her face as the lens becomes bloodied, and her head begins to collapse.[3] This moment is significant in turning the neutral and observing tool of a camera

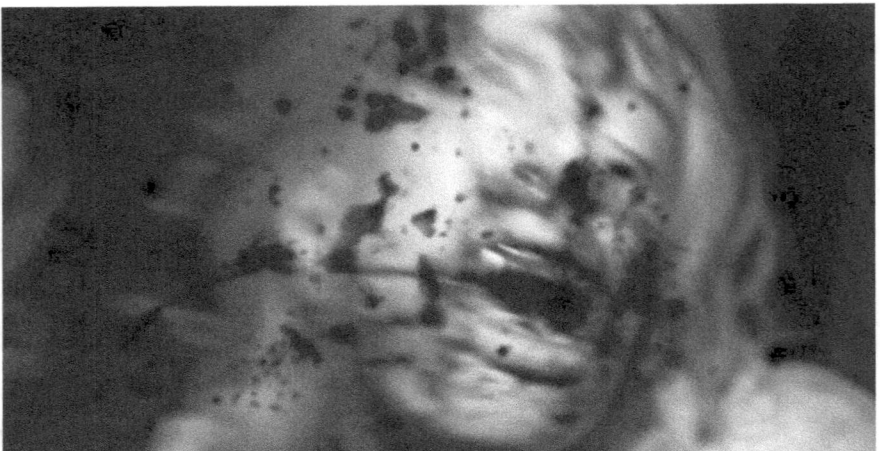

**Figure 6.3** The camera as a tool in found footage horror: the bludgeoning of Elise in *Quarantine*.

into a literal implement of violence, and making the connection between filming and violence explicit, underlining Susan Sontag's assertion that 'there is aggression implicit in every use of the camera' (1977: 7). In found footage horror – as well as in bystander footage of 9/11 – the physicality or physical presence of the camera is emphasised stylistically – for example through the use of specialist lenses or camera lights – or by aspects of the environment altering or impacting upon the lens of the camera.

One of the ways in which the camera is used as a tool, particularly in *Quarantine*, is through night vision. Agnieszka Soltysik Monnet has previously illustrated that the use of night vision in horror is a specifically postmodern aesthetic, and proposes that it resonates particularly with the anxieties of the post-9/11 militarisation of the American gaze. Monnet argues 'night-vision sequences quickly became a standard feature of images of the war shown to television viewers and have been particularly important in documentaries of the recent wars' (2015: 125). Specifically, night vision calls to mind the 'shock and awe' aerial bombardment campaign of the Iraq invasion, with the distinctive green and black footage being shown in nightly news broadcasts. The last scenes of *Quarantine* are filmed solely in night vision, after Scott's floodlight is damaged. By being the person holding the camera, Scott is afforded privileged information, whereas Angela has to rely on Scott for instruction. This is the second time in the film that this operator privilege occurs, the first time being when Scott is able to watch what is happening in the surgery room – which I will discuss in more detail below – while Angela is only able to ask what is happening.

As Stef Craps notes, in his analysis of *9/11*, some of the most dramatic sequences of the film are when 'reality physically imprints itself upon the camera instead of merely being recorded by it' (2007: 198). There are, for example, several scenes where the Naudet brothers have to stop to clean their camera lens, which becomes covered in dust and ash. When Scott bludgeons Elise with his camera her blood splatters over the lens, and in a following scene Scott spends time cleaning it, while having a quiet emotional breakdown over what he has just had to do. During *Quarantine*, Scott continually uses the camera as a tool, for instance, when Jake and Officer Wilensky enter the makeshift surgery room in the basement along with the officials from the Center for Disease Control. Within this scene, Jake realises that Angela and Scott are attempting to record what is being discussed with the CDC official and slams the door on them, blocking their view. Undeterred, Angela and Scott enter the adjacent room, where Scott climbs on a table and lifts his camera to look through a high internal window to document what is happening, therefore using the camera as an extension of his witnessing. Throughout *Quarantine* the camera is dropped, thrown, hit, dirtied and bloodied, but despite this it keeps running and serves as Angela and Scott's record of their night in the apartment block. At the end of the film, Scott has been mauled by a humanoid creature and is presumed dead and Angela pulled backwards into the darkness of the attic. The camera continues to record without an operator, and is the last witness standing. The use of the camera in *Quarantine* as an unblinking witness to the truth connects it to the status of the camera as a tool for observation of the physical world, and this is also a recurrent concept in *9/11* too, where Jules and Gédéon repeatedly discuss the act of witnessing.

## Conclusion

In conclusion, although *Quarantine* is a remake of a Spanish horror film, its striking similarities to the documentary film *9/11*, both visually and narratively, imbue it with a substantial flavour of specifically American cultural anxiety. As stated previously, *Quarantine* is often overlooked in horror scholarship in favour of *[Rec]*. For example, Andy Willis asserts that the remake is less connected to its cultural context because of a desire to make 'globally marketable films' (2017: 56). Willis moves on to argue that there is a removal of the tension surrounding immigration in *Quarantine*, which was present in *[Rec]*, and that this is an aspect which 'could have been retained in the remake' (2017: 59). Willis then describes a scene in *[Rec]* where the character of Cesar attempts to scapegoat an East Asian family in the apartment block. Willis insists that Cesar 'just wants to simplistically blame these "others" for the virus present in "his" apartment block' (2017: 59), with his complaints gaining little traction with the other residents. However, in his analysis, Willis overlooks a similar narrative exchange in *Quarantine*, where a black family are similarly scapegoated and racially Othered. In *Quarantine*, it is established early in the film that the family cannot speak English, and once the outbreak begins, it is mentioned that an unwell elderly relative is still in their apartment, whereas everyone else is downstairs. At this point, some of the residents suggest that this relative could be the source of the outbreak. While some residents propose that he should be brought downstairs with everyone else, a character named Kathy strongly objects. As the family are the only black residents, and visually, are dissimilar to the others due to both their race and Jwahir's hijab, this scene can be read as a reference to racial tensions and immigration in America, particularly in light of anti-Muslim sentiment post-9/11. Despite this, Willis constructs *Quarantine* as a 'less culturally engaged piece of work' (2017: 60), which 'ignores the contexts within which the originals were conceived and produced and their particular engagement with social and political issues arising from these historical moments' (2017: 64).

Willis's refusal to engage with the possibility of *Quarantine*'s relevance to its own social and political context is part of a definable trend in both critical and theoretical engagement with horror cinema, to dismiss remakes in favour of the original films. For example, American remakes of East Asian horror films, particularly those of Japanese horror cinema in the early 2000s, were presented as being 'inferior' (McRoy, 2008: 82), and 'in keeping with the US film industry's longstanding colonisation of Japanese cultural products' (Blake, 2008: 57). This dismissal can also be seen in the reception of the reimaginings of 1970s horror in the middle of the 2000s. For instance, the remake of *Dawn of the Dead* (2004), which Christopher Sharrett notes was 'effectively shorn of politics' (2014: 64) or *When a Stranger Calls* (2006), described by Steffen Hantke as a 'pointless exercise in style' (2010: x). I contend however – with *Quarantine* as my evidence – that remakes are completely capable of resonating with their own sociocultural and political production context.

By reading *Quarantine* as not only a remake of *[Rec]*, but also as being referent to collective images that emerged from the events of 9/11, and by its use of camerawork that is reminiscent of 9/11 bystander footage, we can see how the film references 9/11's trauma, confusion and panic. My decision to compare *Quarantine* to the Naudet brothers' *9/11* was due in part to the fact that *Quarantine* has close visual ties to the mediated event of 9/11, and as such, also closely resembles the Naudets' documentary account of that day. This is seen in *Quarantine*'s frantic camerawork, and the camera being dropped, abused and dirtied during its use as both a tool for truthful documentation and, more pragmatically, as a tool for illuminating areas or as a weapon. This is part of *Quarantine*'s appeal, and its contribution to the found footage horror subgenre is underlined by its eschewing of the qualities of suggestion and ambiguity cited by commentators as being key to subgenre pioneer *The Blair Witch Project* (Phipps, 1999; Colburn, 2015), in favour of high energy, graphic, horror. In approaching this film as a text that re-culturalises the Spanish specificity of *[Rec]* to an American setting, this case study allows us to examine the ways in which *Quarantine* utilises images reminiscent of those from 9/11 to present a narrative that resonates with the anxieties engendered by that event in American society.

I have spoken throughout this chapter of the additions and changes made to the narrative of *[Rec]* by *Quarantine*, and highlighted a number of key alterations or points of expansion that *Quarantine* includes. I have not done this in order to somehow evaluate which of the films is more effective or well crafted, but because I follow Jennifer Forrest and Leonard R. Koos's argument that remakes are interesting 'for what they reveal, [. . .] about different cultures [. . .] about different social-historical periods' (2002: 4–5). The remake is potent because changes can tell us much about audience expectations, shifts within genres and changing contexts.[4] A particularly striking addition to *Quarantine*, for instance, is Bernard's death, which I detailed above. In *[Rec]*, the trapped characters' engagement with the outside world is limited, and characters are attacked or killed only by the infected; Bernard's death in *Quarantine* – by a bullet fired by a government agent – is a departure from this. Although *Quarantine* is full of rampaging, infected individuals tearing (quite literally) through an apartment block and its residents, in the spirit of the cinema of George A. Romero, Bernard's death shows us that another significant threat is governmental agencies following orders from above. This is a theme that is recurrent throughout the next chapter, in which the media and powerful institutions are held accountable in tales of contagion, panic and lies.

## Notes

1 Where *Quarantine* lacks a direct reference to biological terrorism save for a brief moment, the sequel film *Quarantine 2: Terminal* (2011) contains explicit references

to both terrorism and the bioweapon potential of the virus. However, as *Quarantine 2: Terminal* is not a found footage horror film, I have not included it within this book.
2 In *[Rec]*, interestingly, we are shown two women in the firehouse; it is not clear however if they are acting firefighters, as they are stationed behind a reception desk and do not speak to the reporters at any length.
3 This is an action repeated in *Spree* – one of the case studies of Chapter 9 – although in this later film it is a phone (and its camera) that is used as a bludgeoning tool.
4 For an excellent discussion of the post-9/11 remake, see Mee (2022).

# 7
# 'What if they're not even listening?': truth in found footage horror

A key characteristic of found footage horror – and an element that is central to its appeal – is its tendency to blur the line between reality and fiction. In Chapter 2, for instance, I discussed how *Cannibal Holocaust* played with this line to such a degree that audiences questioned the truth status of its narrative. The films that form the focus of this chapter – *Diary of the Dead*, *The Bay* and *The Conspiracy* – also adhere to this subgeneric feature, most notably through their inclusion of actuality footage in their opening frames. Among the first scenes in *Diary of the Dead*, for example, Deb – the protagonist – narrates over real-life footage of violence and looting from around the world; she explains, 'This is what we were getting from the news networks' and in doing so begins to frame her documentary as the converse 'truth'. *The Bay*, meanwhile, begins with a montage of images and clips, including authentic news broadcasts relating to then recent environmental oddities bearing the logos of well known news networks such as CNN. These broadcasts include a 2011 incident where millions of dead fish washed up at Sebastian Inlet State Park in Florida, and when over a thousand blackbirds seemed to spontaneously perish and fall from the sky in Arkansas that same year: both of these events baffled scientists. This montage in *The Bay* ends with a title card that reads 'Those events were covered by the media. The following story was never made public.' The implication present in both *Diary of the Dead* and *The Bay* is that although the mainstream media is reporting on some events, a specific 'truth' in both narratives is being withheld from the general populace. This is also discernible in the first sequence of scenes in *The Conspiracy*. Opening with images that gaze up at huge buildings framed by beautiful clear blue skies, the voice of a man – who we are later introduced to as Terrence, a conspiracy theorist – is heard before we are shown he is in a busy metropolitan street using a megaphone. The man urges us to realise that

> We are human beings! We're not symptoms of overpopulation for you to deal with! We're not cannon fodder for your wars! We will fight for our freedom, because we know what freedom feels like – and this is not it! This is not it!

The screen abruptly cuts to black, and then to the Zapruder footage of President John F. Kennedy's assassination. Following two very short talking head segments, any vague connection we may have made between the skyscraper imagery that opened the film and 9/11 is then solidified, as we cut to a clip from actual bystander footage of the terror attacks captured by Evan Fairbanks. Fairbanks's footage was taken in close proximity to the South Tower of the World Trade Center: it looks up at the Twin Towers and we can see a plume of smoke belching from the North Tower. Flight 175 suddenly enters the frame from behind a building on the left and hurtles into the South Tower. The low angle of this footage – the audience gazing up at these impossibly tall buildings against a bright blue sky – brings this image sharply in line with the footage that opened the film, in a moment that is jarring and combines 'familiarity and shock – resonance and violation' (Phillips, 2005: 8). The audience may not be familiar with the Fairbanks footage precisely, but may well be au fait with footage very much like it that was broadcast on 11 September 2001 and continues to be circulated through various memorial products. It is the placement of this very real shocking moment that resonates with audiences and violates the fictional frame of the film.

All three of these films situate their faux reality side by side with authentic images borrowed from real life events, and the proximity of reality and fiction is used to break down the barrier between their filmic worlds and our own. Donald L. Anderson, in his analysis of what he terms as 'hyperreal horror', has previously examined the inclusion of authentic footage of animal cruelty and death in *Cannibal Holocaust*, noting that 'Genuine death in the horror film stands out as a confrontational signifier of the real, because images of genuine death dare to become part of the viewer's pleasure' (2013: 113). The use of real footage in found footage horror is, of course, not unique to this chapter's case studies, but I argue that there is a distinction to be drawn between the footage of death in *Cannibal Holocaust* – which was captured on set and is therefore unique to that film – and the images that *Diary of the Dead*, *The Bay* and *The Conspiracy* feature. They function as similar signifiers of the real, but they have a resonance that reaches beyond the confines of their diegesis as they blur the line between reality and fiction through their use of images from specific real-world events. And, just as Anderson argues that the authentic footage of animal death in *Cannibal Holocaust* 'may easily provide credibility to the staged human deaths' in that narrative (2013: 116), the inclusion of actuality footage in *Diary of the Dead*, *The Bay* and *The Conspiracy* lends them an air of authenticity (albeit in a much less problematic way than Deodato's film). These films, then, bed themselves down in their opening scenes into a space of the 'real', and this is underlined by – in the case of *The Bay* and *The Conspiracy* at least – their basis in reality. Barry Levinson, the director of *The Bay*, was initially developing a documentary regarding the poor state of the Cheasapeake Bay, but decided that weaving facts into an ecohorror film would be a more effective way of reaching viewers (Vejvoda, 2013), while the Tarsus Club in *The Conspiracy* is a thinly veiled substitute for organisations such as the Bilderberg group, around whom real life conspiracy theories abound.

Trust and truth are the key themes the films examined in this chapter revolve around, and they do this through an engagement with the act of editing, and a palpable fear that those in power cannot be trusted. This chapter will first explore how *Diary of the Dead*, *The Bay* and *The Conspiracy* encourage their audiences to question visual evidence, and how these films presciently relate to the emergence of 'post-truth'. I will then investigate how the films directly reference various world events and put forward narratives where characters remain faithful in their belief that everything will be ok, despite a growing chasm between what they have been taught to believe about their country, their government and their media, and actuality. In doing so, I wish to be clear that I am not presenting these texts as films that are unique within the horror genre in their engagement with fears around politics, society or powerful institutions: the enormous amount of scholarship available on politically-charged horror is testament to the genre's long standing engagement with these anxieties. I do however present them as perhaps the clearest cut cases in this book of found footage horror's ability to engage with cultural trauma and anxieties.

## 'There's a little thing called the first amendment?': the found footage truth teller

Within *The Bay*, *Diary of the Dead* and *The Conspiracy*, the recording and documentation of events is presented at times as something of a noble act. In *The Bay*, Donna notes her reverence for her cameraman by explaining –

although he died later that night – that 'a lot of this footage is thanks to him'. Donna makes it clear that she and others have been trying to get their version of events to the public for years, but that 'sometimes, words have no impact', and that it is only since she got help from a website – govleaks.org – and obtained footage previously confiscated by authorities that she feels able to tell her story. The footage Donna narrates over throughout the film comes from a wide variety of different cameras and follows several disparate characters simultaneously during the outbreak of flesh-eating isopods in the Claridge, Maryland bay area. These include a young couple and their baby who are sailing to Claridge for the 4th of July celebrations, a trauma doctor in the local emergency room who is holding a Skype conversation with a Center for Disease Control official during the outbreak, two police officers from their dashboard camera footage, a young girl abandoned by her parents who is communicating with her friend using iPhone's Facetime feature, and two oceanographers who are seen in retrospective footage as they died before the events of the film take place. *The Bay* includes footage that is water-damaged, professional and amateur, surveillance and personal, and as such represents a key moment in the found footage horror subgenre at a point where the sheer amount of cameras that could capture an event was higher than ever before.

In *Diary of the Dead*, while Deb is shown at first to be sceptical of her boyfriend, Jason, and his motives for documenting the zombie outbreak, she later explains that she 'can now understand why he was so anxious to upload his footage', and that she believes the cause of the initial panic was 'not knowing the truth': a truth she now believes that Jason was attempting

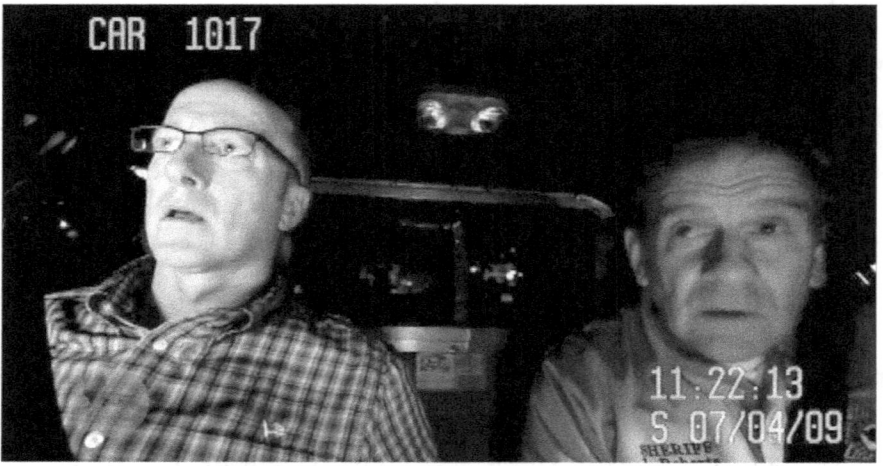

Figure 7.1 *The Bay* contains a vast array of varied footage, including a police dashcam.

to show the wider public through his film. However noble the aim of these characters, the act of truth telling is simultaneously framed as a dangerous pursuit. Early in *The Bay*, Donna nervously admits that 'I don't know if anything is going to happen to me as a result of putting this out there' as there has been money exchanged with various public figures for their silence, and an embargo on any digital information regarding the events she experienced. Although we are not shown the fallout of Donna's truth telling, the film ends with her alive. Jason in *Diary of the Dead*, however, ends up dying due to his compulsion to document the truth. Jason's death is partially due to his hubris but also his inability to stop recording. By the end of the narrative, Deb has taken on the role of documentarian and completed Jason's documentary with his aims in mind. It is in *The Conspiracy*, however, that truth telling is depicted at its most dangerous and perhaps its most impotent, as it is shown that even if you have evidence of the truth, this can be spun in whatever way suits those in positions of power. At the climax of the film, documentarians Aaron and Jim have managed to infiltrate a Tarsus Club meeting, capturing evidence on their hidden tie clip cameras, and take part in a strange initiation ceremony where members' wrists are bound and a mask is placed over their face. We learn there is a hierarchy to the club, with older members being 'Lions' and initiates being 'Ravens'. Jim goes through the ritual first, and we are shown through his camera that he has been given a black raven mask. Aaron, however, is given a bull mask and 'hunted' through the surrounding woods by the assembled Tarsus members. Aaron makes it back to his and Jim's arranged rendezvous point and is relieved to see Jim inside. This is, however, a trap: Jim's presence is a lure, and Aaron is pursued again through the woods before falling and – seemingly – being stabbed multiple times with the club members' ceremonial daggers. The film ends with several talking head segments I will return to below, including one with Jim. Jim explains that he and Aaron were captured by the Tarsus members, questioned and released. Despite this, he goes on to say, Aaron remained upset by the experience and this was the last time Jim saw him. A following segment shows Jim sitting with his wife and child: his wife looks upset and nervous. Jim is asked by an offscreen interviewer where he thinks Aaron might be, as footage is shown of Jim clearing out Aaron's apartment. *The Conspiracy* is in keeping with the found footage convention of unresolved endings, but several key narrative threads – such as the Tarsus Club centring on the worship of the Roman God Mithras, who is often depicted slaughtering a bull – implies that Aaron was murdered in his pursuit of the truth, and his death then covered up by this powerful, shadowy, elite.

## 'With an underlying threat of social satire': editing

Although – as explored in Chapter 2 – found footage horror cinema relies on the historical indexical relationship between photography and reality, several films within the subgenre encourage audiences to question the truth status of film more widely. In *Diary of the Dead*, there is a focus on the sinister potential of editing in particular, which is expressed through the repetition of one piece of footage. This faux reality footage is seen three times within the film: the first time, it functions as the opening scene, and this is framed as being the point at which the footage is in its most raw, unedited and truthful form. As the footage plays, Deb explains by way of a voiceover that

> We downloaded this video off the net sometime in the last three days, I can't remember exactly when. Some of this footage was never broadcast; it was uploaded secretly by the cameraman that shot it. It was his way of trying to tell the truth about what was happening.

The footage itself begins with a shot of an apartment block. The cameraman steps into frame to clean the lens, reminding us of the camera's physical presence in the diegetic environment. The camera documents a conversation between two police officers and an ambulance pulling up. The cameraman runs over to the ambulance and asks the driver to pull the vehicle forward as it is blocking his shot. As they oblige and move, we see two covered bodies being brought from the apartment building. A reporter – from Channel 10 – begins to address the camera and tells us that she is reporting live from the scene, where 'tragedy befell an immigrant family'. The cameraman directs her attention to one of the covered bodies, which is now moving, and tells her to get out of the way so he can capture this on film. The moving female corpse lunges at and bites one of the medical staff and the cameraman swings his shot towards the other covered body, which has begun to move too. The second corpse – a young man – grabs at a different medic, who manages to fight him off while the zombie woman advances on the camera. The cameraman films the police shooting at the male zombie, the bullets uselessly hitting him in the torso, before they shoot him in the head. The zombie woman suddenly lurches into the frame from the left, her hand outstretched towards the camera, which knocks it to the ground. There is a quick burst of static before the camera – now filming from its canted position on the pavement – captures the reporter being attacked by the remaining zombie: we can only see her torso and legs as blood pours to the ground. The police finally dispatch the zombie as the cameraman rushes to the reporter's aid, and holds her as she falls. There is another sharp bust of static as he begins to scream: 'This can't be happening! This can't be fucking happening!' This footage, which I will henceforth refer to as the 'Channel 10 footage', is then seen for the second time around twenty minutes later on Deb's laptop, when Jason reaches her dorm room. As the clip plays, Deb does not directly address it, but her voiceover mentions that the outbreak was 'all over the news, all over the web'. We can assume that this footage is the same, uncut, clip that opened the film. The final time the footage appears, it is in the context of a mainstream news broadcast and this time with commentary from a local police chief (played here by George A. Romero himself). Jason remarks that it is different from the raw footage he saw in Deb's room, and that 'they changed it, they recut it'. The police chief insists that the attackers – 'a bunch of illegal immigrants' – were not dead, at least not until his men shot them. Deb notes in her narration that 'they were trying to make it sound like everything was going to be alright', and that 'the media were lying to us, or the government was lying to them'. Regardless of who is lying, *Diary of the Dead* makes much of how media channels can be used to spread false information, and in these scenes directly implicates the media as a sinister tool of governmental agendas.

The media and government are both proved to be ineffectual institutions in the film, underlining Jason's insistence that 'all that's left is to record what's happening for whoever remains when it's over'. Outside of the Channel 10 footage, the act of editing is also continually returned to in the

**Figure 7.2** 'They changed it . . .': tensions around editing arise for the students of *Diary of the Dead* as they watch the recut Channel 10 footage.

film; for example, Deb advises the audience at the outset of her narration that she has edited what we are about to watch and added music 'hoping to scare' us. Later on, in the interests of transparency, Deb's voiceover explains once the group arrive at her family home that she 'thought long and hard whether to leave this footage in the film. I decided in the end to let you see what happened.' We are then shown that her mother and younger brother are zombies, and we witness their elimination at the hands of Deb's friends. The act of recording is equated with violence throughout *Diary of the Dead* and the narrative's apparent positivity around capturing the 'truth' is complicated by the way the film compares shooting with a camera to shooting with a gun. Throughout the film, Jason refuses requests for his help from his friends by explaining 'I'm shooting', for instance, but the comparison is made abundantly clear in a sequence within a hospital with the repeated line 'Take this, it's too easy to use.' The first time this happens is when Maxwell shoots the infected Mary and immediately hands Tony his gun, delivering the line as he hands over the weapon. This exact line is repeated less than ten minutes later during the zombie attack as the group leaves the hospital, when Deb, having impassively filmed the zombie attacking her friend Gordo, hands the camera to Maxwell, equating the easy danger of documenting with a lethal weapon. This comparison is made even clearer in one of the final scenes of the film, where Jason, who has been up until this point behind the camera capturing the fate befalling his friends, is bitten by Ridley, another infected student. In his last moments, Jason asks Deb to shoot him, not making it clear whether he wishes for her to literally kill him with her gun and save him from zombification or to shoot him with his discarded camera. Perhaps aware of this, Deb does both.

Whereas the act of editing is directly addressed in *Diary of the Dead*, it is perhaps the lack of attention editing receives in *The Conspiracy* that troubles its audience. We have, from the beginning of the film, believed that we are watching a documentary created by Jim and Aaron. Initially focusing on conspiracy theorists more broadly, the aim of the documentary changes when Terrence – their first subject – goes missing, and Aaron begins to decode and understand Terrence's research. Aaron is now determined to infiltrate the Tarsus Club, bringing an interested but reluctant Jim along with him. Tensions flare as Aaron becomes more consumed by their investigation; he expresses on camera to their crew that 'I really don't think Jim's mind is capable of accepting that the world doesn't work the way that he was always told it works'. Jim angrily argues that it doesn't really matter, because even if Aaron is right, 'that there are these people that secretly run things. Then they've always run things, ok? And they always will.' I argued earlier that although the film ends with Jim explaining that Aaron is missing, clues laid throughout the narrative point towards Aaron's murder and a subsequent cover-up by Tarsus. This is underlined by the two talking head interview segments that accompany Jim's in the closing scenes, both from senior officials of the Tarsus Club: the Chief Operating Officer, William Jensen and the Senior Vice President of Public Relations, Nicole Higgins. After we witness the final piece of footage from Aaron's camera, we see Jim in a room with Higgins, silently reviewing what was captured on film. The following to camera interviews by Jensen and Higgins address the 'crazy conspiracy theories' that circle around Tarsus, with Higgins admitting that meeting infiltrations have become so common in recent years that 'it's almost become part of the ritual to scare people off'. I mentioned earlier too that Jim is posed a question as to Aaron's whereabouts by an offscreen interviewer. the interviewer's voice is female, and has not been a feature of the documentary until this point. This voice, along with several other elements: the blurred out faces of Tarsus Club members throughout, the bleeping out of members' names and Jim responding to the question of where he believes Aaron went with 'I guess he ended up in the same place Terrence did, didn't he?' suggests that although the film began as Aaron and Jim's project, it is now under the control of Tarsus. Although this reading of the film sounds like a conspiracy theory itself, it is supported by an earlier conversation in which the character of Mark Tucker notes that having some information available about the Tarsus Club serves their interests, and by the chilling, casual admittance by Jensen that

> to the people screaming about conspiracy, I'll let them in on a little secret: it's true. Global leaders do get together and collaborate. Many of them, including my boss, Murray Chance, are working hard to create a new world, where all nations of all people can come together in one global community. That's what it's all about, the creation of single global community. If that's a conspiracy . . . if that's a conspiracy, well then yes, we're guilty.

Terrence states early in the film that 'the genius of these rulers is that they've created a society that's conditioned to deny what's right in front of its eyes', and the denouement of *The Conspiracy* carefully constructs its unease around the visual evidence we have seen and how it has been presented to us. As such, *The Conspiracy* connects to Susan Sontag's analysis of photographs emerging from the War on Terror, where she cautions that we must continue to ask 'what pictures, whose cruelties, whose deaths are not being shown' (2003: 44). This encouragement to question the official line, and to be sceptical of how evidence is conveyed is at the centre of *The Bay* and *Diary of the Dead* too. In these films, taped does not always mean truth, and the limitations of the camera as a tool for the truth are placed at the forefront of these narratives. Neil McRobert notes the recurrence of this theme in found footage horror cinema, and proposes that 'Where once media-coverage was regarded as a reassurance – a suggestion that some authority, somewhere, was in position – now it is a medium synonymous with horror' (2015: 147). Similarly, these films suggest that we live in an era where, as argued by Brigid Cherry, 'even though we all now have the ability to record all that we witness, this does not provide us with answers' (2009: 194).

It is significant that each of the films featured in this chapter are collections of footage edited after their respective narrative events take place, and this puts them in opposition to the previous chapter's case study film, *Quarantine*, which is presented as a more 'in the moment' account. Connected to the area of editorial control, both *The Bay* and *Diary of the Dead* use privileged positions in an intriguing way, because of their imagined status as edited collections of real footage. The Donna and Deb that the audience watch in these films are in a decidedly unprivileged position – much like Angela in *Quarantine* – they do not have a wider sense of what is going on and are caught up in their inadvertent witnessing. However, the Donna and Deb that we hear as voiceovers in these films are in a position of comparative privilege, having knowledge of how the events we are watching will play out from their position after the fact. The audience is, in a sense, simultaneously positioned with both the privileged versions of Deb and Donna and the unprivileged versions. Our privilege comes from the knowledge that both characters have survived to tell their story, and we know we will not witness their deaths. We are, however, also aligned with their unprivileged counterparts within the footage as it plays out, and our perspective is conflated with these versions of Deb and Donna too. This element places these two films apart from the majority of found footage horror cinema, which is usually presented as (more or less) uncut footage from one or more cameras, such as the narrative of *Quarantine*. Because, more often than not, found footage horror has an 'as it happens' status, foreshadowing is uncommon in the subgenre. However, in both *The Bay* and *Diary of the Dead*, because of the temporal difference between the visuals of the characters and their voiceovers, there is a great deal of foreshadowing present, especially in *The Bay*. In the early part of this film, where footage is seen of the townspeople of Claridge enjoying their Independence Day celebrations, Donna continuously and almost obsessively notes which of the people seen on screen would die throughout the day. Similarly, in *Diary of the Dead*, the fact that Deb tells us that we are watching the completed version of her boyfriend Jason's documentary, called 'The Death of Death', and that she is speaking about him in the past tense, implies that Jason is either dead, missing or grievously injured, and thus unable to complete the documentary and its voiceover himself. This aligns these films with the nihilism often present in found footage horror narratives; although *The Bay* and *Diary of the Dead* are unusual in that we know at least the narrators will survive events, giving the audience a sense of security about their fate.

It is clear that all three of the films analysed in this chapter engage with a specific anxiety around editing, or more accurately, the act of manipulative editing to mislead the public and serve an agenda. In this sense, although debates around the fallibility of media and the ability of media agencies to manipulate footage are not new, the films predate the popular use of the term 'post-truth' to describe partisan media reportage and how the new media ecosystem means, in the words of President Barack Obama, 'everything is true and nothing is true' (quoted in Remnick, 2016). There is a palpable paranoia in *The Bay* and *Diary of the Dead* that the media has an ability to be complicit in governmental agendas, or at the very least, the media has a recurrent inability to be balanced and impartial. This is demonstrative of Baudrillard's suggestion that there is 'no inherently good use of the media, it is part of the event, part of the terror' (2012 [2002]: 31). These allusions to media complicity and manipulative editing connects the films in this chapter to wider debates around newscasting, the media industrial complex and the reliability of mainstream reportage. In *Diary of the Dead*, it is various news agencies who we are told are recutting raw footage to sell a certain narrative about the outbreak, in *The Bay*, we are informed from the outset that the Claridge event was supressed from the public – presumably with the help of media agencies – but in *The Conspiracy*, it is not until the end of the film that we begin to question how information has been presented to us. In both *The Bay* and *Diary of the Dead* we are told explicitly who these documentaries were created by: Deb tells us it is Jason's project that we are watching, and it is clear that Donna has some form of influence over the in-universe narrative of *The Bay* that is being conveyed. The questions raised at the end of *The Conspiracy* bring a specific fear into sharp relief – whose version of the truth are we watching?

## 'We need to keep this in perspective': on being collateral damage in post-9/11 found footage horror

A point of difference between the films in this chapter, and a great number of horror films that have been read as engaging with fears around terrorism and the trauma of 9/11, is the direct references made in *Diary of the Dead*, *The Bay* and *The Conspiracy* to world events. For example, the footage of United Airlines Flight 175 striking the South Tower of the World Trade Center is repeated no less than three times in the first twenty minutes of *The Conspiracy*. Throughout the film, real footage of political figures such as George H. W. Bush and Gordon Brown is included where they mention a 'new world order', and Terrence's protest in a local park – complete with signs that read '9/11 was an inside job' – is interspersed with footage of the strike on the Pentagon.

*The Bay* and *Diary of the Dead* both highlight the possibility of terrorism as the cause for their respective crises. In *The Bay* this is through the inclusion of a conversation between a local radio show host and a caller, who suggests that Al-Qaeda may have poisoned the bay's water, and that this is what is causing the lesions and sickness the townspeople are suffering from. Meanwhile an early scene shows a news website featuring an image of Osama Bin Laden, although this is not commented on. While *The Bay* drops the terrorism explanation from the narrative to focus on the wilful ignorance of local and national governments as the cause of mass death, *Diary of the Dead* is even more direct in its reference of post-9/11 events

**Figure 7.3** *The Conspiracy* repeatedly forefronts 9/11.

and the trauma caused by them. In one of the first scenes in the film Tony, one of the students, dismisses reports of strange occurrences on the radio by saying 'We get this every day. A terrorist is going to drop a dirty bomb on the White House, or your house. You're going to get a disease from opening your mail.' This is, of course, a clear reference to the panic caused by the still unsolved mailing of Anthrax spores shortly after 9/11, as discussed in Chapter 5. This scene could also be seen to reference how the first explanation news reports will often arrive at whenever a suspicious event occurs is terrorism. For example, in reportage of a 2017 car crash in Times Square, New York City, in which one person died and a further twenty were injured, it was noted that the incident 'instantly raised the specter of terrorism' (Rosenberg and Stack, 2017). Whereas *The Bay* raises the idea of terrorism as an explanation early in the film and then moves away from this as it becomes clear that pollution of the bay is the culprit, *Diary of the Dead* keeps the spectre of terrorism in focus, occasionally reminding the student group of this possibility with reports on the radio that encourage 'American people' to 'stay vigilant' against terrorist attacks.

In all of the films discussed in this chapter, a recurrent theme is that the characters place faith in help that never comes. If assistance ever does arrive, as it does in *The Bay* and *Diary of the Dead*, it is shown that the very institutions that have been put in place to protect and serve end up playing either a significantly negative role in the narrative, or are instrumental in character deaths. As Susan Faludi stresses, 9/11 reminds us that the institutions of America failed to protect its people from death, destruction and tragedy (2007: 142), and this failure is writ large in the narratives of both *The Bay* and *Diary of the Dead*. For example, in *The Bay*, one sequence shows footage from a young infected girl's Facetime account, where she is communicating with her friend, who has stayed at home but who is in pain and probably also infected. The girl urges her friend not to come to the hospital, as 'they won't help you, they're not helping me'. These scenes are intercut with footage from a Skype conversation between the Center for Disease Control and a trauma doctor in the local hospital, with the doctor battling to receive help from the government. He argues against their suggestion that he leave the hospital to save himself, and eventually succumbs to the same infection he is trying to help the townspeople against. In *Diary of the Dead*, Tony is the character who clings to the idea of rescue for the longest, advising everyone that the National Guard will soon have the outbreak situation under control. When the National Guard eventually do appear near the end of the film, they first meet the camera with hostility and aggression before intimidating the group, relieving them of the majority of their weapons and leaving, with Jason hissing to Tony angrily that 'there's your fucking National Guard'. This scene is best viewed in comparison to an earlier sequence in which the students are given shelter, fuel and weapons by a group of black men and women. Although the group members outnumber the students and could easily take advantage of them, they appear to be establishing a respectful and cooperative community, and allow the students to take what they need, with these items later being stolen by the National Guard. It is not that the narrative portrays this group as completely and unproblematically heroic, as the scenes in which they interact with the students are imbued with tension, but there is a clear distinction made between their actions and the actions of the National Guard. The National Guard also feature in the narrative of *The Bay*, albeit briefly and not visually, when Donna explains towards the end of the film that in the early hours of 5 July, 'the National Guard came and confiscated every camera'. The National Guard's seizing of both weaponry and cameras in *Diary of the Dead* and *The Bay* respectively responds to a post-9/11 paranoia regarding a political climate in which 'the authorities can search and seize personal effects without probable cause and when American citizens may be subsequently jailed without charge or trial' (Blake, 2008: 139). Indeed, one of the many 'significant events' flagged up in *The Conspiracy* by Terrence when he shows Aaron and Jim his self-styled 'War Room' is the Military Commissions Act of 2006, which Terrence states 'allows US citizens to be detained in undisclosed locations indefinitely'. He then highlights a later 2009 Bill – identified in the film as Bill HR 645 – that 'authorises the Department of Homeland Security to set up a network of FEMA

**Figure 7.4** Aaron becomes obsessed with Terrence's research in *The Conspiracy*.

camps to intern U.S. citizens in the case of a national emergency'. Both the 2009 Military Commissions Act and Bill HR 645 exist in real life, and in *The Conspiracy* take on a level of threat and menace perhaps unintended by their creators.

It is evident that there is a tension present in *Diary of the Dead*, *The Bay* and *The Conspiracy* between the image that the characters have of America, the government, the army and the media and the role they actually play within these films. There is a growing disparity displayed between self-image and actuality. There is also a sense of anger at having misplaced one's trust in these institutions, such as when Donna explains in *The Bay*, narrating over footage from her interview with the Mayor before the outbreak, that she had 'no idea how culpable he was for what was about to happen'. Donna suffers with a lack of evidence to prove culpability because, as she explains at the end of the film, 'Silence was part of the agreement' made between the survivors of the outbreak and unknown agencies, with Donna mentioning that she is not sure how much money exchanged hands to buy that stonewall of silence. It is, paradoxically, governmental silence that Donna uses to advance her accusations of negligence. For example, with the oceanographer's footage that is interspersed throughout the film, it becomes clear that they were documenting changes in the water surrounding the town, and were recording a video diary, of which they sent excerpts to local agencies in order to illustrate the state of the water. After each instalment of their video diary, which serves to give the audience some exposition about what is happening, title cards inform viewers when that particular report was sent and to whom. Invariably, the title card also details the lack of response that the video received from these institutions. In *The Bay*, silence underlines complicity and after one such video diary instalment, Donna interjects by saying 'The question we continue to ask is did the authorities not look at this footage, or did they choose not to reveal it'.

Towards the end of the film, the audience receives an answer of sorts to this question, during a Skype exchange between the Center for Disease Control official, Dr Williams, and a representative of Homeland Security, Officer Slattery. The Skype conversation takes place after the worst of the outbreak has passed, and Officer Slattery states he is replying to a message Dr Williams sent. As Officer Slattery explains, 'it turns out we did hear something a few weeks back, about a couple of divers' bodies being found in the water' and that as they were not sure what had caused it, they did not pursue their investigation. He then asks if Dr Williams would like the Homeland Security report on these deaths sent over. Dr Williams summarises what Officer Slattery has told him, that 'nobody knows what happened and it takes sixteen days to get this information to us', and when Officer Slattery responds in the affirmative, Dr Williams angrily explains that he now has a town full of dead bodies due to this lack of information. Officer Slattery is quick to defend Homeland Security's actions by reminding the doctor that Claridge is 'a small town. I think we need to keep this in perspective here.' *The Bay*, *Diary of the Dead* and *The Conspiracy* all have very clear perspectives on who should be held accountable, and invariably this is those who hold positions of power, whether this be the government, the media or the wealthy elite.

## Conclusion

In Chapter 5, I posed a question in response to Mark Bernard's statement that horror films are first and foremost commercial commodities rather than vehicles to carry any political or cultural message (2014: 5), in asking why horror cannot be both. I could have, essentially, cited the three films that formed the focus of this chapter as an answer to my own question. Within *Diary of the Dead*, *The Bay* and *The Conspiracy*, the found footage horror format is used in order to put forward very clear statements or ideas that relate closely to key anxieties virulent in North American society post-9/11. *Diary of the Dead* presents us with an anxiety around the goals and agendas of the media, *The Bay* sets its sights on critiquing ineffectual governmental agencies and their actions in a crisis, while *The Conspiracy* picks at the scab that covers our latent fears around who is really in control of our politics, media and fate. Earlier in this chapter I highlighted how these films are presented as 'after the fact', edited products, which sets them apart from the common conception of found footage horror films as 'in the moment' accounts. Just as *Diary of the Dead*, *The Bay* and *The Conspiracy* are placed in a position of 'after' their narrative events, these films deal with the 'after' in terms of their relationship to their production context. Linda Ruth Williams has stated that there is something of a 'B.C/A.D. effect of 9/11' (2012: 42) and released in 2007 (*Diary of the Dead*) and 2012 (*The Bay* and *The Conspiracy*), these films were created in and emerged from a culture that was still working through the 'A.D.' of significant traumatic events in the early part of the twenty-first century, where civil rights were being suspended, wars were being fought and society was still reeling from unprecedented terrorist attacks. The films I have examined in the second part of this book as a whole are, to borrow Brigid Cherry's phrase, updated 'documents of anxiety' (2009: 175), which engage with the culture of fear North America found itself mired within. Of course, with *Diary of the Dead* this is perhaps not a surprise, given George A. Romero's history of producing horror cinema that functions as sociopolitical commentary and critique. After the release of the film, Romero suggested that the emergence of found footage horror as a definable subgenre was part of a 'collective subconscious' (Smith, 2008), which gave him the opportunity to return to 'cheap, local, and studio free' filmmaking (Onstad, 2008).

An aspect that runs through all three films that I have engaged with in this chapter is the presence of the internet, a factor that perhaps links the films in this chapter to those I will explore in the third and final part of this book, which examines the rise of social media horror as a subset of found footage horror cinema. Within *Diary of the Dead*, *The Bay* and *The Conspiracy*, the internet is framed in varied ways and we can begin to discern the anxieties around online communication that will become central to social media horror. *Diary of the Dead*, for example, presents two competing views of the internet through the characters of Deb and Jason. Deb is initially sceptical of Jason's claim that he wants to upload his 'truth' to the internet in order to help the general public, and laments that 'the more voices there are, the more spin there is, the truth becomes that much harder to find. In the end, it's all just noise.' This is a viewpoint that closely aligns with the director's own thoughts, as George A. Romero, in an interview with Newsblaze.com shortly after the film was released, cautioned against the dangers of the internet and believing everything you may read on it. Romero stated that, in his opinion, the internet is

> full of dangers wherein any lunatic can post anything. If Hitler was around now, he wouldn't have to go into the town square, he would just throw up a blog. If Jim Jones were here now, all of a sudden there would be a million people drinking Kool-Aid. (Quoted in Miller, 2008)

This sits uncomfortably next to the characterisation of Jason's beliefs, as he argues it is his duty to get the truth out to the wider populace, and the only avenue he has available to do this through is the internet.

This conflicted interpretation of the value of the internet in *Diary of the Dead* is not present for the most part within *The Bay*, which lacks a character with the balancing sceptical view of the internet Deb has, and instead the borderless communities of the internet as characterised in *The Bay* are seen as positive places for truth sharing. This view concurs with Mark Freeman's argument that the internet is a place where 'portals function as a space for social and cultural mobilisation, for declarations of 'truth' in its capacity as an apparently uncensored public forum for the airing of that which state-controlled media may restrict' (Freeman, 2015: 115). However, it is also a place in *The Bay* where, as the closing down of the Ecospy.com website in the narrative proves, governmental control can still reach. Within the narrative, the Ecospy website, which featured a video documenting the proximity of chicken waste to the bay, was shut down the day after the incident in Claridge, alluding to the government's ability to monitor digital communication and the authorities' ability to erase information that they deem to be at odds with their official version of events. Despite this, the characterisation of the internet in *The Bay* does overarchingly conform to Freeman's ideal of a 'delimited virtual space' (2015: 108), as it is through Donna's affiliation with Govleaks.org that she is able to obtain the confiscated material, and is able to broadcast her version of events. Finally, *The Conspiracy* lays out these conflicting views of the internet explicitly, as a conspiracy theorist named Ron explains to Aaron and Jim that

> The internet may be a threat to those in charge, but it's also their greatest weapon. Every single thing you do on the internet is monitored. Every email you send, every website you visit, every picture you look at on your wife's Facebook, all of it is. George Orwell predicted that Big Brother would be watching us one day, but what he didn't predict is that we'd create Big Brother ourselves and then willingly give ourselves over to it.

In the wake of the traumatic opening years of the new millennium, new fears were coming into focus and anxieties that centred around the internet specifically were rising. The ways that *Diary of the Dead*, *The Bay* and *The Conspiracy* present online communication can be seen perhaps as an earlier incarnation of the ongoing assimilation of new technology in the found footage horror subgenre, as can the inclusion of the wide variety of types of footage in *The Bay*. The emergence of 'post-truth' politics, and a wider trend towards uncertainty in who the public can actually trust for unbiased information since these films' release dates, stands as evidence of their continued relevance. However, the idea of the internet as a place where you can find unfiltered truth and sanctuary now seems – as I will explore in the next part of this book – rather naïve.

# Part III

# 8

# Death in digital: found footage horror and the internet

In *Pulse* (2006), an American remake of the Japanese film *Kairo* (2001), we learn that ghosts are using the borderless landscape of the internet to sap users' will to live, tempting them with the promise of a chance to see a real ghost, before driving them to suicide. *Pulse*, which can only very loosely be termed as a found footage horror film – as it has a few sequences which are framed as 'live' footage – engages clearly with the idea that the internet is a dangerous place. It is a film emblematic of what Mikita Brottman suggests is a societal anxiety regarding the reach and content of the internet, and the computer as 'a kind of magical portal – the gate of hell – through which computer viruses can escape to infect your home, turning your husband into a porn fiend and your children into the potential victims of drooling pedophiles' (2004: 169). The horror genre more broadly has featured the internet as a locus of fear for decades, and the found footage horror subgenre in particular has become a space where discomforts around developing technology are being articulated through both themes and form. It should be noted that this chapter and the one that follows will not use a large-scale cultural trauma as a focus point – as was the case with the previous part of this book – instead, they will centre around the pervasive cultural anxiety that surrounds internet use in contemporary society. The internet has been mediating traumatic events for years, and is central to several concurrent societal anxieties around the mediation of violence and the effects of living in an increasingly digital society. This chapter and the next will, therefore, examine the ubiquitous unease that surrounds the internet and its (as yet) unrealised potential for large scale trauma.

As Gary D. Rhodes argues, 'traditionally, even if not necessarily intentionally, horror has been a generic engine for cinematic advancements and experimentation' (Rhodes, 2002: 50). Rhodes goes on to highlight that the second all-dialogue talking picture was indeed a horror film, as was one of the first feature length widescreen films: respectively, these were *The Terror* (1928) and *The Bat Whispers* (1930). The horror genre is not only an early adopter of technological advancement, but has often been the site of early engagement with fears around new technology too, and Jeffrey Sconce's (2000) concept of haunted media highlights how the idea of malevolent technology often resurfaces during periods of technological advancement. This is certainly true of the horror genre. The humble telephone, for example, is used as an instrument of fear in the long running *Scream* franchise (1996–), as well as in *When a Stranger Calls* (1979). In *Poltergeist* (1982), a television functions as a gateway between our world and a realm of the dead, and TV can also be seen as a transmitter of horror in *Halloween III: Season of the Witch* (1982) and *Videodrome* (1983). A fear of technology was also at the heart of several Japanese horror films emerging in the late 1990s and early 2000s, such as *Ring* (1998).[1] Even within this body of films though, there is a distinction to be made between texts which frame the technology itself as having a supernatural presence, such as *Beyond the Gates* (2016), and those that use technology to generate horror. *Ghostwatch* (1992), for example, based its construction of paranoid fear on the suggestion that every television in the United Kingdom showing the programme had been turned into a spectral conduit during the broadcast. Lorna Jowett and Stacey Abbott (2013) propose that *Ghostwatch* is an example of technology being presented not only as a site for horror but as an object of horror, with the

> live television broadcast [...] itself the threshold through which the ghost escapes the boundaries of the house and into the unbounded television airwaves, reinforcing not only the liminality of the television but of the invisible airwaves that form the broadcast network. (Jowett and Abbott, 2013: 124–5)

Given the technological advancements since *Ghostwatch*'s broadcast, then, it must be asked what horror can be found in the internet as a site for, and object of, terror. The particularities of how the internet itself mediates horror, trauma, death, dying and the dead are multitudinous. It is no wonder, as it is a subgenre that is so enormously engaged with its cultural context – at both a narrative and formal level – that these representations would find a home within found footage horror cinema.

Found footage horror's engagement with the internet is not simply 'a novel twist on the so-called found footage cycle that had, by 2015, more or less run its course' (Hart, 2019: 1), not least because this perspective ignores the repeated return of the horror genre to stories involving new technology as a horrific object, and the intertwined history of the internet and the subgenre. In the first half of this chapter, I will outline Jeffrey Sconce's concept of haunted media and build on his framework to include the ways in which computer technology continues this tradition. I will then move to illustrate the ways in which the computer can be framed as horrific, with particular attention paid to the ways in which death is increasingly being mediated through the internet. The second half of this chapter is concerned with the relationship between the internet and found footage horror through the model of viral marketing that can be traced back to *The Blair Witch Project* in 1999. Within this latter part of the chapter, I do not wish to retread the ground so thoroughly excavated by previous research. Instead, I aim to move beyond the tendency in accounts of found footage horror to focus on the marketing campaign of this one film and examine how subsequent found footage horror films have used the internet to create immersive online worlds, fabricate backdrops to films through transmedial storytelling and invite audiences to play into the fantasy that these films and their footage might just be real.

## Ghosts in the machines: new media/new horror

With each major development in new technology, whether this be wireless radio, television or the internet, two strands of reception develop simultaneously. The first of these is that the new technology will overcome communicative obstacles and lead us all to a more peaceful and cooperative society, heralding wonder and enlightenment. Examples of this can be traced back to early Spiritualists, who were astounded by the power of the telegraph, which allowed long distance communication in a world in which this was not only previously impossible, but inconceivable. An article from *Tiffany's Monthly* in 1857, for instance, frames telegraphic communication in fervent religious tone:

> The members together in spirit – in communication, and yet in body seven hundred miles apart! [. . .] Could such a meeting have been predicted forty years ago, wo[e] to the prophet who should have dared to have uttered his vision. But the event has taken place; it is one of the FACTS, proclaiming an ETERNAL TRUTH. (1857: 142, emphasis in original)

This first strand of reception, as Jeffrey Sconce remarks, 'eagerly linked Spiritualist phenomena with the similarly fantastic discourses of electromagnetic telegraphy' (2000: 35). Conversely, the second strand of reception sees new technology as a harbinger of threat and doom, pointing towards the obsolescence of humanity, or opening channels of communication that should stay closed. From ghostly voices on radio waves to apparitions inside television screens, new technology and ghost stories are inextricably linked, and Sconce traces the history of what he terms as 'haunted media' back to the mid-1800s. After proposing that electricity has been understood traditionally as an agent of the uncanny, and that early anxieties surrounding its use are still present in contemporary culture (2000: 7), Sconce tracks three enduring elements of these anxieties through different incarnations of haunted media. The first is the concept of the 'in between', which refers to the unknowable area between two points of electronic communication. It is in this nowhere place that spirits or entities can reside or can, along with the living, become trapped. The idea of the in between space features in a great deal of early speculative fiction and functions as a spectral conduit, or an enabler of communication between the supernatural and natural worlds. If we exist at one end of this conduit, then at the other end is the second element in Sconce's schema: the electronic elsewhere. Early Spiritualists were the first to focus on this concept: a plane of electronic existence which exists just beyond the bounds of our comprehension, like an invisible and intangible blanket over the world. Sconce distinguishes the electronic elsewhere as a 'utopian realm generated and accessed through the wonders of electronic media' (2000: 57). The third and final element featuring in haunted media is new technology having an invariable uncanny quality. Sconce is not alone in connecting hauntings to new technology, and Tom Gunning has worked to relate the uncanniness of mediumship, spirit photography and magic theatre to early cinema. Gunning notes that the uncanniness we can feel around new technology is because of 'a short-lived wonder based on unfamiliarity' (2003: 47) and concludes that although we quickly assimilate new technology into our everyday lives, a trace of the uncanny always remains. The uncanny endures then as new technology involves 'magical operations which greater familiarity or habituation might cover over, but not totally destroy' (2003: 47).

Although both Sconce and Gunning laid the foundations of scholarship into haunted media and uncanny technology, their engagement ends with the personal computer, and they do not go on to analyse the communicative potential of the internet as a form of haunted media in depth. This is likely due to the internet's fledgling status at the time of their work's publication. Sconce does note, however, that '[The Spiritualist's] unbridled enthusiasm for the wonders of an "electronic elsewhere" would have no real equal until the recent emergence of transcendental cyberspace mythologies in our own cultural moment' (2000: 57). Sconce suggests too, earlier in his volume, that

> owners of personal computers make [...] animating investments in their media, of course, but here the interactivity and intimacy of the computer more often transform the machine into a friend and confidant (albeit one with which we often have a stormy relationship). (2000: 3)

If we are to construct the personal computer as a friend and confidant as Sconce suggests, then this definition implies that the computer knows your secrets; it holds details regarding websites you have visited or even the ones you think you have cleared from your browser history, and which words or terms you have entered into your search engine. The computer perhaps only appears to be a friend, but is aware of intimate aspects of your life in a way that previous forms of electronic media were not. If we are to accept that the computer has a living presence, as Sconce prescribes to accounts of new technology, and if it is like live television, which Jane Feuer claims is 'alive [...] living, real, not dead' (1983: 14, emphasis in original), then it has the awareness – and possibly the inclination – to turn on us at any point. This anxiety can be furthered by the idea that the internet can be used to track an individual's movements and activity as a form of surveillance. Kevin Wetmore Jr (2012) for example has noticed a trend in horror cinema to meditate on the idea that our own technology manipulates us, and Neal Kirk (2015), too, discerned this insidious potential of the internet as a source of horror in his analysis of *In Memorium* (2005) and *Pulse*. Although rejecting Wetmore's own analysis of *Pulse*, stating that it is too reliant on the anxiety model, Kirk's analysis of the two films, one of which – *In Memorium* – is a found footage horror film, proposes that there is a 'culture of fear' that exists around the internet and moreso the attention economies of networked new media more broadly (2015: 55). It is clear, then, that computer technology and the internet hold within them the potential for horror as video, television and radio technologies did before them.

The specificities of internet-based horror are manifold. Firstly, and perhaps most importantly, whereas previous forms of haunted media were essentially one directional for the majority of users, who would receive broadcasts or transmissions through them, the communicative potential of the internet is two-directional. As we receive information through our computer screen, we also transmit information about ourselves. Secondly, the internet has a quality of liveness (and life) to it: whereas live news used to be strictly the territory of broadcast media, we can now follow along with events in real time through our internet connection, and we now have the capacity to communicate with large numbers of strangers, leaving us open to unknown threats. Thirdly, the internet has, in the last decade or so, become inescapable for a significant percentage of humanity. We live in an increasingly mediated world, where the internet – and social media in particular – can now be a constant companion in our lives. There are now national 'unplugged' days, designed for hyperconnected individuals to make a pledge to switch off the never ending stream of information from their mobile devices and step away from social media for a period of time.[2] Whereas the playful coda at the end of *Poltergeist* sees Steve Freeling ejecting the television – the source of horror in the film – from the motel room his family has travelled to, there is no such easy avoidance of the ubiquity of the internet for modern audiences. Finally, and as is central to my analysis of social media horror in the following chapter, an aspect that distinguishes the internet from previous forms of haunted media is the level to which it is used as a mediator of death.

As Julian Petley argues, 'there is nothing essentially new' in imagery of death (2016: 27) that can be found online, and the general public engaging with these images is by no means a new development in society. Real death footage can be linked historically to post-mortem photography for instance, whereby photographs were taken of deceased persons and kept by their loved ones as a memento. News footage of death such as the Zapruder film of John F. Kennedy's assassination, and mondo documentaries like the *Faces of Death* series (1978–), in which archival footage of real death is mixed with fake gore footage, are two other ways that audiences have been exposed – and willingly exposed themselves – to real death. However, although it has always been possible to find images of death, the ease of access to these images has grown in the wake of the internet. The ways in which the internet is mediating death, exhibiting death and – in the cases of suicide due to cyberbullying – causing death, are key concerns to the found footage horror subgenre. There are three strands of online death central to this: real death websites, death memorialisation or social media as a grief space, and live trauma broadcast through the internet.

One of the most graphic ways to present death and dying on the internet, and one which grew rapidly in the mid-2000s, is through the proliferation of real death, shock and gore websites, such as Bestgore.com (now defunct), Goregrish.com, Rotten.com (also defunct), and Seegore.com. These websites host(ed) footage and photographs of real death, war atrocities, suicides and accidents. Jeff Jacoby, writing for *The Boston Globe* regarding the ease of access these sites allowed to beheading videos from terrorist groups in the early 2000s, notes that 'for generating a spectacle that will be noticed – and shuddered at – the world over, sawing the head off an American journalist or a European relief worker, then uploading the video to the internet, is hard to beat' (Jacoby, 2014). This rise of real death sites has also been debated in terms of the celebrity it could bestow, for example, whether they could function as 'a new, even dirtier road to celebrity for those with latent sadistic urges' (Anderson, 2012). The internet, and real death websites in particular, afforded extremist groups a kind of visibility unheard of before the widespread use of the internet, with videos of murders carried out by militant Islamic groups, such as the beheadings of Daniel Pearl, James Foley and Nicholas Berg, presented in full and uncensored form on various real death and shock websites. More surprisingly, however, was how social media was also showing this content. Facebook, for instance, allows users to exhibit beheading videos on their timelines, following a temporary ban on graphic videos from May to October 2013, which was due to user complaints regarding how easy it was to access this kind of content. A change to Facebook community standards was made, and the website now allows graphic videos again (Harrison, 2013), with the site stating that this content is permissible as long as the context of the video is condemnation, outlining that 'we remove graphic images when they are shared for sadistic pleasure or to celebrate or glorify violence'.[3] As of 2015, Facebook introduced the addition of click through content warnings at the beginning of graphic videos (Gibbs, 2015). This demonstrates how easy it was, and still is, to watch real death online.

Since the early 2000s, there has also been a sharp rise in death memorialisation online. Wherewereyou.org is a website that was set up in the days after 9/11, and although it is now closed to new submissions, it acts as an online repository for both domestic and international traumatic memories of the event. As mentioned in a previous chapter, Lee Jarvis (2011) analyses the content of posts on Wherewereyou.org, noting that the website's refusal to finalise or correlate a greater meaning from 9/11 allows us to think through mnemonic practices. Jarvis proposes that the entries on the site, which come from a broad variety of different countries and number over 2,500, work as an alternative memory to the official line of mainstream news and reportage. Other accounts, such as Foot et al. (2005) explore web-based memorialisation, and Aaron Hess (2007) explores the relationship between vernacular memory and the construction of such memorial websites. In a different manner, Legacy.com allows users to create an online space to immortalise their lost loved ones, while maintaining breaking news of celebrity deaths. There has also been the creation of websites such as Eterni.me, which pledges to create a digital soul that will live on after the user's demise. The website claims that 'eventually, we are all forgotten', and promises 'Eterni.me collects your thoughts, stories, and memories, curates them and creates an intelligent avatar that looks like you. This avatar will live forever and allow other people in the future to access your memories'.[4] Eterni.me represents an interesting shift in death culture, and is intriguing precisely because it allows "ordinary" people to curate their memories and leave a lasting digital legacy for future generations.[5] Social media websites have also begun to shift around the areas of death and grieving. Facebook used to delete deceased users' profiles, but in the wake of the Virginia Tech shootings of 2007, the website changed its policy to allow the memorialisation of accounts (Hortobagyi, 2007). In doing so, Facebook positioned itself as having the ability to be reframed as an online grief space, and introduced an additional option to set up RIP pages, which can gain followers. A report in *The New York Times* even claims that in the near future, accounts for deceased users of Facebook will outnumber those still living (Wortham, 2010). This would make Facebook a form of digital cemetery, where the dead are still a visible presence among the living: an undoubtedly uncanny space.

Guo-Ming Chen, writing in 2012, proposes that the widespread use of the internet and social media has 'significantly affected humans' perception of the media, the usage of time and space, and the reachability and control of the media' (2012: 1). Just as Facebook led the charge when it came to death memorialisation, social media has also been central to live reportage of traumatic news events through the internet and the mobilisation of citizen information gathering during these incidents. BBC journalist Paul Mason suggests that there are subtle differences in relation to this according to different social media platforms, in that

> Facebook is used to form groups, covert and overt – in order to establish those strong but flexible connections. Twitter is used for real-time organization and news dissemination, bypassing the cumbersome "newsgathering" operations of the mainstream media. YouTube and the Twitter-linked photographic sites – Yfrog, Flickr and Twitpic – are used to provide instant evidence of the claims being made. (2012: 75, emphasis in original)

While Gerbaudo (2012) has looked at the links between social media and activism, Jay Rosen suggests that the internet has given normal people a platform on which to tell their stories, essentially destablising the traditional one directional broadcast news and reframing it into more of a conversation. As Rosen puts it, pre-internet and social media, 'a highly centralized media system had connected people "up" to big social agencies and centres of power but not "across" to each other. Now the horizontal flow, citizen-to-citizen, is as real and consequential as the vertical one' (2006: 14). We see here the echo of that first strand of reception to technological advances, with the internet being positioned as a utopian place of equitable communication that removes or diminishes the role of (possibly corruptible) mainstream news reporting. Social media applications can be used as knowledge tools, allowing users access to points of view or alternative versions of events which may have remained unknown to them before the expansion of the internet. And, as Martin Randall claims, the internet is often seen as 'a vital and flourishing alternative news outlet that is unmediated and unregulated and therefore, at least to a percentage of people, inherently more "true"' (2011: 10). These kinds of claims, however, have come under extensive scrutiny following the proliferation of fake news, particularly in the wake of Donald Trump's presidential campaign and subsequent election (Allcott and Gentzkow, 2017; Persily, 2017), with users being urged to be more critical of the content they are exposed to on social media (Glavin, 2016; Carson, 2019).

Although the internet may well have given historically excluded voices a platform, it has also been central to the formation and organisation of hate groups, and allowed them a place to mobilise. Christian Fuchs reminds us that 'the collective intelligence and activity of cultural communities [. . .] can easily turn into a fascist mob, especially in situations of capitalist crisis that are prone to advance the growth and radicalization of right-wing extremism' (2013: 60). Fuchs's argument has become ever more relevant in the years since he advanced it, with the Christchurch Mosque shootings in New Zealand of early 2019 being said to have been part of an 'internet-driven evolution of nationalist hatred' (Marsh and Mulholland, 2019), as well as 'made to go viral' (Warzel, 2019), with the gunman livestreaming the first 17 minutes of the massacre on Facebook. Other livestream tragedies include the shooting at West Freeway Church in Texas in 2019, which was captured and broadcast live due to the church using YouTube to stream its services, and the mass shooting at Arizona's Westgate Entertainment District in May of 2020, where the gunman filmed the attack with his mobile telephone's camera and streamed it via Snapchat. After murdering Bianca Devins in 2019, Brandon Andrew Clark posted images of her corpse to Instagram and Discord, a popular messaging site for gamers (Zoellner, 2020), before stabbing himself in the throat and posting photos of his injuries online (Cooper, 2019b). The internet is also charged with being instrumental to the radicalisation of Jake Davison – the gunman in a mass shooting in Plymouth, England – who frequently visited websites affiliated with the 'incel' subculture (Das et al., 2021) and posted multiple videos on YouTube expressing his misogynistic views (Griffin, 2021).[6]

The internet, then, can be situated as a contradictory place, as a place that is, as argued in *Vice* magazine, traumatising in and of itself, through the presence of a distressing 24-hour news cycle, the retraumatising capacity of movements such as #MeToo, and the ubiquitous threat of trolls (Gillespie, 2018). While it can function as a 'borderless virtual community' (Freeman, 2015: 107), it also, arguably, allows unlimited access to indulge sadistic curiosity (Atkinson and Rodgers, 2015: 1). Although primarily focusing on video games, Atkinson and Rodgers proclaim that the internet is a place

> providing access to a wave of material detailing and allowing us to interact with a phantasmagoria of pain, suffering and humiliation – extreme pornography, videos of beheadings or animal torture, rapes and fights, archives of 'fails' involving human injury, game worlds based around the bodily destruction or murder of simulated victims and so on. (2015: 1295)

While I would caution against instigating any kind of media effects debate regarding the access the internet provides to violent images, this idea – that the internet is a lawless and potentially dangerous domain – is one that horror cinema has taken on with aplomb.

It makes sense that found footage horror in particular – as a subgenre that is both able to adapt and respond quickly to broader shifts both cultural and technological – has turned towards online fear in a world where the internet has impacted so completely on our everyday life. The changing face of the internet has influenced the found footage horror subgenre in multiple ways, including the way in which these films are marketed, as more diverse ways of communicating online become available. The overarching element that has remained, however, is an attempt to infiltrate the audience's real world, and an encouragement towards a call to play.

## 'Is it real?': internet-based paratexts and found footage horror

A few days before the general release of *The Blair Witch Project* in North America, the Sci-Fi channel broadcast a documentary entitled *Curse of the Blair Witch* (1999). As Jane Roscoe notes, this documentary was made up of unused footage from the film itself (2000: 3), and it also included faked archival footage, interviews with 'experts' such as a Blair Witch historian and an ominous voiceover. Within the documentary, which functions to underline the truth claims of *The Blair Witch Project*, various pieces of the Blair Witch story are presented as fragments of a mystery to be solved. The narrative of *The Blair Witch Project* is similarly a puzzle, with parts of the story scattered across various ancillary products. Although the particulars of this campaign are now well known (or at least, easily found out with a quick Google search), it is worth briefly recapping its various aspects to demonstrate just how extensive it was. In addition to *Curse of the Blair Witch*, missing posters depicting the lead actors of the movie were hung around Sundance film festival before the film's premiere, but the backbone of *The Blair Witch Project*'s marketing was carried out online, with tidbits of information drip-fed into various internet-based message boards in the months before the film's opening. Anyone curious enough to look up the film on the Internet Movie Database would also find the principal actors listed as 'Missing – Presumed Deceased'. Most relevantly for this chapter, however, is the website Blairwitch.com, which became a central paratext in the film's viral marketing. The website[7] was arranged into sections entitled 'Mythology', 'The Filmmakers', 'The Aftermath' and 'The Legacy' and took care to construct and underline the authenticity of the filmic text. The website included a timeline of pertinent events in the Black Hills Forest, candid photographs of Heather, Josh and Mike before their disappearance, crime scene photographs, scanned pages of Heather's journal which was 'found with the filmmakers' equipment', audio files and details of the ongoing search for the missing students. There was nothing on the website to suggest that *The Blair Witch Project* was a work of fiction, carrying on the illusion of reality presented in both *Curse of The Blair Witch* and the tie-in book *The Blair Witch Dossier* (Stern, 1999). The success and subsequent influence of *The Blair Witch Project* marketing cannot be overstated, but although the idea of a viral campaign was remarkable and innovative in 1999, there is a critical need in scholarship surrounding the found footage horror subgenre to move on from a tendency to focus on the marketing of this one film. In contrast, an under-researched area is how internet-based marketing for found footage horror films has subtly adapted to move with the ever expanding and evolving world of online interaction.

In 1999, the internet was in a fledgling stage, with slower dial-up connection speeds, and without YouTube, Facebook and other user-generated content websites or social media applications in the form we now recognise. The truth claims of the Blair Witch website were therefore not easily undermined. In our age of 'fake news' it is highly unlikely that a film ever will, or ever could, achieve an effective blurring of the line between fact and fiction in the same way that *The Blair Witch Project* did. Released when it was, before the widespread use of internet communication, before social media and before the found footage horror style had gained a significant saturation level in mainstream American horror cinema, *The Blair Witch Project* was uniquely positioned temporally. The film was able to use a 'look' of reality through a handheld lens and the infancy of the internet to market its horror in a way that has been often emulated, but never equalled.

The extraordinary success of *The Blair Witch Project*, however – aided by its internet-based marketing campaign – is perhaps the reason why the internet and the found footage horror subgenre have become indisputably linked. This connection has expanded beyond marketing methods, and use of the internet outside of narratives now often moves to encourage audience interaction both before and after viewing. With a plethora of new instruments of engagement and marketing at their disposal – social media, livestreaming, user-generated content websites and more – recent found footage horror films have used new and innovative ways to engage with potential audiences, offering a level of interaction that was unimaginable at the time of *The Blair Witch Project*'s release. The question I wish to answer here, however, is what has changed since the marketing of that film, due to the evolution of the internet, and what – if anything – has remained the same.

Xavier Aldana Reyes has previously discussed *[Rec]* and the way in which that film immerses the viewer within the horror onscreen through affective techniques. Reyes also suggests that part of the film's success was due to its marketing campaign, which gathered momentum through videos on YouTube, and what Reyes terms as its 'strong paracinematic output' (Reyes, 2015b: 151).[8] Another found footage film that possessed this – and one that can be closely tied to the model set by *The Blair Witch Project* – is *Cloverfield*, with several websites being created around it. For example, a website was launched at 1.18.08.com (sadly no longer available), which hosted a series of time-coded images for user interpretation. Another site, Whencloverfieldhit.com, encouraged users to upload five-minute videos they had produced on consumer grade cameras, responding to the question 'Where were you when the monster hit?' (Wessels, 2011: 78), inspired perhaps by the presence of the 9/11 memories website Wherewereyou.org. Further websites, such as one for a fictional Japanese carbonated drink called Slusho that featured in the film and a fake corporate site for a deep sea drilling company, delivered obscure clues towards an explanation of the narrative. In addition to Myspace.com profiles for the main characters, Homay King explains that these enigmatic websites served as 'an extra-diegetic example of *Cloverfield*'s reflexive relationship to digital media forms' (2011: 135). These websites also helped to integrate the world of *Cloverfield* into our reality, through their 'deft insinuation of a movie world into the "real" pages of the internet' (Walters, 2007: 67). Alexandra Heller-Nicholas makes much of the way in which *Cloverfield* does not align itself with previous found footage films, as its marketing did not appear to be aiming to present the film as a 'genuine found footage artifact' (2014: 179). I argue that with the possible exception *of The Blair Witch Project* and, as I will demonstrate below, *The Upper Footage* (2013), the intention of internet-based marketing for found footage horror films, such as that for *Cloverfield*, is not necessarily to do this at all but rather can be simply to pull audience members into a call to play, by encouraging engagement with the filmic text both pre- and post-viewing.

James Castonguay views the interactive element of *The Blair Witch Project*'s viral marketing negatively, noting that he sees this use of the internet not as a form of progressive interactivity but 'instead as forms of inter-*passivity* in which Internet users actively embrace the pleasures of consumerism and celebrate the profit-driven practices of Hollywood film production and distribution' (2004: 72, emphasis in original). The perspective that Castonguay speaks from is a somewhat traditional (and outdated) view of fans or media consumers being passive recipients, and is influenced by the Frankfurt School of scholarship on mass media. Castonguay's position on the passivity of the audience and their framing as vacuous puppets playing into the Hollywood machine is somewhat reductive, and this kind of framework has been refuted by several cultural studies and fandom scholars previous to (see Bacon-Smith, 1992; Hills, 2002) and since (Larsen and Zubernis, 2012 among others) Castonguay's account. My own response to Castonguay's assertion is that a fan or consumer's relationship to a media text cannot be broken down into such binary terms. Following Matt Hills, I contend that just because a fan/consumer enjoys and engages in the commodification of a text, 'it does not mean that fans are *really* "passive" because caught up in commodification or that they are *really* active in their online fan activities' (2002: 206, emphasis in original). In other words, the ways in which fans/consumers engage with media products is becoming more and more complex in the internet age, and understanding this relationship as a one-directional flow is no longer accurate nor relevant. Henry Jenkins has proposed that since the expansion of the internet, interactions between fans and producers of content have become more intricate, 'especially as media industries have had to embrace more participatory strategies to court and maintain relations with their fans at a time where logic of "engagement" shapes many of their policies and productions' (2013: xxiii). This can be seen particularly clearly in journalistic debate around the power that fans now wield; for instance the online backlash surrounding the physical appearance of Sonic in a trailer for *Sonic the Hedgehog* (2020), which led to the film being delayed for extensive character redesign (Stuart, 2019). The intention of found footage horror marketing since *The Blair Witch Project* is not necessarily to inspire debate over filmic veracity, and to assume that all users will passively believe anything they see on the internet is simplistic.

Lars Krautschick suggests that there has been a wider movement in recent horror cinema towards the infiltration of 'safe zones' within narratives. A safe zone, in Krautschick's analysis, is a place that we feel secure in our everyday life, and his example of one of these being infiltrated is the breaking of the boundaries between the television and the living room in *Ring* and its American remake *The Ring* (2002). What this infiltration strategy does, Krautschick advances, is simulate a 'common, global cultural habit – such as dreaming or watching TV – or sphere – such as bedroom or living room – and then presents it as fearsome or gruesome', often through a rupture of boundaries in a moment of 'transparent immediacy' (2012: 9). Krautschick compares this to previous horror films, where the threat was constructed as being external to the characters' home, such as a haunted house or area – what Carol Clover would call 'the terrible place' (1992: 30). Whereas Krautschick's analysis proposes that audiences might seek out films in which horror infiltrates safe zones within the narrative in order to feel a 'live threat' (2012: 16), I expand his concept within this chapter – and this book more broadly – to include the infiltration of safe zones outside of the films themselves. Moving away from the puzzle-based interaction with their respective films that the websites of *The Blair Witch Project* and *Cloverfield* offered audiences, several subsequent found footage horror films extended their scares outside of their narrative.

*The Last Exorcism*, arriving two years after *Cloverfield*, is one such film that, through its marketing, infiltrated a safe zone outside of its filmic world with the utilisation of Chatroulette, a video chat website where users are randomly paired with other users for a webcam conversation. *The Last Exorcism*'s campaign video shown on Chatroulette was of an attractive young woman who begins to unbutton her top – playing on the often sexual content of the hosting website – before looking directly at the viewer as her face becomes demonic and she leaps at the camera. There were additional campaign videos for the film that ran along similar lines, such as one where the woman appears to break her own neck. These videos, which run for under a minute in length, then cut to black and direct viewers to the official website for the film.[9]

Chatroulette users did not actively seek out the viral marketing video for *The Last Exorcism*; it was shown at random, eliciting often terrified reactions.[10] The users who were lucky/unlucky enough to receive the viral video had the safe zone of their computer screen violated by the marketing campaign. Although the video did not attempt to underline the authenticity of the narrative of *The Last Exorcism* per se (the woman in the viral video does not appear at any point during the film), its positioning on Chatroulette and the random nature of its appearance there troubled the line between reality and fiction. A separate website, created at Churchofstmarks.com (now sadly defunct), however, did make some attempt to claim authenticity. The website proclaimed to be the online home of the Church of St Marks, where Reverend Cotton Marcus – one of the film's protagonists – was the minister. Along with the inclusion of service times, a biography for the Reverend and an email address for the church, the website also hosted articles regarding the history of demonic possessions, an online application form to request the services of the church for an exorcism, a quiz to determine the presence of demons, and links to Reverend Marcus's Twitter feed. Although it uses new forms of social media to give the film more reach, the marketing of *The Last Exorcism* still adheres to the online marketing template set out by *The Blair Witch Project*, in that Churchofstmarks.com actively tries to engage the viewer in a participatory make-believe experience before the release of the film. The websites of *The Blair Witch Project*, *Cloverfield* and *The Last Exorcism*, then, work to further the mythology of their respective narratives and encourage audiences to consume the films as cult objects. This use of internet-based marketing can, however, backfire completely if it does not serve its purpose properly, with a notable example of this being *The Devil Inside* (2012).

*The Devil Inside* is styled as an in-progress documentary following the character of Isabella Rossi, who wishes to document an investigation into exorcisms. Isabella feels compelled to determine the veracity of demonic possessions as her mother, Maria, was placed in a mental institution after committing three murders while under exorcism conditions. She meets with two priests, Ben and David, who allow her to record an exorcism they carry out before they join her to visit Maria. In the final sequences of the film, Isabella suffers a seizure and Ben accompanies the camera operator, Michael, as he drives for help to exorcise Isabella. During the journey,

Isabella attempts to strangle Michael, who then shows signs of being possessed himself and drives at high speed into oncoming traffic. The screen abruptly cuts to black, with sudden bursts of footage showing the characters during the chaos of a resulting car crash before ending on a title card, which directs viewers to the (no longer operational) Therossifiles.com. Although anti-endings are common to found footage horror cinema, neither *The Devil Inside* nor Therossifiles.com provide any information about what ultimately happens to the characters and the film was largely critically derided (Haglund, 2012; Faraci, 2012).[11] Audience members inclined to visit the website after viewing the film would find their frustrations compounded by a website that only featured backstory for the narrative – which had already been given during the film – instead of the conclusion they may have expected or desired.

Arriving later that same year, and using a different form of online interaction in user-generated content websites, *The Upper Footage* was marketed initially through video clips posted on YouTube to garner interest from potential audiences. The most notorious of these was a clip uploaded in 2012 titled *NYC Socialite Overdose*, which showed several individuals with pixelated faces at a party implied to be snorting cocaine. YouTube subsequently removed this video, and there was confusion from several media outlets as to the veracity of the footage, as well as speculation as to which celebrities may have been involved. Eventually, director Justin Cole released a statement through the popular horror news website DreadCentral.com, where he denied the footage was real. Cole stated that his goal was to make a found footage film that 'really went for it as *The Blair Witch Project* did in 1999', explaining that 'my intention wasn't to fool people for the sake of fooling them but to give them an experience where they could leave a movie theater, discuss the film, [and] wonder if the footage was real or not'. Cole's admiration for the marketing campaign of *The Blair Witch Project* is further made explicit when he continues that 'I knew to really pull this off I not only had to make a realistic film, but also create a world for it to live on the internet' (quoted in Barton, 2013). Of particular note is Cole's caveat later in the article that he was admitting the fictitious status of *The Upper Footage* 'with much hesitation'. Cole was seemingly only moved to debunk the veracity of the footage because of the controversy that had ensued after ex-Disney Channel actress Chelsea Kane was rumoured to be one of the partygoers in *NYC Socialite Overdose*. Although we can never know for sure, this suggests that if this debate had not occurred, Cole may have continued to make a sustained attempt at convincing audiences that both *NYC Socialite Overdose*, and by extension *The Upper Footage*, was real.

The discourses around the marketing for *The Upper Footage* possibly come the closest to replicating the debates around the veracity of *The Blair Witch Project* – seen as the pinnacle of found footage horror narratives' ability to skillfully blur the line between fact and fiction – while using a different form of internet-based communication to its predecessor. The confusion over the truth status of *The Upper Footage* appeared to ignite from how little information audiences had to go on: a few hastily removed videos on YouTube and a very simple website – its lack of information particularly apparent when compared to the rich and extensive website for *The Blair Witch Project* little over a decade earlier. In the age of information saturation online, however, less may indeed be more for suggesting the authenticity of such footage. The uneasiness inspired by many found footage horror films is often predicated on how firmly one can vouch with absolute certainty that the events in the film are fictive, or how easy it is for an audience to play into the idea that the events depicted really occurred. Of note in the case of *The Upper Footage* is Justin Cole's stated desire to create a 'world' for his narrative and to lure audiences into it. It would seem however that the desire is not so much to create a world for a found footage horror narrative, but to be able to seamlessly integrate the narrative into our real world. Whether this be by building an interactive website for the main character's place of work, as is the case of *The Last Exorcism*, or by using an enigmatic lack of information to offer interested audience members a space to imagine possibilities.

## Conclusion

As this chapter has made clear, the connection between the internet and found footage horror is strong. Although the subgenre's distinctive aesthetics would later appear on television (for example in *The River* (2012), and *American Horror Story: Roanoake* (2016)) it is on the internet that its format has been most enthusiastically adopted by content creators. The long running YouTube series *Marble Hornets* (2009–14), for example, inspired by the internet-created urban legend Slenderman, is told entirely through the found footage style, and its narrative centres around a set of tapes containing footage from an unfinished student film. In the tradition of found footage horror films of the past, the creators of *Marble Hornets* skilfully utilised social media (most notably Twitter) to expand the universe of the story and give clues to viewers as the mystery of the tapes unfolded.

Social media has of course become a pronounced and commanding presence in society within the last decade or so, not only through platforms such as Facebook, which enable users to connect with others through status updates and photograph posting, but also with the emergence of microblogging websites such as Tumblr, which allow users to share as much or as little original content as they desire, and then have this content 'reblogged' by other users. Other social media websites and applications such as Twitter, Instagram and TikTok have ensured that users have a platform and can use it how they wish. Although the kind of marketing used by *The Blair Witch Project* and *Cloverfield* has broadly come to an end, more recent found footage horror films such as *Unfriended* and *Spree* – both of which are explored more thoroughly in the following chapter – have taken advantage of new forms of internet-based communication to market their films. *Unfriended*, for example, made use of Kik messenger, on which users could have a conversation with the character of Laura Barns (through automated responses). Additionally, after the film's premiere at South by Southwest Festival, attendees were friended on Facebook by Laura Barns's account. *Spree*, meanwhile, made use of Instagram, with the account @kurtsworld96 – belonging to the main character Kurt Kunkle and heavily referenced in the narrative itself – being created around a month before the film's release on Netflix and featuring footage not present in the released film.[12]

It would seem, then, that older found footage horror films used the internet to provide the audience with what John Fiske (1989) would term as 'producerly' texts. Following Roland Barthes (1975), Fiske outlines that readerly texts are characterised by their invitation of a narrow interpretation to an essentially passive audience, with the predetermined meaning of the text being easy to uncover and enjoy. Writerly texts, meanwhile, resist coherence and closure, requiring more interpretative effort from the audience to uncover the meaning of the text. The producerly text, then, combines both the more narrow reading encouraged by readerly texts and the 'open' characteristic of writerly texts which 'replaces the pleasures of identification and familiarity with more cognitive pleasures of participation and production' (Fiske, 2010: 95). Producerly texts resist closure by incorporating gaps in the narrative (such as what is going on in the characters' lives in between episodes of a television show). Moreover, Fiske identifies that a producerly text is one that 'has loose ends that escape its control, its meanings exceed its own power to discipline them, its gaps are wide enough for whole texts to be produced in them' (Fiske, 1989: 104).

In this way, we can understand a number of found footage horror narratives as producerly. The numerous paratexts presented by *The Blair Witch Project*, and then the marketing of such later films as *The Last Exorcism*, offer audience members an invitation to continue to suspend their disbelief, fill in the narrative gaps and play into the idea of the narratives being real. More recent found footage horror films have perhaps recognised the perils of giving audiences an abundance of information, however, and work to convince us of their realism – if only for a short time or as part of a call to play – because they already fit into our reality, being aesthetically similar to a multitude of user-generated videos that can be found on YouTube.com, or other various content websites. There is no need to create an overly complex and furnished world to house these narratives, because that world already exists as our – ever more mediated – world. These narratives are heteroglossic; they invite viewers to play into the performance, and as Angela Ndalianis evaluates, 'the key words in this instance are "play" and "performance": the participant is invited to literally play and become part of the performance *as if it's real*' (2012: 172, emphasis in original). As such, the online marketing of these films seeks to pull the viewer into their call to play, and engage with the viewer both pre-viewing, in the case of *The Last Exorcism* and *The Upper Footage*, and post-viewing, as is seen in the marketing of *The Devil Inside*. With the exception of *The Upper Footage* there is a lessening focus in recent marketing campaigns on underlining the authenticity of found footage horror narratives or the veracity of the footage within them, but it could be argued that the time for this kind of paratextual play, given the rise of fake news and deepfakes, is over. Yet still, found footage horror is not ready to stop playing with the horrific potential of the internet.

## Notes

1 See Mitsuyo Wada-Marciano (2007) for an examination of this tradition in Japanese horror cinema.
2 Nationaldayofunplugging.com is one such site that encourages a two-day period of disconnection.
3 Information from Facebook community standards, accessed 19 September 2016.
4 Available on Eterni.me.
5 A website such as this was the focus of the *Black Mirror* (2011) episode 'Be Right Back', where a bereaved woman accesses an online service to use her deceased boyfriend's social media accounts to duplicate his voice so she can talk to him on her telephone. Eventually she allows a synthetic body to take on his appearance. Since this episode aired, the possibility of speaking to an AI version of deceased individuals has become a reality (MacDonald, 2016).

6   In addition to live streaming murder, live streamed suicides have also occurred; for example the deaths of Erdoğan Ceren in 2016 and Angel Hernandez Grado in 2021. A video detailing the suicide of Gleb Korablev in 2019 has gained a level of notoriety due to it being framed as a 'cursed' video (see Cleary, 2019).
7   The original website for *The Blair Witch Project* has since been taken down, but various archival websites such as web.archive.org have preserved the pages for posterity.
8   Although I have found no official tie-in to the film itself, the independently produced game *[Rec]: Shutter* (2012) features a first-person perspective through a camera. The player can activate night vision to enable them to see into dark areas, and if they are killed by the monsters that inhabit the game, the screen cuts to black and text reads 'You failed to record'.
9   This advert can be seen as a version of the once popular 'Screamer' videos that populated YouTube in the early to mid-2000s, where idyllic or innocuous footage would play only to be sharply interrupted by a blast of noise and a frightening image.
10  YouTube hosts a variety of reaction videos to this marketing campaign, showing user responses ranging from hysterical laughter to outright terror. However, given that these reaction videos are taken from the official marketing for the film, and fed into the hype that was being generated around it, their veracity has to be considered as questionable.
11  For a defence of the ending of the film by William Brent Bell (the writer/director) and Matthew Peterman (co-writer), please see Cornet (2012).
12  A YouTube channel was created too, with more footage not present in the film.

# 9

# 'You have committed a fatal error': social media horrors

Xavier Aldana Reyes proposes that 'horror appropriates the structures of fear already in circulation' (2013: 150) and, as I argued in the previous chapter, anxieties began to revolve around the communicative potential of the internet as its use became more widespread. As this book so far has made clear, a wide variety of reality aesthetics sit under the umbrella of 'found footage horror': from documentary framing and bystander videos to the more inhuman gaze of dashcam and CCTV. After the phenomenal success of *Paranormal Activity* – once it was widely released in 2009 – the found footage format exploded: new stories made use of its distinctive (and low cost) style and a host of old scares were updated through a found footage frame. Just over the horizon, however, was a group of found footage horror films that would move the subgenre into new territory entirely, and the aim of this chapter is to provide an account of this subset of the subgenre, which I have tentatively termed 'social media horror'.

Several other terms have been put forward to describe the kind of films this chapter will analyse, including ones proposed by their producers, with Timur Bekmambetov advancing the term 'Screenlife' to describe *Unfriended* (Kohn, 2018). It is important at this point, therefore, to outline my own use of 'social media horror' and to highlight the differences between this term and 'desktop horror', as put forward by Lindsay Hallam (2021). Although 'desktop horror' is a term that works well for the central film of Hallam's discussion – *Open Windows* (2014) – and there is clear overlap between my term and Hallam's, there are multiple factors that suggest that 'social media horror' is a more appropriate term to describe the particular body of films discussed in this chapter: *The Den, Unfriended* and *Spree*. The most significant difference between desktop horror and social media horror is the way in which these films use their internet-based aesthetics. Although

*Open Windows* takes place on a laptop, it does not emulate the first person perspective of a laptop user, containing movements – such as the almost 'ping pong' action of the frame moving to different parts of the screen and zooming in and out at significant moments – that a laptop user is not able to do in real time. In contrast, even though *Unfriended*, *The Den* and *Spree* break with the found footage conceit in their very final moments, the majority of these films' runtime takes place as if the laptop (or in the case of *Spree*, phone) screen is our own. *Open Windows* also, crucially, contains camera footage that is not adequately explained as being achievable diegetically. In contrast, *Spree*'s movements between different cameras and apps are explained within the narrative, as it is shown to be a curated fan video at the end of the film. *Open Windows* does not include commonly used social media apps or websites, or even proxies of them, which stands in contrast to a social media horror film such as *Sickhouse* (2016), which was the first film to be made and presented on Snapchat.[1] Films coming under the term social media horror, then, can be characterised as found footage horror films that consist of footage filmed on, intended to be viewed on, or made to resemble in its aesthetics, social media applications or websites. The emphasis of desktop horror, and *Open Windows* particularly, is on the advances that computer-based technology affords us and the dangers inherent therein; in contrast, social media horror constructs fear around the specific areas of social media and internet-based communication, and engages with cultural anxieties relevant to these particular spheres such as digital witnessing, access to extreme content and the rise of potentially damaging subcultures.

The internet has, in social media horror, become a fundamental part of the narrative. Understanding the specific cultural fears that this body of films engages with is essential to furthering academic investigation into the constantly evolving nature of found footage horror cinema, as well as in examining how the internet has influenced and changed the content of the horror genre more broadly. In the previous chapter, I discussed three key ways in which death, dying and the dead are being mediated online, and each of the films discussed here correlates with these varied representations in turn: *The Den* relates to real death websites, *Unfriended* to social media as a grief space and *Spree* to the trend towards livestreaming death. A chronological approach to these case studies – which were released over a period of seven years – allows an overview of the changing face of found footage horror cinema, but also sketches how internet-based anxieties have shifted too. The films in this chapter mark the next logical step for a subgenre keenly involved with its cultural context and our experience of the world more broadly. Beginning with *The Den*, this chapter will discuss how the ostensibly disparate subgenres of torture horror and found footage horror began to blur, and how the proliferation of real death websites has impacted on the subgenre with their promise to present an uncensored truth to their users. Although these websites feature too in *Unfriended*, they take a supporting role as anxieties shift to fears around digital anonymity and the permanence of mistakes recorded on the internet – a subject that presciently predates debate around 'cancel culture'. Here I will discuss how the uploadable aesthetics of user-generated content websites are used to update the found footage horror subgenre and the traditional ghost story. If *Unfriended* focuses on the isolating qualities of online interaction, then the final case study, *Spree*, deals with the dangers of living in a world driven by the desire for constant, changing, fresh content and how murder may just become the next internet sensation.

## 'It's the internet, you should have expected something like this': real death, the internet and *The Den*

*The Den*, which is presented through webcam and mobile phone footage, follows the character of Elizabeth, a PhD student who wins a research grant at the start of the film in order to carry out a study of video chat websites. Her research questions are concerned with how this particular form of communication has changed interpersonal interaction, and why people choose to share their lives in this way. Elizabeth's computer is hacked after she exchanges instant messages with the user Pyagrl*16 on the video chat website 'The Den' and witnesses the brutal murder of a girl – who she (and we) assume to be that user – on a video call with them. As part of her research, Elizabeth has been recording all of her online interactions and shows this particular video log to the police, who do not investigate it in any depth. Although Elizabeth admits that the video could have been, as the police suggest, some 'viral prank', she asks her friend Max to track the location from where the video was transmitted. A masked assailant then incapacitates Elizabeth's boyfriend Damien and kills one of her other friends before kidnapping Elizabeth and taking her to a disused warehouse. The close of the film shows us that the stalking, kidnapping and eventual murder of Elizabeth was to provide content for an online pay-per-view website.

In terms of gore, found footage horror is often positioned as being relatively tame. *The Blair Witch Project,* for example, was argued to have taken 'a "less is more", psychological (as opposed to visceral) approach to horror' (Aloi, 2005: 188); Peg Aloi has noted that *The Blair Witch Project* 'puts horror in the psychological realm rather than in the "actual" realm of blood and guts' (2005: 192). Just as *The Blair Witch Project* was positioned as a salve to the horror genre that surrounded it in the late 1990s, *Paranormal Activity*, some ten years later, was also characterised as a bloodless alternative to the gore of films such as the *Hostel* series (2005–11) and the *Saw* franchise. One of the most interesting initial aspects of *The Den*, then, is its incorporation of gore-led elements more commonly associated with torture horror. This complicates an assumption around found footage horror cinema: that it elevates the concept of suggestion above the display of bloody carnage. The realism of the torture and execution of Elizabeth in the last scenes of *The Den*, for example, where she is first hanged by masked men and struggles to breathe for over twenty seconds before being cut down and shot in the head, is closer to the bloody scenes shown in *Hostel* than the virtually bloodless affair of *The Blair Witch Project*.

Bestgore.com, which was indefinitely shut down in November 2020, was a repository of footage and photographs of extreme gore. During its lifespan, Bestgore's creator, Mark Marek, repeatedly strove to position the website as a place that actively tried to present uncensored reality to its users, and as working towards the public's best interests. Marek – who was arrested and charged under obscenity laws in 2013 (Purdy, 2013), which he eventually pleaded guilty to in 2016 (Reith, 2016) – noted in reference to users of his website that 'They want to know the truth and are not afraid to face it. They want the real truth, the raw truth, the uncensored truth. Not the played down one presented by the media with an agenda' (Jeffries, 2013). These claims were underlined on the October 2021 landing page of the website, on which testimonials from users noted how much they would miss Bestgore and the 'truth' it presented to them. While Marek's claims regarding his website can be disputed – to say the least – due to the sensational way real death was presented on the website, what is true is that in the aftermath of 9/11, footage of people falling from the Twin Towers was deemed too upsetting to be screened during news broadcasts on mainstream media, and is still usually strangely absent from retrospective discussions of the event;[2] this footage first reappeared on fringe internet websites such as Bestgore.com. The website was also the first to host *1 Lunatic, 1 Ice Pick*, showing the dismemberment of student Jun Lin, which was recorded and uploaded by his murderer, Luka Magnotta. Beheading videos, such as those of Daniel Pearl, were also first seen on real death websites before being shown in edited form on mainstream news channels. In a sense, then, these websites were presenting a form of hidden 'truth' to their users that they would not have been able to access otherwise.

Catherine Russell, in her book *Narrative Morality: Death, Closure and New Wave Cinemas*, talks of fictional representations of death, and assesses that brutal death in fictional films presents 'a special crisis in believability, a threshold of realism and its own critique' (1994: 23). Although Russell is discussing fictitious death, her thoughts on fictive horror do echo through journalistic reactions to the proliferation of real death websites. Journalist Caitlin Moran (2009), after watching the video *3 Guys, 1 Hammer* – which shows the torture and murder of a man by men later known as the Dnepropetrovsk Maniacs[3] – explains that she was struck with how she was carrying out something as mundane and normal as collecting her children from school after bearing digital witness to the video. She writes that while she, 'in a pair of bourgeois Ugg boots', was at the school, she was 'thinking of a man being murdered in a wood'. Moran summarises that she has not felt quite the same since watching the video, and ends her account by urging her readers to 'take great care in what you chose – often in a cavalier moment – to place in your memory [. . .] A very tiny part of me now, and will always, consist of an elderly man dying in a wood in Ukraine.' Moran notes that after switching off the video, she feared that the footage might have damaged her computer in some way; her actions were to turn it off, unplug it and then cover it with a cloth. This irrational urge connects this particular account of watching real death videos to the concept of haunted media. There is an anxiety, evidenced in Moran's actions, that somehow clicking onto a real death video might leave the individual open to not only computer viruses, but also the possibility that, somewhere, someone knows you have viewed it and has placed your name or IP address onto a 'watch list' of deviants, or may now have access to your files or webcam. *The Den*, and the following case study, *Unfriended* (as well as its sequel), are essentially haunted by the possibility of sinister surveillance. When we log into a website, we are receiving the information that is on the screen, but conversely, with HTTP cookies and other web analytics, the average internet user is also transmitting information to the internet, such as their location and shopping preferences. As Kevin Wetmore Jr explains, 'The idea that one is simply a passive user of the internet with no data flowing in the other direction is hopelessly naïve' (2012: 188). In *Unfriended*, as will be explored more fully below, this multi-directional element is used by the ghost of Laura Barns to gain control of laptops, and in *The Den*, it is the creators of the pay-per-view torture website revealed at the film's conclusion who have used the internet to gain control of and spy on Elizabeth.

After her computer mysteriously connects to the video chat website while she sleeps, Elizabeth asks her friend, Max, if computers can just switch themselves on, to which he jokingly suggests 'Maybe it's a ghost?'. Although *The Den* does not feature the supernatural at any point, Elizabeth's computer and the internet work against her throughout the film: her files are deleted because she clicks on a malicious link, and a video of her having sex is sent to a Professor at her institution without her knowledge. They are not haunted per se, but the internet and Elizabeth's laptop are haunting presences in her life, as Elizabeth's friends and family flag up to her several times that she is becoming obsessed with internet-based communication and that they never see her in real life. Elizabeth appears exasperated as she video calls her sister, explaining 'You're seeing me now, why doesn't anyone get that?' and argues that her sister will need to embrace internet communication at some point. As the audience only ever sees Elizabeth through her webcam, and does not have access to her without it, she does seem to only really 'exist' online, and this is a theme that will reoccur in the subsequent social media horror films in this chapter.

Temporal discrepancies in *The Den* are also a haunting presence and trouble the 'liveness' the audience may have come to expect of internet-based communication. Early in the film, Elizabeth's boyfriend Damien goes missing. The audience sees – although Elizabeth does not because she momentarily turns away from the screen she is chatting to him on – that someone in the backseat of his car attacks Damien. After trying in vain to contact Damien the next day, Elizabeth receives a request for a video chat from him. Opening the video chat, the images of Damien safe in his apartment reassure her. When Damien starts speaking, however, Elizabeth realises that she has seen this footage before, when Damien video chatted with her earlier. This video chat is, then, a ghostly remnant of the past, returning to haunt Elizabeth before cutting to a live feed of Damien's now empty apartment. Later in the film, after Elizabeth is kidnapped and placed in front of her laptop, Damien again invites her to a video chat. As the chat connects, Elizabeth receives another incoming call from Max and the screen splits into three. Max is suffocated with a plastic bag in front of Elizabeth and Damien, and as Elizabeth screams and sobs, Damien tells her that he has already watched this footage the previous day, and that Max is already dead.[4]

The aesthetic of real death websites is most clearly evoked in the final sequence of *The Den*, where we first see the website hosting the video of Elizabeth. Although *The Den* does stay in the found footage format for the majority of its run time, the end scene breaks with this conceit most disruptively, when the camera pulls back from Elizabeth's corpse to reveal the laptop of someone else, who has been watching events unfold with the audience. This laptop-within-a-laptop reveal is jarring and alters the relationship between the spectator and the screen. We watch as the unnamed man starts to type in his credit card details to access another 'murder feed', which, like Elizabeth's, promises a full webcam takeover and home surveillance feeds. It also assures it contains over 120 hours of footage, friends and family, interactive torture and nudity. We can see that the website contains a 'like' system for the murder feeds, with this feature tying the website to Goregrish.com, which features a user voting system for their videos similar to that found on Reddit.com and Youtube.com, where users can 'upvote/like' or 'downvote/dislike' a video depending on how much they enjoyed it. We can also clearly read various categories of video hosted on the website, which include 'axe play', 'cannibal' and 'blowtorch', and learn that Elizabeth's narrative has over 12,000 likes. A click-through advert on the website shows a GIF of a woman having her throat slit, as our unnamed companion viewer ponders spending $99 to access another feed. Aside from the inclusion of buying more extreme content, the visual aesthetic of the murder website within *The Den* is very similar to real death websites such as Bestgore, which included categories such as 'Autopsy', 'Beheading', 'Drowning' and 'Hanging' for perusal. When the audience finally sees the unnamed user's face, we find a completely unremarkable middle-aged white man, who is accessing the website in what appears to be his home office,

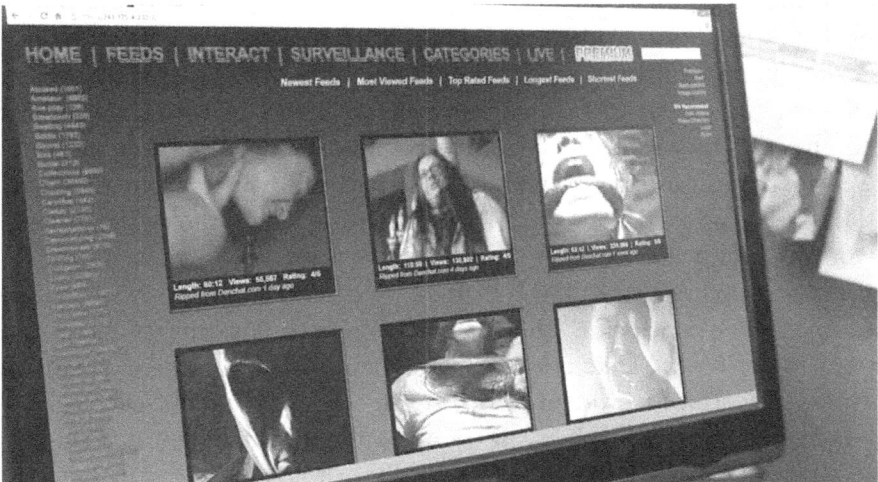

**Figure 9.1** The pay-per-view torture website in *The Den* includes categories for 'axe play', 'blow torch' and other niche interests.

before his child enters the room and interrupts his viewing. The question that Elizabeth poses at the beginning of the film, that of 'who is really out there', is responded to in this scene, with a clear indication that the answer is 'us' – the average, unremarkable user of the internet. Adam Charles Hart argues that 'The camera of the horror film is not one that the viewer easily identifies with' (2019: 47) but it is precisely our forced identification with the unnamed user at the end of *The Den* that amplifies our fear.

Neil Jackson proposes that, historically, 'snuff has been present within popular and subcultural discourse, yet absent as a "proven" artefact', and that 'any study dealing seriously with the phenomenon is immediately obliged to stress the malleable nature of the debate' (2016; 1). With internet death videos, the enduring cultural myth of the snuff film becomes a reality, as any internet user can, with the click of their mouse, watch recorded footage of real death. The malleable nature of the debate now moves towards an argument over the definition of snuff. One such discourse is how snuff is often framed as being sexual in nature. The sexual element that surrounds the debate of snuff films seems lessened in the case of internet death videos. Although many gore sites include advertisement banners from pornographic businesses, the videos hosted by these websites themselves can be seen as more of an endurance test, or a limit experience, as the majority of the real death videos available online are distinctly unsexualised, with the exception of the necrophiliac aspects of *1 Lunatic, 1 Ice Pick*. Another discourse around the definition of snuff is regarding an element of commerce that needs to be present. In other words, that people are being killed specifically because someone has paid for that to happen, or that footage of a death is recorded to then be sold, rather than be seen as simply a recording of death. The torture and death pay-per-view website featured in the close of *The Den* touches upon these debates, both with its emphasis on the erotic aspect of these murder feeds and the clear drive the website has towards profit, with the murder feeds being pay-per-view and the advertising strip along the side of the screen. This is the easily accessed world of real death websites, and the journalistic response to them (see Harkin, 2006, Lillebuen, 2012, Anderson, 2012 and Dewey, 2014), taken to an extreme conclusion. This is a place where real death aficionados can pay a modest fee to watch the actual moment of death, complete with the option of 'interactive torture'. Real death websites, and the videos contained within them, which can be uploaded, downloaded, deleted and reuploaded, are demonstrative of how difficult it is to police digital communities and how it is almost impossible to remove something from the internet forever.

## 'What you've done here will live forever': the haunted (social) media of *Unfriended*

*Unfriended* follows the fictional events surrounding the one-year anniversary of the death of Laura Barns, a teenage girl who committed suicide after a 'shaming' video of her at a party was uploaded to social media.[5] The shaming video plays an important role in *Unfriended* and is shown to the audience several times; each time it is played for a different duration, with more visual information being revealed. The first time we see this video it begins at a party full of teenagers, and shows Laura Barns lying on a table talking to a young man. Val, one of the other characters in the film, is involved in a short altercation with Laura before the footage abruptly cuts to show a girl passed out and face down beside a trailer. The camera approaches the girl and the operator crouches down to slowly pan over her legs. It lingers over the girl's inner thighs, which are covered in excrement, as are her crotch and white shorts. As the operator of the camera moves to film the girl's face, it becomes clear that it is Laura who has passed out, and she raises her finger to her lips in a hushing motion. The camera sweeps back to a close-up of Laura's crotch before ending on a freeze frame of her soiled legs and shorts, with the text 'LEAKY LAURA, KILL URSELF' superimposed on top of the frame. The shaming intention of this video is not Laura's inebriated state, but clearly her loss of control over her bowels and the subsequent spectacle. As the narrative progresses, we learn that this video was uploaded to YouTube anonymously from the account 'Laura Exposed' and a mass shaming campaign began, with the comments on the video urging Laura to commit suicide. *Unfriended*'s narrative is deliberately self-contained, with the entirety of the film – bar a few seconds at the end – taking place on the laptop screen of Blaire, Laura's best friend. The film is presented as a Skype group chat between Blaire and several of her peers: Mitch, Adam, Jess, Ken and Val, and documents the spectral revenge of Laura Barns as it becomes clear that this group of characters was behind the shaming campaign that caused Laura's death. The film uses the uploadable aesthetics of social media and user-generated content websites to engage with and update both the tradition of the ghost story and the found footage horror subgenre.

These uploadable aesthetics are continually evoked throughout the film, particularly within two further videos. The first of these opens the film, with grainy footage showing Laura committing suicide. This fictional suicide video was, until recently, still available to view on Liveleak.com, a now defunct shock website which often featured videos of real fatal accidents, and the video is situated on this website within the film itself too. It is low resolution footage of a girl standing in a basketball court and the camera, which is moving in a way that suggests a human onlooker is holding it, is unsteady and zooms in and out of focus, but stays trained on the girl as she lifts a gun to her face. We hear voices shouting 'Laura!' before there is a loud bang. The camera abruptly tilts upwards, suggesting the operator either jolted at the noise or was jostled by another onlooker. As the camera moves back down we see the girl, who we now know as Laura, lying on the floor. This video not only uses the kind of bystander footage aesthetics I explored in Chapter 5, but is also – through its positioning on Liveleak.com – evocative of the real death sites explored above. The third and final key video is one that is shown to have been uploaded to YouTube by Laura herself before her death. This video, in which Laura holds up flash cards instead of speaking, is remarkably aesthetically similar to the real-life pre-suicide video of Amanda Todd, a girl who committed suicide after she was subjected to an extended online bullying campaign. In addition to the use of flashcards instead of speech, both girls wear black vest tops, both have long dark hair and both videos are in black and white.[6] All three of the videos in *Unfriended* carefully recreate video aesthetics common to the time of the film's release: bystander footage in the shaming and suicide videos, and videos made by the victims of bullying – such as Amanda Todd and Jonah Mowry – that were uploaded to YouTube and went viral.

The videos within *Unfriended* are not the only connection to uploadable aesthetics. Image macros,[7] for example, are also referenced in the scene where Laura kills Jess. In this scene, Blaire is alerted by a Facebook notification that a photo has been uploaded to Jess's profile and clicks to take a look. The image shows Jess with her face upturned towards the camera in the style of a selfie (a photographic self-portrait) with her hair straighteners smouldering in her throat. The distinctive white block text of an image macro proclaims 'LOOKS LIKE SHE FINALLY STFU'.[8] These references to internet culture within *Unfriended* are presented as less of a critique of social media, or indeed of a generation that has been said to be 'addicted to the internet' (Cassidy, 2014), but more to build a sense of realism through the incorporation of various visual aspects of internet culture that it assumes viewers may be familiar with. Adam Daniel, for example, has discussed how *Unfriended* uses 'the frozen frame' (the bane of an internet user's life) to great effect, with 'the eerie stillness' of these unmoving, glitched out frames heightening the viewer's engagement with the screen as they wait for movement to recommence (2020: 152). The

Social media horrors    179

**Figure 9.2** Ken's death in *Unfriended*, the horror emphasised by violent glitching, is witnessed digitally by his friends.

traditional ghost story hinges on the idea of the unfamiliar or supernatural appearing as a rupture into the reality of everyday life: a ghostly happening in a credible setting. The credible setting in this film is Blaire's laptop screen. Whereas *The Den* uses proxy versions of popular websites, within *Unfriended* Blaire's laptop clearly displays the recognisable logos and functionality of websites such as Google, Chatroulette, Facebook, YouTube, Liveleak and Facebook Messenger. She also uses software such as Skype and Spotify. These are websites and applications that audience members themselves might use. Indeed, the inclusion of familiar and arguably mundane icons and sounds, down to the tapping of Blaire's fingers on her keyboard, act as a marker of authenticity and also of continuity. They marry our reality to the fictitious setting of the film and pull us into its call to play. *Unfriended* turns the quotidian reality of internet communication into a site of threat and horror.

It is not immediately apparent within *Unfriended* that the threat is supernatural, and in the first part of the film the fears of the group of friends circulate around anxieties relating to hacking and cyberstalking, with the malevolent communication thought to be originating from another internet user. After it becomes clear that the threat is supernatural, the internet and social media are coded in *Unfriended* as having potential for vindictive communication from the ghostly realm, directly linking it to earlier films such as *Poltergeist*, but with an updated engagement with contemporary internet-based fears. Within the film, Laura Barns inhabits the electronic elsewhere, overtly tying the film to Sconce's concept of haunted media. As the narrative progresses, Laura uses the internet and the way it links the group of friends to each other to gain control of other technology, similar to the way Sconce describes stories of radio waves seemingly possessing ordinary household implements – such as a metal spade or a mirror picking up radio transmissions (2000: 68). Laura – who is initially presented as an unknown avatar within the friend's group chat on Skype – gains control of telephones so the group cannot call for help, their printers to further her torment of them, and at several points in the narrative disables laptop functionality for the characters. When the group members turn off their microphones and call each other on their mobile telephones, Laura simply switches the microphones back on. When she terrorises Blaire through her Spotify software, playing a song at high volume to taunt her, Blaire mutes her speakers and we see onscreen how Laura turns the volume back up. Laura also often types messages on different characters' behalf on the Skype chat, causing fractures to appear in friendships.

The concept of the internet as a site of both hauntings and the haunted is also emphasised in the film's marketing taglines. These include 'online your memories last forever, but so do your mistakes' and 'every comment, share, message, like, post, can come back to haunt you'. These taglines underline the false security of digital anonymity in the film and more widely tie into societal fears around internet predators, identity theft and hacking. Whatever the teenagers did or said on the internet anonymously, or under the guise of a fake profile, is now known to Laura's ghost. Near the end of the film, Laura uploads a longer cut of the shaming video onto Blaire's Facebook timeline. This version shows her former best friend Blaire as the operator of the camera, adding to the previous reveals of each of the characters having had a role in getting the video online and the subsequent cyberbullying, with one character going as far as to deface Laura's grave after her burial. After this video is posted, Blaire's Facebook friends begin to berate her with messages similar to those sent to Laura, expressing disgust and urging her to kill herself for her part in Laura's death. The users of Facebook within the film recalibrate what Whitney Phillips calls 'RIP energies' (2015) to focus on Blaire, showing Facebook as a place with a changeable moral code, where social media can be used as a form of behaviour policing.

I have discussed in previous chapters how suspense is often built around the offscreen space in found footage horror, how threats are often obscured by the limitations of the camera and how we are at the mercy of where the operator decides to point the lens. Most often in watching a found footage horror film, we are placed in the same distinctly unprivileged position as the operator and are given information and visual confirmation at the same time as them. Although – as discussed in Chapter 4 – found footage horror has previously played with spectator privilege, it is fair to say this is relatively rare in the subgenre. In *Unfriended*, we follow Blaire's cursor as it allows us access to her personal emails, her Google searches and the files she opens, actions which give the audience information that the other members of the Skype group chat are not aware of, nor do they have access to. In the final moments of the film for instance, Blaire condemns her boyfriend Mitch to death in an attempt to save herself, by confessing his sins to Laura via Facebook Messenger. As I have demonstrated thus far, the offscreen space in found footage horror is used as a place in which potential dangers lurk, and as Matthew Raimondo proposes, the audience's curiosity about the offscreen space is capitalised on 'to create immediate horror, suspense and fear' (2014: 72). Although in *Unfriended* we have access to information that characters other than Blaire do not have, we are still restricted by only having access to Blaire's screen. When her friends are attacked, and their Skype feed deleted from the chat, we are given no more information about what happened to their bodies. This demonstrates that *Unfriended*, although constructing its fear primarily around the contemporary communicative technology of the internet, has a good deal in common with the traditional spectatorial privileges seen in earlier horror cinema, and as such is not a complete departure from it.

Although *Unfriended* may work towards evoking traditional privileged spectatorial positions more common to the slasher subgenre, where it is innovative is in how it supplants older ghost story traditions with internet-based replacements. In films such as *Psycho* (1960), characters walk down dark hallways or open doors while audience members wait for something to appear out of the darkness and deliver a jolt. In social media horror, this becomes the tense act of waiting for a gruesome image to load, with the audience leaning into the screen in anticipation, and engaging in a heightened act of active viewing. This leaves audiences vulnerable to receive a jolt (see Chapter 2) when the image is eventually revealed. Elsewhere, the panic of a character running from an apparition and trying to lock themselves somewhere safe is supplanted by Blaire's mounting panic as she waits for antivirus software to finish running on her laptop, before the timer that Laura's ghost has placed on her screen runs down. The spectral quality of online interaction contributes to the tension within the film. The way it is used also emphasises the idea of 'the in between' put forward within Sconce's concept of haunted media. For example, when we converse online, we often find ourselves waiting for replies; on Facebook, we are reassured that a friend is typing a response on Messenger when we see three dots appear in the chat to signify this. In this moment, we are together in our online interaction, even if we are geographically apart. The other party, and their message, are temporarily travelling in the in between. Similarly, the group of friends in *Unfriended* are together online; as in their group Skype chat, they can even see each other. However, their geographical isolation from each other becomes ever more apparent as the film progresses. At various points in the narrative, characters are unable to relay a friend's address to a police call handler because they do not know it instinctively, and more than once have to helplessly watch as a friend is brutally murdered on their screen.

Temporal delays are a convention that has been previously used in horror films such as *Saw 2* (2005), where the character of Detective Eric Matthews watches what is assumed to be a live feed of a group of people, one of which is his son, trapped in a house and at the mercy of the Jigsaw Killer. *Saw 2* plays with the temporality of the narrative by revealing towards the end of the film that this footage was pre-recorded and not live. Similarly, in *Scream* (1996), a scene depicts characters in a van watching the antagonist Ghostface approaching the character of Randy without his knowledge and they run to his house to raise the alarm. It is only after most of the characters leave the safety of the van that it is revealed the footage has been received with a substantial time delay. In both *Saw 2* and *Scream*, temporal delays reduce the characters to helplessly watching what has already passed. *Unfriended* does not use delays, but more the liveness of images as a source of horror. The panic of the victims in *Unfriended*, and their deaths, are transmitted live to their friends, who act as real-time digital witnesses to their performative murder-suicides, moving this convention into even more horrifying territory. The urge that audiences of horror cinema may feel to shout at characters, and warn them that splitting up in a dark and haunted space is a bad idea, is now irrelevant. These characters are already completely alone, linked only by their fallible internet connection and a compulsion to stay logged on. In this way, the internet is presented very much like Sconce's analysis of wireless communication, where

> alone at their crystal sets and radios, listeners felt an electronic kinship with an invisible, scattered audience, and yet they were also acutely aware of the incredible distances involved in this form of communication that ultimately reaffirmed the individual listener's anonymity and isolation. (2000: 62)

These characters are often painfully aware of their isolation, with Jess at one point begging the others to stay online with her, as they start to call each other on their mobile telephones instead of interacting online. Laura is alone too, and when the group members realise that someone has hacked Jess's account to post photos, and deduce that it is 'Billie' – the interloper in their group chat – Val threatens to come to wherever Billie is and fight her. Billie/Laura's reply is simply 'You wouldn't like it here.' This is reminiscent of the sad and foreboding warnings given by supposedly spectral voices in Konstantins Raudive's experiments with electronic voice phenomena in the 1960s. During these experiments, scientists attempting to make contact with the dead reported receiving messages of suffering and penance from the electronic elsewhere, as detailed in the book *Break Through: Electronic Communication with the Dead May Be Possible* (1971).

It is true that if we are to pull back the aesthetic layers of the film, Laura's story is that of revenge, a long standing narrative structure used in the horror genre. As such, the basic storyline of *Unfriended* does not stand out as particularly noteworthy or innovative. However, it is the film's centralisation of the internet and social media as a locus of fear that marks it as an important landmark in the found footage horror subgenre, and the horror genre more widely. *Unfriended* provides a filmic space for investigating emergent anxieties around social media, cyberbullying and digital anonymity. Since *Unfriended*'s release, several films engaging with fears around cyberbullying have been made, including the documentary film *Audrie & Daisy* (2016) and the genre film *#Horror* (2015). *Unfriended* updates the tradition of the ghost story and stands as a film which is a perfect example of both a genre and a subgenre in transition.

The internet in *Unfriended* is characterised as being haunted as much by the characters' mistakes and digital footprint as it is by the supernatural. The friends in the group are shown as being especially preoccupied with the way they are perceived online. For example, when Laura posts photos of Val getting drunk at a party from Jess's Facebook account, Val's fury is less that these incriminating photos of her exist, but more that they are being posted without her permission on social media and that they will alter her carefully constructed digital identity. Much like Elizabeth in *The Den*, these characters only really 'exist' online. We watch as they are murdered both physically and digitally, as once they are killed their camera feed is removed from the video chat. In this way, Laura Barns snuffs out their internet identities as well as their lives. *Unfriended*, being released in 2014, emerged around the time that the idea of a social media 'celebrity' was beginning to take hold, and the importance of the internet to the construction of identity began to rise. It is this connection between internet celebrity and selfhood that the next case study circles around.

## 'If you're not documenting yourself, it's simple. You don't exist': content, identity and audiences in *Spree*

The horror satire of *Spree*, described in a positive review as 'a lurid and soulless entertainment spectacle' (Lattanzio, 2020), centres around a social media-obsessed rideshare driver who, in an attempt to go viral and become internet famous, livestreams his series of murders. As Alice Marwick has explained, in relation to internet-enabled celebrity status, 'To many, the distinction between those famous for doing something and those famous for simply being famous is unimportant. What matters is the fame' (2013: 116), and this is certainly true of Kurt Kunkle, *Spree*'s lead character. Since the founding of YouTube – its motto being 'broadcast yourself' – there has been an increase in what Theresa M. Senft (2001) termed the 'micro celebrity', meaning an individual who has cultivated and gained a niche following or audience through the internet. Although Senft coined this term in relation to 'Cam girls',[9] it could also be broadly applied to a variety of individuals who have built sizable followings on social media websites and applications such as YouTube, Instagram and TikTok.

Arriving on Netflix seven years after the first case study of this chapter, *The Den*, it is perhaps not surprising that *Spree* – as an example of social media horror – looks completely different to the earlier film. Instead of through a laptop, we watch the narrative unfold primarily through the lens of a phone camera, through which Kurt livestreams his murder marathon. The aesthetics of YouTube and Instagram are instantly recognisble, as are various terms and phrases characters use. The characters and action of *Spree* are near constantly in motion, and the ever changing landscape and parlance of the internet is reflected, for instance, in the character of Jessie Adams – who becomes something of a final girl in the closing moments of the film – when she asks Kurt if he is a 'Twitter bot' after he utters the outdated enquiry of 'Follow for follow?'. Rather than simply marking a movement in aesthetics however, *Spree* is an important entry in the cycle of social media horror films due to its shift in anxieties. While real death websites were the concern of *The Den* seven years previously, the lack of sustained interest in these can be seen in the defunct status of many websites that were key to that subculture, and the anxieties around cyberbullying and digital anonymity shown in *Unfriended* – although still a minor concern in the horror genre – are no longer front-page news. *Spree*, instead, seems to be a response to (often sensationalist) reports that social media is linked to narcissism (Fishwick, 2016), is addictive (Andersson, 2018) and creates attention deficit disorder and concentration issues for users (Howard, 2018; Griffey, 2018). *Spree* is about the role social media plays in the construction of identity, celebrity and the fickle attention span of online interaction.

Journalist Jeff Sneider has advanced that *Spree* is essentially 'an *American Psycho* update for the digital age' (Sneider, 2020). I would agree that there are clear similarities: just as Patrick Bateman states that although there is 'an idea of a Patrick Bateman. Some kind of abstraction [. . .] there is no real me. Only an entity', we are similarly not presented with a clear idea of who Kurt Kunkle is, other than an individual who is trying to carve a niche for himself as – in his words – 'an influencer and content creator'. As Rebecca Lewis proposes, 'The participatory affordances of social media have shifted the nature of celebrity online' (2020: 205) and Crystal Abindin describes influencers as 'the epitome of internet celebrities given that they make a living from being celebrities native to and on the internet' (2018: 1). Kurt's failure to make his mark as an influencer can be seen in the clips from his YouTube videos that open the film, which feature several past and present trends of YouTube content creators, such as unboxing videos, life hacks, tutorials and reviews. Kurt has tried to reinvent himself in several different ways, from an online gamer to a musician, and is shown too attempting to piggyback on his father's minor fame as a DJ. Early in the film, Kurt's voice-over notes that 'It's not always easy making great content day after day' and a title card straight after this statement relates that Kurt has spent over ten years posting content, but has remained in obscurity. This is a fact made especially striking given his relationship with Bobby Bud Lee – a boy he used to babysit for who is now a successful content creator.[10] Bobby, in fact, is the person who tells Kurt that he is not suited to internet celebrity, given that 'Some people are born with influencer vibes and some people are not.' Kurt is in his mid to late twenties,[11] has a slight stutter and is not terribly remarkable in terms of appearance or personality. It is perhaps not surprising, then, that Kurt opts to follow in the footsteps of many unremarkable white men before him, and decides his path to fame is murder. In order to reach his potential as a record-breaking livestream murderer, however, Kurt must both commodify his self and build his audience.

As Lindsay Hallam argues, in our digital age 'our identity and sense of self, and certainly our fears, are now bound to the digital realm' (2021: 184). In terms of internet-based microcelebrities, identity is often structured around a cultivation of authenticity (Marwick, 2013: 114), whereby influencers stress that they are presenting their 'real' relatable selves. The line between authenticity and fakeness, particularly in terms of identity, is commented upon directly several times in *Spree*. After Kurt kills his first passenger of the day – a white supremacist named Frederick – his only audience member, Bobby, messages him declaring 'FAKE NEWS!!!', which Kurt brushes off by explaining that actually 'No one should be able to tell what you are doing is real at first. Because you want to get as many done undetected, for maximum attention down the road.' At various points in the film, once Kurt's viewer count begins to grow, the scrolling comments at the bottom of his feed include debate over the veracity of what is going on, with one user evaluating that the 'Blood is fake af'.[12] Bobby's comments on the authenticity of Kurt's actions return to haunt him, when Kurt – tired of Bobby's constant criticism – turns up at Bobby's house and after being humiliated online, stabs Bobby. As he bleeds, Bobby gives one more piece of feedback – 'What the fuck, dude? This shit isn't supposed to be real!' – before Kurt slashes him to death. Bobby's earlier deduction that Jessie Adams has a huge following because 'She's got great energy and an authentic brand', and his focus on keeping his own stream close to reality, are undercut by this line. They are undermined earlier in the film too, when he shows Kurt that a popular video he created, of a 'homeless hero' finding money and buying supplies for his friends, was faked. Kurt appears to care less for authenticity and more for visibility, and seemingly assumes everyone around him has this same fixation. At one point, where Kurt displays his multiple camera set up in his car, he notes to us that 'If you're not documenting yourself, its simple: you just don't exist', and later becomes incensed by a homeless encampment under a bridge, yelling that the residents there have 'zero social media presence. They don't even care that the whole world doesn't know they exist.' Kurt, a previous self-described 'zero', starts his stream with one, reluctant, viewer in Bobby, but by the close of the film – and through the hijacking of several different feeds – amasses 58,321 viewers in the moment of his death – fittingly – by his own phone, wielded by Jessie. Bobby remarks early on that 'the thing about Kurt is, he really wants attention' and the stark metric of fame provided by viewer count underlines his achievement of this aim.

With *The Den*'s construction as a pay-per-view murder feed, and *Unfriended*'s position as a Skype call between friends, the footage in both of these narratives can be figured as being for a private – or at least paying – audience. *Spree*, however, has the diegetic audience play a significant role. Alice Marwick advances that social media is 'intrinsically focused on individuals [. . .] who produce and consume content' (2013: 7) – the consumer is positioned as being just as important as the creator – and before Kurt begins his murders, he is careful to flag up the benefits of being a subscribing member to his feed, and that 'For my premium subscribers [. . .] you can choose your own angles'. However, we can assume a large percentage of his audience is receiving the stream for free. After Kurt learns that Jessie has a large following on Instagram, he becomes almost giddy with excitement, asking her how she grew her audience and positioning himself as her peer. Before Kurt murders Bobby, his maximum viewer count is six, and later, two of his victims – Kendra and Richard – each have a higher viewer count than Kurt at the time of their own livestreamed deaths. After Bobby's death, Kurt's stream has just over 100 viewers, mostly curious about what just happened. Perhaps aroused by his increasing viewers, Kurt asks if they want to see 'his boner'. He then redirects Bobby's feed to his own, and it is after this that his viewer count rapidly grows.

To keep an audience interested online, 'content' is key. This word is repeated dozens of times during the film, and it is not just Kurt who is obsessed with creating fresh content. Kendra, London and Richard are charmed by Kurt when he notes that 'I think I know what you guys want. Get people to think you're having an adventure, a total WTF moment. Am I right?' shortly before he kills him. As soon as another passenger, Mario, realises he is liftsharing with Jessie Adams, he jumps straight onto his stream to document the encounter, and DJ uNo, after ignoring Kurt's pleas to tag him in her Instagram post, demands that he take her to a taco truck and be the photographer in an impromptu shoot for her own curated experience. Murder is Kurt's preferred content and he is, in his words, 'literally out here killing people', but even this may not be enough to make a mark in the attention economies of online interaction. This is because, as Bobby remarks, murder is 'stale content, happens every day'. The diegetic social media audience members of *Spree* are not passive consumers; they tip Kurt various amounts of money, engage in his poll to decide whether he should 'Fuck, Marry or Kill' Jessie Adams and give him suggestions and demands as to what they want him to do next. At one point Kurt even reprimands them, informing them that they 'led him astray'. The audience members are implicated in several missives from Jessie, who functions for the most part as a moral compass within the narrative. The first of these is during her comedy set, when she berates her live audience that no matter your follower count 'we're all being watched and judged and hated. And you love it, you love it. You need it, you're all addicted to it.' Another occurs after Jessie kills Kurt, when she picks up his phone and chastises the online audience, screaming 'Whoever the fuck is watching this, you are sick! What is wrong with you? This is not a fucking tv show.' *Spree*, then, is not a film without explicit social commentary and even Jessie Adams, who rejects social

Figure 9.3 Content, content, content: a triumphant Jessie with a dead Kurt.

media both verbally and by smashing her phone, cannot resist requests from the audience for a selfie with the dead Kurt, which she promptly posts on Instagram.

Although we primarily view the action through Kurt's mobile phone, this is not the only screen in *Spree*. At times, multiple screens fill the frame and are intercut with CCTV footage and YouTube videos. The constant barrage of comments at the bottom of the screen means that the frame of *Spree* is a complex, multifaceted one, with these comments in particular updating so fast that they are – at times – impossible to read before new comments take their place. This frantic action was criticised in reviews, with it being said that

> a proliferation of screens, phone screens within phone screens within phone screens, rapidly unfurling comments sections, text messages coming in, DMs [. . .] feels like a day spent entirely on the internet [. . .] and I'm not sure that's a good thing. (O'Malley, 2020)

However, this abundance of screens, content and comments accurately provides 'an account of what it feels like to live in the early twenty-first century' (Shaviro, 2010: 2, emphasis in original). We live in a screen society, where 'film, TV, and videogame consumers might only have one screen of their own, or they might have five' (Hart, 2019: 12) and it is through these screens that Kurt provides '#TheLesson' – his manifesto on how to create content, grow followers and achieve insta-fame. Kurt's fame is recognised within the narrative at the end of the film, where we realise that *Spree* is narratively a fan-made compilation of Kurt's night of mayhem. We are shown

**Figure 9.4** Hyperconnectivity: screens upon screens and constant comments in *Spree*.

internet-based articles on Kurt from such outlets as Vice.com and message boards – including 4chan[13] – where Kurt's fans – 'Kurties' – chat about their hero and share content on him, bringing the film in line with the presence of the true crime community of websites such as Tumblr. Early in the film, Kurt mentions the word 'Legacy', and although he does not survive his spree, and Jessie Adams through murdering him becomes the heroine of the piece and gains the kind of fame Kurt could only dream of, his fans keep his legacy alive. Kurt may not be the hero of *Spree*, but he emerges the victor.

## Conclusion

This chapter has demonstrated that social media horror cannot be dismissed as a cheap gimmick that moves the subgenre into 'found footage 2.0', which is 'sure to become as tired and overused as the original found footage genre' (Debruge, 2014). Instead, I argue that this subset of films marks a significant step in the subgenre – which has a need to maintain a connection with the audience's experience of reality in order to stay relevant – in terms of both form and themes. Although the subgenre had begun to play with the idea of internet-based aesthetics as early as *The Collingswood Story* (2002), later building on this specific 'look' with *Paranormal Activity 4* (2012), *The Sick Thing That Happened to Emily When She Was Younger* (2012) and *The Den*, it was with *Unfriended* that the marriage of uploadable aesthetics and found footage horror was sealed. Early social media horror such as *Unfriended* led to a flurry of imitators both within and outside of the found footage horror subgenre. *Searching* (2018), for example, drew critical acclaim for its use of an internet-based aesthetic in reviews that downplayed this style's presence in the horror genre several years before (see Debruge, 2018; Erbland, 2018; Travers, 2018), and perhaps this speaks to the maligned position that horror still finds itself in.

Each of the films considered in this chapter relates to wider debates surrounding internet use and misuse. *The Den*'s terror stems from fears regarding the lawless or borderless nature of the internet, and the multidirectional surveillance it can provide, while crafting a horror around real monstrosity rather than ghostly revenge. *Unfriended*, arriving just a year after, engages with the idea of digital anonymity, calling into question the privacy of the internet when controlled by a vengeful spirit. It resonates with the rising fears during the time of its creation and release about how the internet was being used to cause destruction and death through cyberbullying, while reminding us how hard it is to police digital communities. A review commented that with *Spree*, 'the point is that there isn't one' (Lattanzio, 2020), and I must disagree. I have demonstrated here that the film functions as a pointed critique of internet-based celebrity culture, and calls into question not only the need for validation that social media engenders but issues around accountability and authenticity in an online space that troubles the line between the real and the fake. The seven years between the first and the final case studies of this chapter show, therefore, not only significant aesthetic shifts in the found footage horror subgenre, but its ability to quickly adapt to a constantly changing cultural milieu. If in *The Den*, the internet enabled horror to take place, and in *Unfriended* it functioned as a conduit for horror, then the link between death and the internet finds its zenith in *Spree*. Horror finds a home in this film as part of the constant stream of never ending content, and a digital world in which we are no longer watching people get hurt by the internet but watching them be killed for the internet, for the likes and for the lulz.[14]

## Notes

1. *Sickhouse* was originally presented on lead actress (and social media celebrity) Andrea Russett's Snapchat account.
2. Although at least one documentary exists – *9/11: The Falling Man* (2006) – which addresses this kind of footage directly, it is fair to say that this is the exception to the overarching exclusion of this footage in retrospectives of the event.
3. The Dnepropetrovsk Maniacs – Viktor Sayenko and Igor Suprunyuk, who were both 19 at the time of their killings – murdered twenty-one people between 25 June – 16 July 2007. *3 Guys 1 Hammer* refers to the video, which is just over four minutes long, detailing the torture and murder of 48-year-old Sergei Yatzenko, which was hosted on several shock websites.
4. Although found footage horror films overarchingly present themselves as 'in the moment' and emphasise the idea of 'liveness', temporal discrepancies are played with in an interesting way both here in *The Den* and in *Home Movie* (2008), which features onscreen rewinding of footage.
5. 'Shaming', in this context, is when an individual is targeted for humiliation online through the use of social media, or videos/photographs/information shared in online spaces. Internet shaming often plays a significant role in cyberbullying. For example, the deaths of Tyler Clementi, Amanda Todd and Audrie Pott were due to extended cyberbullying campaigns, which used shaming or private photos and footage of the individuals.
6. Amanda Todd's 2012 video, entitled *My Story: Struggling, bullying, suicide, self harm* is still available to watch on Amanda's YouTube channel: TheSomebodytoknow.
7. Image macros are still photographs or images overlaid with white block text for

humorous effect. These images are not the same as, but often become, internet memes – another internet-based form of communication. It is usually when a macro has reached a high level of saturation and popularity that it achieves meme status.
8  STFU is common internet shorthand for 'Shut the fuck up'.
9  A cam girl is a woman who performs on webcam for an audience. These performances are paid for by 'tips' from audience members and will often include erotic acts. Cam girls will often maintain sizable online audience fanbases.
10  Bobby Bud Lee is portrayed by Joshua Ovalle, who became internet famous after posting a series of videos on Vine – a social media short-form video hosting service.
11  At least, that is what we can surmise from how he relates his experience of watching 9/11 on television as a child.
12  In this context, 'af' meaning 'as fuck'.
13  The website 4Chan has often been the subject of controversy, including the posting of illegal content.
14  Lulz is an internet-based term used to convey to a high level of amusement, especially at someone else's expense.

# 10

# The footage yet to be found

> It's obvious this sub-genre isn't going away. (Turek, 2014)

Released in February of 2017, *Savageland* follows the fictional trial of Francisco Salazar during the aftermath of the 2011 massacre in Sangre de Cristo: a small town located near the United States/Mexico border, of which Salazar was the lone survivor. The trial of Salazar is presented as being biased in favour of the prosecution – who accuse Salazar of being the perpetrator of this murder spree – and littered throughout the narrative are interviews with residents of the nearby town of Hinzman. In these clips, locals proclaim that they 'know what these people are capable of' and that – as a Mexican person – Salazar's culture 'worships death', 'celebrates violence' and he is part of the 'tide' of illegal immigrants coming over the border to 'wipe us off the map'. We learn that video footage supporting Salazar's innocence – which has captured strange occurrences at the border – has been barred from the trial. This suppression of evidence is underlined by the existence of a roll of photographs showing images captured by Salazar during the massacre, which have similarly not been submitted as evidence and around which debates regarding authenticity circulate.

Distilled within *Savageland* are certain themes this book has explored. It blurs the line between fact and fiction through its aping of documentary form (like the films analysed in Part 1 of this book), but also through the appearance of testimony from Lawrence C. Ross Jr, a real-life writer of historical texts, and in this inclusion situates the fictive next to the real (like the three films explored in Chapter 7). The roll of film in *Savageland* stands as a counterversion of events being suppressed by morally ambiguous government officials (akin to several of the films covered in Part 2) and it focuses on discussions around America's borders and tensions around immigration – showing a clear engagement with its contemporary cultural moment (as, I have argued, all of the films in this book do too). Moreover, Salazar's use of the camera in *Savageland* is noted by the character of Len Matheson as being a defence mechanism, when he explains that 'so long as you are behind that lens, so long as you are shooting through that lens, you are indestructible [. . .] while you're shooting, you can't be hurt': this brings the film in line with discussions in Chapter 5 regarding the compulsion to tape in crisis situations. Meanwhile, Salazar's position as a person accidentally caught up in horrific events and choosing to record them, taking the pictures – as Matheson comments – 'because someone has to', situates him as an inadvertent witness: a recurrent character convention and theme of the analysis contained in this book (that was explored at length in Chapter 6).

To return to an argument I made in Chapters 5 and 7, *Savageland* is a film that is both political statement and commercial commodity. After the execution of Salazar, the Mexican community in the area positions him as a martyr: the film ends with characters displaying their tattoos of his face while posing in front of a giant mural that depicts Salazar in a Christ-like pose. The racism espoused by characters earlier in the film is then further highlighted by their comments following Salazar's demise, that 'even in death he avoids being deported'. This is in addition to references regarding a 'great wall of America' that needs to be built at the border, which oddly and presciently echoes the 'impenetrable and beautiful' (quoted in Moore, 2016) wall between America and Mexico that President Donald Trump called for during his 2016 election campaign. Above all, then, *Savageland* purposefully and consciously positions itself as a piece of social commentary, which uses the horror genre to comment upon racial tensions at the United States/Mexico border.

In placing *Savageland* as part of the found footage horror subgenre – which I do because of its framing as a true crime documentary and use of the subgenre's conventions – I should admit that the emphasis of the film is not on footage of the massacre at all, but rather on still photography and the aforementioned roll of film. The photographs developed from this film are black-and-white, occasionally marred by overexposure or motion blurring and within them a narrative of the massacre emerges. We can make out strange and frightening figures closing in on Sangre de Cristo from the desert and their subsequent rampage through the town. The effect of the photographs is eerie and unsettling and their inclusion – as a return to an older form of documentary evidence, and one that recalls arguments made in Chapter 2 regarding the original uses of photography – marks *Savageland*

Figure 10.1 Haunting images: the found photography of *Savageland*.

as an intriguing addition to the subgenre. Although it returns to video footage in its final moments and as such aligns itself to the shaky, handheld aesthetic the subgenre is known for, it is through *Savageland* that we see clearly how found footage horror seeks to continually reinvent itself and – perhaps now more than ever – how it is a subgenre thoroughly engaged with its sociopolitical context.

Throughout this book, I have demonstrated that a key element of found footage horror's endurance is due to its ability to adapt to emerging technology and adopt new reality looks or, in the case of *Savageland*, utilise different technology within its narratives to reinvent itself. Part of found footage horror's appeal is that it has no loyalty to a specific look or framing device, even within the same series of films. This can be seen in *Unfriended: Dark Web* (2018), the sequel to *Unfriended*. Within this film, a group of friends is swiftly dispatched by a team of hackers called 'The Circle', after protagonist Matias comes into possession of a laptop left by them in a coffee shop as bait. Although *Unfriended: Dark Web* touches upon similar anxieties around online communication to those films featured in Chapters 8 and 9, it presents these even more overtly. Primarily this is done through the character of AJ: an online commentator, content creator and conspiracy theorist. Taking the fears of *The Conspiracy* (discussed at length in Chapter 7) and placing them in a strictly online space (like the settings of the films in Chapter 9), AJ rants to his friends that

> It is not just the government. It's the Circadians, and the Bilderbergs, and the Illuminati, and corporations. Why do you think Facebook and Twitter are free? Because you're the product. They own every single thing you

post! [. . .] But the internet as you know it, is just the surface [. . .] it is a deep goddamn ocean and there are sharks swimming below you [. . .] It's not just sharks down there, guys. There are leviathans and krakens and colossuses [. . .] It is total integration of Wi-Fi and cell towers, GPS, IP address detection, Bluetooth device tracking, even those Fitbit things you like to run around with.

Later still, AJ refers to Silk Road and Lolita City, websites accessed through anonymous networks such as Tor and which operated as marketplaces for illegal drugs and hosted child pornography respectively. *Unfriended: Dark Web* shifts its attention from the supernatural threat of *Unfriended* to one far more corporeal: the internet is still haunted, but this time by cybercriminals, cryptocurrency and the entertaining potential of death on the dark web, all of which were growing concerns around internet use at the time of the film's release. As per its predecessor, the action takes place within the limits of a laptop screen; however *Unfriended: Dark Web* incorporates more varied footage than *Unfriended*, featuring live CCTV feeds and facetime calls, perhaps speaking to our shifting attention spans in our ever more digitally mediated world. Although some commentators have passionately argued that social media horror films are not really found footage horror at all (Merry, 2015), the subgeneric movements demonstrated within *Unfriended: Dark Web* are characteristic of found footage horror as a whole: always shifting, evolving and updating.

Linnie Blake posited that the horror genre is the 'most traumatic and traumatised of film genres' (2008: 1). I would argue that found footage horror stands as one of the genre's utmost traumatic/traumatised spaces and advance that this is because of its level of cultural engagement. Found footage horror is one of the most culturally engaged subgenres through necessity. Our experience of the world has shifted subtly and also seismically through the subgenre's history, both in terms of reportage of events and how we witness and engage with society. Found footage horror is enormously preoccupied with its cultural context because it has to be. As a subgenre based around representations of reality, evolving along with our experience of the real is vital to enable a connection between its audiences, its narratives and its formal aesthetics, and to allow the subgenre to continue to be effective. Adam Lowenstein's concept of the allegorical moment is often crystallised by found footage horror form – as not only does the subgenre frequently forefront a 'collision of film, spectator, and history' (2005: 2), but it often presents traumatic histories by aping exactly how a spectator would have witnessed them had they been there. Although found footage horror uses allegorical representations in a vast majority of its narratives, it also moves beyond them – as I demonstrated in Chapter 3 in terms of *The Sacrament* – and as such, in some ways ties itself closer to participatory documentaries of the 1980s, which would often include 'renderings of traumatic past events' (Nichols, 2017: 151). The swaying, falling, damaged and broken lenses of found footage horror place the spectator within the action, and provide a sense of physicality through their often doomed camera operators that acts as a 'simulation of the twenty-first century experience of trauma, terror, and crisis' (McRobert, 2015: 143). Found footage horror has engaged with traumas historic (Chapter 3), long standing (Chapter 4) and world changing (Chapters 5, 6 and 7) by providing a space in which cultural preoccupations and fears can be articulated, anxieties presented and events relived.

Found footage horror engages with cultural trauma and anxieties not only through form but also through its themes. At the forefront of the films I have examined, there is an insistence on behalf of the characters to witness or gain visual evidence of the unique and unprecedented: whether this be an event, an act or an entity/being. In some narratives – for example, the *Unfriended* films and *Savageland* – the presence of visual evidence or the capturing of this evidence is a significant step in a character's downfall. In other films, the act of witnessing is panicked or confused and is often inadvertent in nature, with characters ensnared by the unexpected as they occupy themselves with the obtainment of evidence, whether this be of the supernatural (*Grave Encounters*), strange events (*The Sacrament*) or the forbidden (*The Den*). The characters of found footage horror are compelled to document what is happening to them, but often let down by their own technology as it fails to provide visual evidence to support what they are experiencing – whether this be through the limitations of the frame or the operator – articulating a certain discomfort around our reliance on technology. The found footage protagonist's quest for the truth and evidence is often undercut, too, by their own inability to record events objectively, as they are either driven to intervene or to help, or shocked into simply letting their camera roll and capture what it can. The vulnerability of the characters in these films is consistently highlighted and they are repeatedly endangered by what lurks in the offscreen space or punished for their desire to see, to look and to know. Their vulnerability is then emphasised by found footage horror's shaky, unstable framing. The seeming visual imperfections of the subgenre – often honed in on in critiques of how found footage horror is 'artless' (Swanson, 2021) – are often its greatest strength and they lend narratives a sense of immersion, immediacy, liveness and danger. These films often end with the failure of the documentary project, where characters disappear, die or are otherwise destroyed. Despite this, the found footage protagonist is always driven to continue to document events – whether this be due to the fact that it is their job, because they distrust mainstream accounts, because no one else will or simply – as Deb in *Diary of the Dead* suggests – 'for the camera, for history'.

On the subject of history, I advance that the found footage horror subgenre is one which both constantly glances back towards the horror genre's longstanding engagement with its cultural context and also looks forward towards emerging new anxieties. This is another key characteristic of the subgenre that has allowed it to endure. Throughout this book I have traced the ways in which the subgenre has both adopted emerging reality 'looks' and adapted to new media and technology, and seamlessly integrated these into its formal characteristics. It has moved in tandem with the evolution of documentary form it first aped, engaged with the changing nature of reportage in the wake of widespread cameras and documentation, and with the contemporary fascination with recording and exhibiting one's life online. Found footage horror has responded to the rise of reality television, and a move towards graphic presentations of death and dying on both mainstream news networks and online spaces. In the final part of this book, I began pulling away from the strictly cinematic and it is fair to say that this more diffused focus reflects the way in which we now live in a post-cinematic world. Still, found footage horror has found a way to navigate this new landscape. Since its early days, found footage horror has flexed its tendrils in varied directions. Not only are there franchises that operate solely within the format, such as the *Paranormal Activity*, *V/H/S* (2012–) and *Hell House LLC* (2015–19) series, but there is now a company, P.O.V. Horror, that produces and distributes found footage horror exclusively, as well as operating the Found Footage Film Channel, which hosts found footage horror films and found footage horror films only. Since the post-cinematic turn, we have seen the release of various videogames, such as *Outlast* (2013), *Outlast: Whistleblower* (2015), *Resident Evil VII: Biohazard* (2017) and *Anatomy* (2017), which have adapted found footage aesthetics into their gameplay mechanics to enhance the player's experience of terror. In other cases, videogames have expanded the subgenre's filmic worlds, such as *Blair Witch* (2019). Indeed, recent work (such as Hart, 2019 and Daniel, 2020) has traced the ways in which found footage horror has moved between, and influenced, various media forms.

In terms of the scope of this book, it was always clear that a selection of ten films – albeit drawn from an initial survey of hundreds – cannot and does not represent an exhaustive account of North American found footage horror cinema, and there are several fruitful areas of research that I have not had the space to discuss here. These include the longstanding recurrence of narratives involving extraterrestrials (such as *The McPherson Tape* (1989), *Slumber Party Alien Abduction* (2013), *Alien Abduction* (2014), *Area 51* (2015) and *Phoenix Forgotten* (2017)) and a more recent trend towards the inclusion of haunts gone wrong (along with the *Hell House LLC* films, *The Houses October Built* (2014) is a key example of this) within the subgenre. During the research and writing of this book, I have begun to trace how found footage horror has started to infiltrate the world of podcasting, and how several online narratives, such as many of those held on the SCP foundation website[1] – have adapted common features of found footage horror into the online realm. More recently, users of the endlessly scrollable social media app TikTok have made dexterous use of the found footage aesthetic to create what could be described as horror vignettes. Some examples of this include videos made by the user Security98, in which demonic noises and images are captured by a security guard, and a video uploaded by the user do_not_go_in_there, which features a haunted basement and is filmed in a way that clearly references its cinematic found footage horror predecessors. The found footage horror subgenre, as this book has conveyed, is a multifaceted place and seemingly one that lends itself well to our post-cinematic moment.

Although the cameras of found footage horror will often fail to assist their operators – and even have the capacity to be used against them – they are often used as tools both metaphorical and literal to navigate horrific landscapes and to extend the operator's field of vision. They are also repeatedly situated as a weapon, through an approximation with violent acts (*Diary of the Dead*) or as a literal bludgeon (*Quarantine* and *Spree*). The physicality of the camera allows it to be both acknowledged as existing diegetically as well as bloodied, dropped, dirtied and – occasionally – completely destroyed. The physicality of the found footage camera also has an effect on spectator engagement, and I have presented the subgenre as one that encourages an active viewing mode. Recurring elements of found footage horror that assist in this are the use of dead time and seemingly inactive frames as well as its use of reality formats that we recognise as truthful (in addition to those that encourage an active viewing experience, such as ghost hunting reality shows). Other key characteristics of the subgenre – the danger of the offscreen space, the limits of the frame and the acknowledgement of the camera's diegetic presence – evoke a simulation of participation for the viewer, prompting them to scan the screen for information. The subgenre encourages the viewer to lean into the screen, thus heightening the impact and affective quality of its jolting scares when they occur. In Chapter 3 I spoke of Susan Sontag's concepts of the accidental and endangered gazes, both of which increase an audience's empathetic fear for their onscreen avatars and affirm an engagement with the immediate and intimate. This is amplified in found footage horror, where the camera acts as an extension of the viewer's gaze, removing one level of detachment between what is occurring onscreen and our proximity to it, and conflating the character's lens with our own vision. The legacy of found footage horror more widely may well be this embodied audience experience, and the wider impact of the found footage format has resulted in its adoption outside of the horror genre within such films as *Zero Day* (2003), *End of Watch* (2012), *Chronicle* (2012), *Project X* (2012) and *Earth to Echo* (2014) standing as entries into the genres of drama, crime, science fiction, comedy and family film respectively.

Even before the format's adoption outside of the genre, however, found footage horror has historically reached beyond its boundaries. The subgenre certainly blurs the line between fiction and fact within its narratives – as various parts of this book attest – but an interesting aspect of found footage horror is how it infiltrates spaces outside of the narrative. A strong link has been present between internet-based viral marketing and the subgenre since the unprecedented success of *The Blair Witch Project*, and in Chapter 8 I responded to a crucial need to move beyond a focus on this film's campaign in illustrating the ways in which subsequent found footage horror films have used paratextual tools such as websites and social media to imbue their narratives with a similar sense of verisimilitude outside of the films themselves. These websites and online tools have allowed the found footage horror subgenre to encourage participation from the viewer both pre- and post-viewing. *The Upper Footage* sparked debate through the release of a scant few highly pixelated YouTube videos, while the ephemeral nature of *The Poughkeepsie Tapes* inspired similar disputes around its truth status online. Overarchingly, however, it is the cameras of found footage horror and its use of forms that often have dubious relationships with 'reality' themselves, such as reality television and true crime programming, that are key to the subgenre's effectiveness.

During the Covid-19 pandemic, when film production all but ground to a halt, *Host* was released on Shudder on 30 July 2020 and captured the prevailing cultural mood. Shot over twelve weeks during the national lockdown in the United Kingdom, the actors in *Host* were directed remotely and set up their own lighting and make up effects, which were posted to them. The film only runs for fifty-six minutes – adhering to the limited time of free Zoom chats. *Host* utilised our life under lockdown, where interaction was often reliant on video chats, friendships were socially distanced and anxieties around digital (dis)connections were rising, and acknowledged 'the difference between hyperconnectivity as a luxury and as a lifeline' (Nayman, 2020). The ancestry of the film is clear, and various scenes and conventions recall *The Blair Witch Project*, *[Rec]* and *Paranormal Activity* along with perhaps the film's closest found footage horror relation, *Unfriended*. Despite criticisms that it added to an 'already played-out trend' towards social media horror (Abrams, 2020), the film connected with its isolated audience. *Host* represents a compelling addition to the subgenre not only because its limitations were forced rather than chosen, but because when the world shut down, it was the found footage horror subgenre that adapted to our new experience of reality, and survived.

At the beginning of this book, I spoke of the disappointing financial and critical performance of 2016's *Blair Witch*. It was perhaps unfair not to mention that the impending decline of the subgenre had already been the subject of various articles before that film's release (such as Meslow, 2012; Misra, 2014; Turek, 2014; Prigge, 2015). *Blair Witch* merely increased their frequency, with some proposing that found footage horror was 'ready to lay down and die' (Glieberman, 2016). Still, the subgenre endured and found new homes in podcasts such as *The Black Tapes* (2015–17) and *Video Palace* (2018), the latter of which has been described as 'found footage audio' (Dass, 2018) and in which glitches and imperfections are used as markers of authenticity.[2] Popular interest in the subgenre is also still high, as demonstrated by the release of a documentary – *The Found Footage Horror Phenomenon* (2021) – and the edited collection *Filtered Reality: The Progenitors and Evolution of Found Footage Horror* (Booth and Griffiths, forthcoming). Moreover, following a downturn in production in the late 2010s, the subgenre seems to be undergoing a renaissance, with *V/H/S/94* (2021) and *Paranormal Activity: Next of Kin* (2021) being released some years after their last respective franchise entries.

Along with these revivals of key series in the subgenre, we have seen older found footage horrors being discovered by new audiences. *Megan is Missing*, for example, experienced a resurgence and caused a minor stir on TikTok nearly ten years after its release, as users who were quite possibly children when the film originally emerged documented on the app how they were 'traumatised' after seeing it. This led to the film trending on Twitter, and its director, Michael Goi, issuing a warning about the film to potential viewers on TikTok himself (Lewis, 2020). The conceit of 'found footage' also continues to be key in more recent horror genre entries such as *Antrum* (2018) and the Netflix original series *Archive 81* (2022), as well as remaining a favoured aesthetic of low/no budget projects like the YouTube short film *The Backrooms (Found Footage)* (2022).

I return then to some of the accusations levelled at the subgenre in the opening chapter: that it is 'tiresome' (Phipps and Tobias, 2014), 'derivative' (Berkshire, 2015), 'unimaginative' (Fontana, 2016) or 'intentionally hard to comprehend' (Ebert, 2012). Throughout this book, I have reframed these arguments and continually refuted these claims. In terms of the future of found footage horror, the recording light still flickers, the battery still has power and the lens remains unbroken.

## Notes

1 Some examples include SCP-4076, which details several 'found' VHS tapes with anomalous properties, or SCP-1757, which outlines the content of footage which, if watched, results in horrific mutilations. These stories and others can be found at SCP-wiki.wikidot.com.
2 The narrative too, revolves around mythical white video cassette tapes that the main character, Mark Cambria, literally finds.

# Bibliography

Abbott, Stacey (2016) *Undead Apocalypse: Vampires and Zombies in the 21st Century*, Edinburgh University Press, Edinburgh.
Abbott, Stacey (2021) 'When the Subtext Becomes Text: The Purge Takes on the American Nightmare', in Mark McKenna and William Proctor (eds), *Horror Franchise Cinema*, Routledge, Abingdon and New York, pp. 128–42.
ABC News (2014) 'EXCLUSIVE: Serial Killer's Home Movies', *ABC News*, online, 9 July, https://abcnews.go.com/Primetime/exclusive-serial-killers-home-movies/story?id=132005 (accessed 9 October 2021).
Abindin, Crystal (2018) *Internet Celebrity: Understanding Fame Online*, Emerald Publishing, Bingley.
Abrams, Simon (2020) 'Host', *Roger Ebert*, online, 30 July, https://www.rogerebert.com/reviews/host-movie-review-2020 (accessed 9 October 2021).
Aftab, Kaleem (2009) 'Don't Lose Your Head', *The Independent*, online, 5 June, http://www.independent.co.uk/arts-entertainment/films/features/drag-me-to-hell--dont-lose-your-head-1697053.html (accessed 25 October 2021).
Allcott, Hunt and Matthew Gentzkow (2017) 'Social Media and Fake News in the 2016 Election', in *Journal of Economic Perspectives*, vol. 31, no. 2, pp. 211–36.
Allio, Kirstin (2018) 'Why Are We So Fascinated by Cults?', *The Paris Review*, online, 21 May, https://www.theparisreview.org/blog/2018/05/21/why-are-we-so-fascinated-by-cults/ (Accessed 25 October 2021).
Aloi, Peg (2005) 'Beyond The Blair Witch: A New Horror Aesthetic?', in Geoff King (ed.), *The Spectacle of the Real: From Hollywood to 'Reality' TV and Beyond*, Intellect, Bristol, pp. 187–200.
Altheide, David L. (2010) 'Fear, Terrorism, and Popular Culture', in Jeff Birkenstein, Anna Froula and Karen Randell (eds), *Reframing 9/11: Film, Popular Culture and the "War on Terror"*, Continuum, London, pp. 11–22.
Anderson, Donald L. (2013) 'How the Horror Film Broke its Promise: Hyperreal Horror and Ruggero Deodato's *Cannibal Holocaust*', in *Horror Studies*, vol., no. 1, pp. 109–25.
Anderson, Lesley (2012) 'Snuff: Murder and Torture on the Internet, and the People who Watch it', *The Verge*, online, 13 March, https://www.theverge.com/2012/6/13/3076557/snuff-murder-torture-internet-people-who-watch-it (Accessed 9 April 2019).
Anderson, Steve F. (2011) *Technologies of History: Visual Media and the Eccentricity of the Past*, University Press of New England, Lebanon, NH.
Andersson, Hilary (2018) 'Social Media Apps are 'Deliberately' Addictive to Users',

*BBC*, online, 4 July https://www.bbc.co.uk/news/technology-44640959 (accessed 9 October 2021).

Arkin, William M. (2021) *On That Day: The Definitive Timeline of 9/11*, PublicAffairs, New York.

Arndt, Jamie, Jeff Greenberg, Jeff Schimel, Tom Pyszcznski and Sheldon Solomon (2002) 'To Belong or Not to Belong, That is the Question: Terror Management and Identification with Gender and Ethnicity', in *Journal of Personality and Social Psychology*, vol. 83, no.1, pp. 26–43.

Associated Press (2014) 'Sacred Pearl Harbor Memorial Scene of Rampant Mismanagement, Report Alleges', *The Guardian*, online, 5 December, https://www.theguardian.com/us-news/2014/dec/05/pearl-harbor-memorial-allegedly-mismanaged (accessed 25 October 2021).

Astley, Mark (2016) 'Snuff 2.0: Real Death Goes HD Ready', in Neil Jackson, Shaun Kimber, Johnny Walker, and Thomas Joseph Watson (eds), *Snuff: Real Death and Screen Media*, Bloomsbury, London and New York, pp. 153–70.

Atkins, Anna (1843) *Photographs of British Algae: Cyanotype Impressions*, Unknown publisher.

Atkinson, Rowland and Thomas Rodgers (2015) 'Pleasure Zones and Murder Boxes: Online Pornography and Violent Video Games as Cultural Zones of Exception', in *British Journal of Criminology*, vol. 56, no. 6, pp. 1291–307.

Atwwalloway (2014) 'Joe Swanberg & A. J. Bowen Talk Thriller "*The Sacrament*"', *YouTube*, online, 23 May, https://www.youtube.com/watch?v=VX3b-Pqp1oc (accessed 25 October 2021).

Aufderheide, Patricia (2007) *Documentary Film: A Very Short Introduction*, Oxford University Press, Oxford.

Awan, Akil N. (2017) 'Why Mark Wahlberg's Patriots Day is a Vanity Project: For a Movie that has Taken Such Great Pains to be Authentic, Walhberg's Casting Defies Reason', *The Independent*, online, 28 February, https://www.independent.co.uk/arts-entertainment/films/features/mark-wahlberg-patriots-day-boston-marathon-bombings-a7603591.html (accessed 9 October 2021).

Bacon-Smith, Camille (1992) *Enterprising Women: Television Fandom and the Creation of Popular Myth*, University of Pennsylvania Press, Philadelphia.

Baker, David B. and Ludy T. Benjamin Jr (2014) *From Séance to Science: A History of the Profession of Psychology in America*, University of Akron Press, Akron, OH.

Barnes, Dustin (2021) '12 Shocking Images that Show how Bad the COVID-19 Crisis is in India', *USA Today*, online, 29 April, http://eu.usatoday.com/in-depth/news/world/2021/04/29/covid-19-crisis-india-display-these-shocking-photos/4886613001/ (accessed 9 October 2021).

Barone, Matt (2014) 'My Biggest Disappointment of 2014: Found-Footage Horror's Haters', *Complex*, online, 10 December, https://www.complex.com/pop-culture/2014/12/disappointment-in-found-footage-horror-movie-haters (accessed 25 October 2021).

Barry, Ellen (2006) 'Lost in the Dust of 9/11', *Los Angeles Times*, online, 14 October, https://www.latimes.com/archives/la-xpm-2006-oct-14-na-cleaners14-story.html (accessed 25 October 2021).

Barthes, Roland (1975) *S/Z*, Cape, London.

Barthes, Roland (1981 [1980]) *Camera Lucida: Reflections on Photography*, trans. Richard Howard, Hill and Wang, New York.

Barton, Steve. (2012) 'Editorial: An Apologists Rant: In Defense of Found Footage', *Dread Central*, online, April 26, https://www.dreadcentral.com/news/33208/editorial-an-apologist-s-rant-in-defense-of-found-footage/ (accessed 25 October 2021).

Barton, Steve (2013) 'Justin Cole Explains that *The Upper Footage* is NOT Real', *Dread Central*, online, 7 March, https://www.dreadcentral.com/news/42080/justin-cole-explains-that-the-upper-footage-is-not-real/ (accessed 25 October 2021).

Barton, Steve (2014) 'Found Footage Flick *The Poughkeepsie Tapes* Found on DIRECTV', *Dread Central*, online, 19 July, https://www.dreadcentral.com/news/55271/found-footage-flick-the-poughkeepsie-tapes-found-on-directv/ (accessed 15 October 2021).

Baudrillard, Jean (2012 [2002]) *The Spirit of Terrorism*, trans. C. Turner, Verso, London.

Baumgarten, Marjorie (1999) 'The Blair Witch Project', *Austin Chronicle*, online, 16 July, https://www.austinchronicle.com/events/film/1999-07-16/the-blair-witch-project/ (accessed 9 October 2021).

Beck, Lia (2019) 'Why the Ending of 'Once Upon A Time In Hollywood' May Leave a Bad Taste in your Mouth', *Bustle*, online, 27 July, https://www.bustle.com/p/why-the-ending-of-once-upon-a-time-in-hollywood-may-leave-a-bad-taste-in-your-mouth-18229949 (accessed 9 October 2021).

Benson-Allott, Caetlin (2013) *Killer Tapes and Scattered Screens: Video Spectatorship from VHS to File Sharing*, University of California Press, Los Angeles.

Berger, James (2003) 'There's No Backhand to This', in Judith Greenberg, ed., *Trauma at Home: After 9/11*, University of Nebraska Press, Lincoln, pp. 52–9.

Berkshire, Geoff (2015) 'Film Review: "The Gallows"', *Variety*, online, 9 July, https://variety.com/2015/film/reviews/the-gallows-review-1201535834/ (accessed 25 October 2021).

Bernard, Mark (2014) *Selling the Splat Pack: the DVD Revolution and the American Horror Film*, Edinburgh University Press, Edinburgh.

Berros, Chris (2017) 'Netflix's New "True" Crime Story you have to Check Out', *The Odyssey*, online, 27 September, https://www.theodysseyonline.com/american-vandal (accessed 25 October 2021).

Bibbiani, William (2014) 'The Sacrament: Ti West on the Horrors of Jonestown', *Mandatory*, online, 4 June, https://www.mandatory.com/fun/699983-the-sacrament-ti-west-on-the-horrors-of-jonestown (accessed 25 October 2021).

Binkley, Timothy (1988) 'Camera Fantasia: Computed Visions of Virtual Realities', in *Millennium Film Journal*, vol. 20, no. 21, pp. 6–43.

Biressi, Anita (2004) 'Inside/Out: Private Trauma and Public Knowledge in True Crime Documentary', *Screen*, vol. 45, no. 4, pp. 401–12.

Biressi, Anita and Heather Nunn (2005) *Reality TV: Realism and Revelation*, Wallflower Press, New York.

Birkenstein, Jeff, Anna Froula and Karen Randell (2010) *Reframing 9/11: Film, Popular Culture and the 'War on Terror'*, Bloomsbury, London and New York.

Bishop, Bryan (2012) 'Why Won't You Die? The Art of the Jump Scare', *The Verge*, online, 31 October, https://www.theverge.com/2012/10/31/3574592/art-of-the-jump-scare-horror-movies (accessed 25 October 2021).

Bishop, Kyle William (2010) *American Zombie Gothic: The Rise and Fall (and Rise) of the Walking Dead in Popular Culture*, McFarland, Jefferson.

Blake, Linnie (2008) *The Wounds of Nations: Horror Cinema, Historical Trauma and National Identity*, Manchester University Press, Manchester.

Blake, Linnie and Xavier Aldana Reyes (2015) *Digital Horror: Haunted Technologies, Network Panic, and The Found Footage Phenomenon*, I. B. Tauris, London.

Bly, Nellie (1887) *Ten Days in a Mad-House*, Ian L. Munro, New York.

Blyth, Michael (2016) 'Found Footage Turns up Bold New Horrors at the LFF', *BFI*, online, 7 April, https://www.bfi.org.uk/news-opinion/news-bfi/features/found-footage-turns-bold-new-horrors-lff (accessed 25 October 2021).

Bogart, Laura (2018) 'Why Our True Crime Obsession is Bad for Society', *The Week*, online, 31 January, https://theweek.com/articles/736073/why-true-crime-obsession-bad-society (accessed 25 October 2021).

Bolter, Jay David (2005) 'Preface', in Geoff King, ed., *The Spectacle of the Real: From Hollywood to 'Reality' TV and Beyond*, Intellect, Bristol, pp. 9–12.

Bond, Gwenda (2018) 'Why Are We So Fascinated With Cults? They Reveal the Dirty Cultural Secrets All Around Us', *Salon*, online, 2 July, https://www.salon.com/2018/07/02/why-are-we-so-fascinated-with-cults-they-reveal-the-dirty-cultural-secrets-all-around-us/ (accessed 25 October 2021).

Bondebjerg, Ib (1996) 'Public Discourse/Private Fascination: Hybridization in "True Life Story" Genres', in *Media, Culture and Society*, vol. 18, no. 1, pp. 27–45.

Booth, Rebecca and Valeska Griffiths (forthcoming) *Filtered Reality: The Progenitors and Evolution of Found Footage Horror*, House of Leaves Publishing, Manchester.

Bordwell, David (2012) 'Return to Paranormalcy', *David Bordwell*, online, 13 November, http://www.davidbordwell.net/blog/2012/11/13/return-to-paranormalcy/ (accessed 25 October 2021).

Boult, Adam (2013) 'Eli Roth answers your questions', *The Guardian*, online, 20 February, https://www.theguardian.com/film/filmblog/2013/feb/20/eli-roth-questions (accessed 25 October 2021).

Boult, Adam (2017) '*Most Haunted* Team Claim to Have Caught "Ghost" on Camera – Are You Convinced?', *The Telegraph*, online, 24 April, https://www.telegraph.co.uk/tv/2017/04/24/haunted-team-claim-have-caught-ghost-camera-convinced/ (accessed 25 October 2021).

Bowie, Adam (2010) 'Inside VICE Magazine's Alternative Travel Guides', *The Independent*, online, 26 February, https://www.independent.co.uk/news/media/press/inside-vice-magazines-alternative-travel-guides-1912087.html (accessed 25 October 2021).

Brady, Sara (2012) *Performance, Politics, and the War on Terror*, Palgrave Macmillan, London.

Brailey, Jeffrey (1998) *The Ghosts of November: Memoirs of an Outsider Who Witnessed the Carnage at Jonestown Guyana*, J&J Publishers, North Carolina.

Bridge, Sarah and Kazi Stastna (2011) '9/11 Anniversary: What Was Lost in the Damage', *CBC*, online, 21 August, https://www.cbc.ca/news/world/9-11-anniversary-what-was-lost-in-the-damage-1.1123528 (accessed 25 October 2021).

Briefel, Aviva And Sam J. Miller (2011) 'Introduction', in Aviva Briefel and Sam J. Miller (eds), *Horror After 9/11: World of Fear, Cinema of Terror*, University of Texas Press, Austin, pp. 1–10.

Bromley, David G. and J. Gordon Melton (2002) *Cults, Religion, and Violence*, Cambridge University Press, Cambridge.

Bronfen, Elisabeth (2012) *Specters of War: Hollywood's Engagement with Military Conflict*, Rutgers University Press, New Brunswick, NJ.

Brottman, Mikita (2004) 'The Fascination of the Abomination: The Censored Images of 9/11', in Wheeler Winston Dixon (ed.), *Film and Television after 9/11*, Southern Illinois University Press, Carbondale, pp. 163–77.

Bugliosi, Vincent and Curt Gentry (1974) *Helter Skelter*, W. W. Norton & Company, New York.

Butt, Aimen Khalid (2013) 'The Vice Approach: Shock First, Explain Later (If Ever)', *World Policy*, online, 16 April, https://worldpolicy.org/2013/04/16/the-vice-approach-shock-first-explain-later-if-ever/ (accessed 25 October 2021).

Byrne, C. A. and D. S. Riggs (1996) 'The Cycle of Trauma: Relationship Aggression in

Male Vietnam Veterans with Symptoms of Posttraumatic Stress Disorder', in *Violence and Victims*, vol. 11, no. 3, pp. 213–25.

Cain, Patrick (2016) 'Empty Skies After 9/11 Set the Stage for an Unlikely Climate Change Experiment', *Global News*, online, 12 September, https://globalnews.ca/news/2934513/empty-skies-after-911-set-the-stage-for-an-unlikely-climate-change-experiment/ (accessed 25 October 2021).

Capote, Truman (1966) *In Cold Blood*, Random House, New York.

Carr, David (2014) 'Its Edge Intact, Vice is Chasing Hard News', *The New York Times*, online, 24 August, https://www.nytimes.com/2014/08/25/business/media/its-edge-intact-vice-is-chasing-hard-news-.html (accessed 25 October 2021).

Carson, James and Michael Cogley (2019) 'Fake News: What Exactly is it – and How Can You Spot it?', *The Telegraph*, online, 3 July, https://www.telegraph.co.uk/technology/0/fake-news-exactly-donald-trump-rise/ (accessed 25 October 2021).

Caruth, Cathy (1996) *Unclaimed Experience: Trauma, Narrative, and History*, John Hopkins University Press, Maryland.

Cassidy, Sarah (2014) 'The Online Generation: Four in 10 Children are Addicted to the Internet', *The Independent*, online, 9 May, https://www.independent.co.uk/life-style/gadgets-and-tech/news/the-online-generation-four-in-10-children-are-addicted-to-the-internet-9341159.html (accessed 25 October 2021).

Castonguay, James (2004) 'The Political Economy of the Indie Blockbuster: Fandom, Intermediality and *The Blair Witch Project*', in Sarah L. Higley and Jeffrey A. Weinstock (eds), *Nothing That Is: Millennial Cinema and the Blair Witch Controversies*, Wayne State University Press, Detroit, pp. 65–85.

Cavanaugh, Carole (2001) 'A Working Ideology for Hiroshima: Imamura Shōhei's Black Rain', in Dennis Washburn and Carol Cavanaugh (eds), *Word and Image in Japanese Cinema*, Cambridge University Press, Cambridge, pp. 250–70.

CBS News (2020) 'Trump Dismisses Question on White Privilege: "You Really Drank the Kool-Aid"', *CBS News*, online, 10 September, https://www.cbsnews.com/news/trump-bob-woodward-george-floyd-black-lives-matter-60-minutes-2020-09-10/ (accessed 9 October 2021).

Chang, Soojung (2002) 'Outburst of Patriotism After 9/11 Still Evident', *The Michigan Daily*, online, 8 March, https://www.michigandaily.com/uncategorized/outburst-patriotism-after-911-still-evident-0/ (accessed 25 October 2021).

Chen, Guo-Ming (2012) 'The Impact of New Media on Intercultural Communication in Global Context', in *China Media Research*, vol. 8, no. 2, pp. 1–10.

Cherry, Brigid (2009) *Horror*, Routledge, Abingdon and New York.

Chidester, David (2003) *Salvation and Suicide: Jim Jones, The People's Temple, and Jonestown*, Indiana University Press, Indiana.

Christiansen, Steen (2015) 'Uncanny Cameras and Network Subjects', in Linnie Blake and Xavier Aldana Reyes (eds), *Digital Horror: Haunted Technologies, Network Panic, and The Found Footage Phenomenon*, I. B. Tauris, London, pp. 42–53.

Clark, Andrew (2010) 'MGM Film Studio Plunges into Bankruptcy', *The Guardian*, online, 31 October, https://www.theguardian.com/business/2010/oct/31/mgm-bankruptcy-spyglass (accessed 25 October 2021).

Clark, Sandra (2003) *Women and Crime in the Street Literature of Early Modern England*, Palgrave Macmillan, Basingstoke.

Clayton-Lea, Sarah (2017) 'A Serial Killer Film So Freaky it was Banned from Cinemas has just been Re-Released', *Lovin*, online, 14 October, https://lovin.ie/entertainment/tv-movies/a-serial-killer-film-so-freaky-it-was-banned-from-cinemas-has-just-been-re-released (accessed 25 October 2021).

Cleary, Tom (2019) 'Video1444: The Viral YouTube "Curse" Video Explained', *Heavy*, online, 11 December, https://heavy.com/news/2019/10/video-1444-youtube/ (accessed 9 October 2021).

Clover, Carol J. (1992) *Men, Women, and Chainsaws: Gender in the Modern Horror Film*, Princeton University Press, New Jersey.

CNN Wire Staff (2011) 'President Obama visits Pearl Harbor memorial', *CNN*, online, 30 December, https://edition.cnn.com/2011/12/30/politics/obama-pearl-harbor/index.html (accessed 26 July 2019).

Colburn, Randall (2015) 'Beyond Blair Witch: Why Found-Footage Horror Deserves your Respect', *AV Club*, online, 28 October, https://film.avclub.com/beyond-blair-witch-why-found-footage-horror-deserves-y-1798286059 (accessed 25 October 2021).

Cole, Leonard A. (2003) *The Anthrax Letters: A Medical Detective Story*, Joseph Henry Press, Washington, DC.

Colesky, Niels (2013) 'Documenting the True Horror: The Unedited NBC Tape', *Alternative Considerations of Jonestown & Peoples Temple*, online, 25 July, https://jonestown.sdsu.edu/?page_id=30234 (accessed 25 October 2021).

Connah, Leoni (2020) 'US Intervention in Afghanistan: Justifying the Unjustifiable?', in *South Asia Research*, vol. 41, no. 1, pp. 70–86.

Cooper, Kelly-Leigh (2019a) 'Is Our Growing Obsession with True Crime a Problem?', *BBC News*, online, 1 April, https://www.bbc.co.uk/news/world-us-canada-47474996 (Accessed 25 October 2021).

Cooper, Kelly-Leigh (2019b) 'Bianca Devins: The Teenager Whose Murder was Exploited for Clicks', *BBC*, online, 21 July, https://www.bbc.co.uk/news/world-us-canada-49002486 (Accessed 25 May 2022).

Corner, John (1995) *Television Form and Public Address*, Edward Arnold, London.

Corner, John (1999) *Critical Ideas in Television Studies*, Oxford University Press, Oxford.

Corner, John (2000) 'What Can We Say About Documentary?', in *Media, Culture & Society*, vol. 22, no.5, pp. 681–8.

Corner, John (2002) 'Performing the Real: Documentary Diversions', in *Television & Media*, vol. 3, no. 3, pp. 255–69.

Cornet, Roth (2012) '"The Devil Inside" Director Defends the Movie's Ending', *Screenrant*, online, 17 January, https://screenrant.com/the-devil-inside-ending-spoilers-discussion/ (Accessed 25 October 2021).

Costello, Sam (2014) 'Ti West's The Sacrament and the Dangers of Fictionalized Horror', *Full Stop*, online, 18 June, https://www.full-stop.net/2014/06/18/blog/sam-costello/ti-wests-the-sacrament-and-the-dangers-of-fictionalized-horror/ (Accessed 25 October 2021).

Craps, Stef (2007) 'Conjuring Trauma: The Naudet Brothers' 9/11 Documentary', in *Canadian Review of American Studies*, vol. 37, no. 2, pp. 183–204.

Critchley, Simon (2011) 'The Cycle of Revenge', *The New York Times*, online, 8 September, https://opinionator.blogs.nytimes.com/2011/09/08/the-cycle-of-revenge/ (Accessed 25 October 2021).

Daniel, Adam (2020) *Affective Intensities and Evolving Horror Forms: From Found Footage to Virtual Reality*, Edinburgh University Press, Edinburgh.

Darer, Michael (2016) 'The Untapped Potential of "Found Footage Horror"', *Huffington Post*, online, 31 October, https://www.huffpost.com/entry/the-untapped-potential-of-found-footage-horror_b_5817c2e8e4b096e87069698c (Accessed 25 October 2021).

Dargis, Manohla (2014) 'A Horror Story Borrows from History', *The New York Times*, online, 5 June, https://www.nytimes.com/2014/06/06/movies/the-sacrament-invokes-jonestown.html (Accessed 25 October 2021).

Das, Shanti, Cameron Charters and Hannah Al-Othman (2021) 'Plymouth Shooting: Thousands of Boys Drawn to 'Incel' Sites Urging Them to Kill Women', *The Times*, online, 15 August, https://www.thetimes.co.uk/article/plymouth-shooting-incel-groups-radicalising-boys-as-young-as-13-8jzffqzn0 (Accessed 9 October 2021).

Dass, William (2018) 'Shudder's "Video Palace" Director Ben Rock on How Podcasting Could be a New Entry Point for Filmmakers', *Film School Rejects*, online, 4 December, https://filmschoolrejects.com/shudders-video-palace-director-ben-rock-on-how-podcasting-could-be-a-new-entry-point-for-filmmakers/ (Accessed 25 October 2021).

Dawson, Nick (2008) '"A Lot of People Settle for the Vanilla": George A Romero on Diary of the Dead', *Filmmaker Magazine*, online, 15 February, https://filmmakermagazine.com/1303-george-a-romero-diary-of-the-dead (Accessed 25 October 2021).

de Moraes, Lisa (2002) 'CBS's Controversial Date With Destiny', *The Washington Post*, online, 9 March, https://www.washingtonpost.com/archive/lifestyle/2002/03/09/cbss-controversial-date-with-destiny/30809f83-f42c-4c5a-bd53-521794f78f7d/ (accessed 25 October 2021).

Debruge, Peter (2014) 'Film Review: "Unfriended"', *Variety*, online, 3 August, https://variety.com/2014/film/festivals/film-review-cybernatural-1201274261/ (accessed 9 October 2021).

Debruge, Peter (2018) 'Film Review: "Searching"', *Variety*, online, 29 January, https://variety.com/2018/film/reviews/search-review-aneesh-chaganty-1202679816/ (accessed 25 October 2021).

Deren, Maya (1960) 'Cinematography: The Creative Use of Reality', in *Daedalus*, vol. 89, no. 1, pp. 150–67.

Dewey, Caitlin (2014) 'When Botched Surgeries and Suicides Go Viral: The Revolting Rise of "Medical Gore"', *The Washington Post*, online, 28 October, https://www.washingtonpost.com/news/the-intersect/wp/2014/10/28/when-botched-surgeries-and-suicides-go-viral-the-revolting-rise-of-medical-gore/ (accessed 25 October 2021).

Dickson, Evan (2014) '[Stanley Fest '14 Review] "The Sacrament" is Highly Effective and Suspenseful!', *Bloody Disgusting*, online, 28 April, https://bloody-disgusting.com/reviews/3290974/stanley-fest-14-sacrament-highly-effective-suspenseful/ (accessed 25 October 2021).

Dixon, Wheeler Winston (2004) *Film and Television After 9/11*, Southern Illinois University Press, Carbondale.

Dixon, Wheeler Winston (2004) 'Introduction: Something Lost – Film after 9/11', in Wheeler Winston Dixon (ed.), *Film and Television After 9/11*, Southern Illinois University Press, Carbondale, pp. 1–28.

Dixon, Wheeler Winston (2010) *A History of Horror*, Rutgers University Press, New Brunswick, NJ.

Doka, Kenneth J. (1989) *Disenfranchised Grief: Recognising Hidden Sorrow*, Jossey Bass, San Francisco.

Donnar, Glen (2020) *Troubling Masculinities: Terror, Gender, and Monstrous Others in American Film Post-9/11*, University Press of Mississippi, Jackson.

Donnelly, Sally (2001) 'The Day the FAA Stopped the World', *Time*, online, 14 September, http://content.time.com/time/nation/article/0,8599,174912,00.html (accessed 25 October 2021).

Dovey, Jon (2000) *Freakshow: First Person Media and Factual Television*, Pluto, London.

Dread Central (2014a) 'THE SACRAMENT Interview with Ti West & Amy Seimetz',

*YouTube*, online, 27 May, https://www.youtube.com/watch?v=30BRdDtdVG0 (accessed 25 October 2021).

Dread Central (2014b) 'THE SACRAMENT Interview with AJ Bowen & Joe Swanberg', *YouTube*, online, 27 May, https://www.youtube.com/watch?v=blR2LrL9pEU (accessed 25 October 2021).

Dredge, Stuart (2013) 'How Vice's Tim Pool used Google Glass to Cover Istanbul Protests', *The Guardian*, online, 30 July, https://www.theguardian.com/technology/2013/jul/30/google-glass-istanbul-protests-vice (accessed 25 October 2021.)

Durham Peters, John (2001) 'Witnessing', in *Media, Culture & Society*, vol. 23, no. 6, pp. 707–23.

Dwyer, Jim and Kevin Flynn (2005) *102 Minutes: The Definitive Account of the Fight to Survive*, Arrow Books, London.

Earle, Harriet (2017) '"A Convenient Place for Inconvenient People": Madness, Sex and the Asylum in *American Horror Story*', in *The Journal of Popular Culture*, vol. 50, no. 2, pp. 259–75.

Ebert, Roger (1999) 'The Blair Witch Project', *Roger Ebert*, online, 16 July, https://www.rogerebert.com/reviews/the-blair-witch-project-1999 (accessed 9 October 2021).

Ebert, Roger (2012) 'V/H/S', *Roger Ebert*, online, 3 October, https://www.rogerebert.com/reviews/vhs-2012 (accessed 25 October 2021).

Ebiri, Bilge (2014) 'Ebiri on The Sacrament: This Should Be Ti West's Final Horror Movie', *Vulture*, online, 6 June, https://www.vulture.com/2014/06/movie-review-the-sacrament.html (accessed 25 October 2021).

Edelstein, David (2006) 'Now Playing at Your Local Multiplex: Torture Porn', *New York Magazine*, online, 6 February, http://nymag.com/movies/features/15622/ (accessed 25 October 2021).

Egan, Kate (2007) *Trash or Treasure?: Censorship and the Changing Meanings of the Video Nasties*, Manchester University Press, Manchester.

Elsaesser, Thomas (2001) 'Postmodernism as Mourning Work', in *Screen*, vol. 42, no. 2, pp. 193–201.

Erbland, Kate (2018) '"Searching" Review: John Cho Stars in Thrilling Abduction Drama that Exists Entirely on a Computer Screen', *Indiewire*, online, 27 January, https://www.indiewire.com/2018/01/search-review-john-cho-abduction-drama-computer-sundance-1201922001/ (accessed 25 October 2021).

Evangelista, Chris (2018) '"The Staircase" Review: Netflix Makes an Old True Crime Doc New Again', *Slashfilm*, online, 4 June, https://www.slashfilm.com/the-staircase-review/ (accessed 25 October 2021).

Faludi, Susan (2007) *The Terror Dream: Myth and Misogyny in an Insecure America*, Picador, New York.

Faraci, Devin (2012) 'Why Everybody Hates the Ending of *The Devil Inside*', *Birth Movies Death*, online, 8 January, http://birthmoviesdeath.com/2012/01/08/why-everybody-hates-the-ending-of-the-devil-inside (accessed 25 October 2021).

Felperin, Leslie (2016) '"*Blair Witch*": Film Review', *Hollywood Reporter*, online, 11 September, https://www.hollywoodreporter.com/movies/movie-reviews/blair-witch-review-927536/ (accessed 9 October 2021).

Fetveit, Arild (1999) 'Reality TV in the Digital Era: A Paradox in Visual Culture?', in *Media, Culture & Society*, vol. 21, no. 6, pp. 787–804.

Feuer, Jane (1983) 'The Concept of Live Television: Ontology as Ideology', in E. Ann Kaplan (ed.), *Regarding Television: Critical Approaches – An Anthology*, BFI, London, pp. 12–22.

Finnegan, Leah (2016) 'Ethics in Stunt Journalism: The Truth Cannot be Created', *The*

*Outline*, online, 16 December, https://theoutline.com/post/584/ethics-in-stunt-jour nalism?zd=2&zi=tacsv4gi (accessed 25 October 2021).

Fishwick, Carmen (2016) 'I, Narcissist – Vanity, Social Media, and the Human Condition', *The Guardian*, online, 17 March, https://www.theguardian.com/world/2016/mar /17/i-narcissist-vanity-social-media-and-the-human-condition (accessed 9 October 2021).

Fiske, John (1989) *Understanding Popular Culture*, Routledge, Abingdon and New York.

Fiske, John (2010) *Television Culture*, Routledge, Abingdon and New York.

Fitch, Marc E. (2013) *Paranormal Nation: Why America Needs Ghosts, UFOs, and Bigfoot*, Praeger, Santa Barbara.

Flynn, Bernadette (2005) 'Docobricolage in the Age of Simulation', in Geoff King (ed.), *The Spectacle of the Real: From Hollywood to 'Reality' TV and Beyond*, Intellect, Bristol, pp. 130–9.

Foley, Malcolm and J. John Lennon (1996) 'JFK and Dark Tourism: A Fascination With Assassination', in *International Journal of Heritage Studies*, vol. 2, no. 4, pp. 198–211.

Fontana, David (2016) '*Blair Witch*: An Unimaginative, Unnecessary Sequel', *Film Inquiry*, online, 28 September, https://www.filminquiry.com/blair-witch-2016-review/ (accessed 25 October 2021).

Foot, Kirsten, Barbara Warnick and Steven M. Schneider (2005) 'Web-Based Memorializing After September 11: Toward a Conceptual Framework', in *Journal of Computer-Mediated Communication*, vol. 11, no. 1, pp. 72–96.

Forrest, Jennifer and Leonard R. Koos (2002) 'Reviewing Remakes: An Introduction', in Jennifer Forrest and Leonard R. Koos (eds), *Dead Ringers: The Remake in Theory and Practice*, State University of New York Press, Albany, pp. 1–36.

Fosco, Molly (2016) 'Is Our Obsession With True Crime Morally Irresponsible?', *Huffington Post*, online, 26 January, https://www.huffpost.com/entry/is-our-obsess ion-with-true-crime-morally-irresponsible_b_9073196 (accessed 25 October 2021).

Foutch, Haleigh (2014) 'Ti West Talks THE SACRAMENT, Shooting a Vérité Film, Taking a Break from Horror, His Upcoming Western IN THE VALLEY OF VIOLENCE and More', *Collider*, online, 4 June, https://collider.com/ti-west-the-sac rament-interview/ (accessed 26 October 2021).

Fowle, Kyle (2014) 'It's Time to Revitalize the Found-Footage Horror Movie', *Esquire*, online, 6 January, https://www.esquire.com/entertainment/movies/a26619/paran ormal-found-footage-horror-movies/ (Accessed 9 October 2021).

Freeman, Mark (2015) 'An Uploadable Cinema: Digital Horror and the Postnational Image', in Linnie Blake and Xavier Aldana Reyes (eds), *Digital Horror: Haunted Technologies, Network Panic and the Found Footage Phenomenon*, I. B. Tauris, London, pp. 107–20.

Friend, David (2011) *Watching the World Change: The Stories Behind the Images of 9/11*, Picador, New York.

Frost, Laura (2011) 'Black Screens, Lost Bodies: The Cinematic Apparatus of 9/11 Horror', in Aviva Briefel and Sam J. Miller (eds), *Horror After 9/11: World of Fear, Cinema of Terror*, University of Texas Press, Austin, pp. 13–39.

Froula, Anna (2010) 'Prolepsis and the "War on Terror": Zombie Pathology and The Culture of Fear in *28 Days Later*', in Jeff Birkenstein Anne Froula and Karen Randell (eds), *Reframing 9/11: Film, Popular Culture and the 'War on Terror'*, Bloomsbury, London and New York, pp. 195–208.

Fuchs, Christian (2013) *Social Media: A Critical Introduction*, Sage Publications, London.

Gerbaudo, Paolo (2012) *Tweets and the Streets: Social Media and Contemporary Activism*, Pluto Press, London.

Gibbs, Samuel (2015) 'Facebook Tackles Graphic Videos and Photos With "Are You Sure?" Warnings', *The Guardian*, online, 13 January, https://www.theguardian.com/technology/2015/jan/13/facebook-tackles-graphic-videos-and-photos-with-are-you-sure-warnings (accessed 25 October 2021).

Gillespie, Katherine (2018) 'Everybody on the Internet is Talking About Their Trauma', *Vice*, online, 16 April, https://www.vice.com/en/article/vbxx88/everybody-on-the-internet-is-talking-about-their-trauma (accessed 25 October 2021).

Glavin, Nicholas A. (2016) 'Facebook, Twitter Users Must be More Critical of Content', *The New York Times*, online, 22 November, https://www.nytimes.com/roomfordebate/2016/11/22/how-to-stop-the-spread-of-fake-news/facebook-twitter-users-must-be-more-critical-of-content (accessed 25 October 2021).

Gleiberman, Owen (2016) 'As "Blair Witch" Flops, is the Found-Footage Horror Film Over?', *Variety*, online, 18 September, https://variety.com/2016/film/columns/blair-witch-is-the-found-footage-horror-film-over-1201864069/ (accessed 25 October 2021).

Godard, François (2002) 'Canal Plus 9/11 Pic Courts Controversy', *Variety*, online, 21 August, https://variety.com/2002/film/markets-festivals/canal-plus-9-11-pic-courts-controversy-1117871633/ (accessed 16 October 2021).

Goldner, Tracey (2014) 'Vice News Thrives With Young Audience, Controversy', *Global Journalist*, online, 25 September, https://globaljournalist.org/2014/09/despite-controversies-vice-news-thrives-young-audience/ (accessed 25 October 2021).

Goss, Brian Michael (2017) 'The Pain in Spain: An Analysis of Horror Auteur Jaume Balagueró's Films', in *Studies in European Cinema*, vol. 14, no. 1, pp. 66–81.

Grant, Barry Keith (2013) 'Digital Anxiety and the New Verité Horror and SF Film', in *Science Fiction Film & Television*, vol. 6, no. 2, pp. 153–75.

Grant, Drew (2013) 'The Vice Guide to Serious Journalism: How a DIY Drug Mag Became Serious Business for HBO', *Observer*, online, 26 March, https://observer.com/2013/03/the-vice-guide-to-serious-journalism-how-a-diy-drug-mag-became-serious-business-for-hbo/ (accessed 25 October 2021).

Griffey, Harriet (2018) 'The Lost Art of Concentration: Being Distracted in a Digital World', *The Guardian*, online, 14 October, https://www.theguardian.com/lifeandstyle/2018/oct/14/the-lost-art-of-concentration-being-distracted-in-a-digital-world (accessed 25 October 2021).

Griffin, Andrew (2018) 'Logan Paul Video: What did Controversial Footage Show and What is Aokigahara, The Japanese "Suicide Forest"', *The Independent*, online, 2 January, https://www.independent.co.uk/life-style/gadgets-and-tech/news/logan-paul-video-what-aokigahara-suicide-forest-show-youtube-post-dead-body-latest-news-a8137561.html (accessed 25 October 2021).

Griffin, Andrew (2021) 'Plymouth Shooting: YouTube Channel Thought to Belong to Shooter Taken Offline', *The Independent*, online, 13 August, https://www.independent.co.uk/news/uk/crime/plymouth-shooting-youtube-jake-davison-videos-b1902017.html (accessed 9 October 2021).

Grixti, Joseph (1989) *Terrors of Uncertainty: The Cultural Contexts of Horror Fiction*, Routledge, Abingdon and New York.

Gunn, Jeff (2017) *The Road to Jonestown: Jim Jones and Peoples Temple*, Simon & Schuster, New York.

Gunning, Tom (2003) 'Re-newing Old Technologies: Astonishment, Second Nature and the Uncanny in Technology from the Previous Turn-of-the-Century', in David Thorburn and Henry Jenkins (eds), *Rethinking Media Change: The Aesthetics of Transition*, The MIT Press, London and Cambridge, MA, pp. 39–60.

Haglund, David (2012) 'Does *The Devil Inside* Have the Worst Ending in Movie History?', *Slate*, online, 9 January, https://slate.com/culture/2012/01/the-devil-inside-ending-is-it-the-worst-ever-and-why-do-people-hate-it.html (accessed 25 October 2021).

Hahner, Leslie A., Scott J. Varda and Nathan A. Wilson (2013) 'Paranormal Activity and the Horror of Abject Consumption', in *Critical Studies in Media Communication*, vol. 30, no. 5, pp. 362–76.

Hale, Mike (2009) 'Consigning Reality to Ghosts', *The New York Times*, online, 10 December, https://www.nytimes.com/2009/12/13/arts/television/13paranormal.html (accessed 25 October 2021).

Hall, John R. (1987) *Gone from the Promised Land: Jonestown in American Cultural History*, Routledge, Abingdon and New York.

Hallam, Lindsay (2010) 'Genre Cinema as Trauma Cinema: Post 9/11 Trauma and the Rise of "Torture Porn" in Recent Horror Films', in Mick Broderick and Antonio Traverso (eds), *Trauma, Media, Art: New Perspectives*, Cambridge Scholars Publishing, Newcastle-Upon-Tyne, pp. 228–36.

Hallam, Lindsay (2021) 'Digital Witness: Found Footage and Desktop Horror as Post-cinematic Experience', in Eddie Falvey, Jonathan Wroot and Joe Hickinbottom (eds), *New Blood: Critical Approaches to Contemporary Horror*, University of Wales Press, Cardiff, pp. 183–200.

Hantke, Steffen (2007) 'Academic Film Criticism, the Rhetoric of Crisis, and the Current State of American Horror Cinema: Thoughts on Canonicity and Academic Anxiety', in *College Literature*, vol. 34, no. 4, pp. 191–202.

Hantke, Steffen (2010) 'Introduction: They Don't Make 'Em Like They Used To: On the Rhetoric of Crisis and the Current State of American Horror Cinema', in Steffen Hantke (ed.), *American Horror Film: The Genre at the Turn of the Millennium*, University of Mississippi Press, Jackson, pp. vii–xxxii.

Harkin, James (2006) 'Shock and Gore', *Financial Times*, online, 29 May, https://www.ft.com/content/1373c930-8325-11da-ac1f-0000779e2340 (accessed 25 October 2021).

Harris, Martin (2001) 'The "Witchcraft" of Media Manipulation: Pamela and *The Blair Witch Project*', in *Journal of Popular Culture*, vol. 34, no. 4, pp. 75–107.

Harrison, Virginia (2013) 'Outrage Erupts Over Facebook's Decision on Graphic Videos', *CNN*, online, 23 October, https://money.cnn.com/2013/10/22/news/companies/facebook-violent-videos/index.html (accessed 25 October 2021).

Hart, Adam Charles (2014) 'Millennial Fears: Abject Horror in a Transnational Context', in Harry M. Benshoff (ed.), *A Companion to the Horror Film*, Wiley Blackwell, Chichester, pp. 329–44.

Hart, Adam Charles (2019) *Monstrous Forms: Moving Image Horror Across Media*, Oxford University Press, New York.

Hatcher, Chris (1989) 'After Jonestown: Survivors of Peoples Temple', in Rebecca Moore and Fielding M. McGehee III (eds), *The Need for a Second Look at Jonestown*, Edwin Mellen Press, New York, pp. 127–46.

Heller-Nicholas, Alexandra (2014) *Found Footage Horror Films: Fear and the Appearance of Reality*, McFarland, Jefferson.

Hensley, Laura (2019) 'Why Are We Obsessed With True Crime and What is it Doing to Our Minds?', *Global News*, online, 26 January, https://globalnews.ca/news/4888508/how-does-true-crime-affect-you/ (accessed 25 October 2021).

Heritage, Stuart (2016) 'Angel Has Fallen: Is Gerard Butler Hollywood's weirdest action hero?', *The Guardian*, online, 22 August, https://www.theguardian.com/film/2019/aug/22/angel-has-fallen-gerard-butler (accessed 16 October 2021).

Hess, Aaron (2007) 'In Digital Remembrance: Vernacular Memory and the Rhetorical Construction of Web Memorials', in *Media, Culture and Society*, vol. 29, no. 5, pp. 812–30.

Hight, Craig (2008) 'Mockumentary: A Call to Play', in Thomas Austin and Wilma de Jong (eds), *Rethinking Documentary: New Perspectives, New Practices*, Open University Press, Maidenhead, pp. 204–16.

Higley, Sarah Lynn And Jeffrey Andrew Weinstock (2004). *Nothing That Is: Millennial Cinema and the Blair Witch Controversies*, Wayne State University Press, Detroit.

Higley, Sarah Lynn and Jeffrey Andrew Weinstock (2004) 'Introduction: The Blair Witch Controversies', in Sarah Lynn Higley and Jeffrey Andrew Weinstock (eds), *Nothing That Is: Millennial Cinema and the Blair Witch Controversies*, Wayne State University Press, Detroit, pp. 11–36.

Hill, Annette (2005) *Reality TV: Factual Entertainment and Television Audiences*, Routledge, Abingdon and New York.

Hill, Annette (2007) *Restyling Factual TV*, Routledge, Abingdon and New York.

Hill, Annette (2010) *Paranormal Media: Audiences, Spirits and Magic in Popular Culture*, Routledge, Abingdon and New York.

Hill, Katherine (2014) 'Horror or Horrible: A Review of *The Sacrament*', Alternative Considerations of Jonestown and Peoples Temple, online, 10 October, https://jonestown.sdsu.edu/?page_id=61702 (accessed 25 October 2021).

Hills, Matt (2002) *Fan Cultures*, Routledge, Abingdon and New York.

Hortobagyi, Monica (2007) 'Slain Student's Pages to Stay on Facebook', *USA Today*, online, 8 May, http://usatoday30.usatoday.com/tech/webguide/internetlife/2007-05-08-facebook-vatech_N.htm (accessed 25 October 2021).

Howard, Jacqueline (2018) 'ADHD Study Links Teens' Symptoms With Digital Media Use', *CNN*, online, 17 July, https://edition.cnn.com/2018/07/17/health/adhd-symptoms-digital-media-study/index.html (accessed 25 October 2021).

Hubber, Duncan (2017) 'Exhuming the Past: Found-Footage Horror and National Wounds', *Frames Cinema Journal*, online, http://framescinemajournal.com/article/exhuming-the-past-found-footage-horror-and-national-wounds/ (accessed 25 October 2021).

Huffington, Arianna (2002) 'Wacko in Waco', *Salon*, online, 17 August, https://www.salon.com/2002/08/16/waco_13/ (accessed 25 October 2021).

Humphries, Reynold (2002) *The American Horror Film: An Introduction*, Edinburgh University Press, Edinburgh.

Hunt, Leon (1992) 'A (Sadistic) Night at the Opera: Notes on the Italian Horror Film', in *The Velvet Light Trap*, no. 30, pp. 65–75.

Hutchings, Peter (2004) *The Horror Film*, Pearson Publishing, Cambridge.

Ip, Chris (2015) 'The Cult of Vice', *Columbia Journalism Review*, online, https://www.cjr.org/analysis/the_cult_of_vice.php (accessed 25 October 2021).

Jackson, Neil (2002) 'Cannibal Holocaust, Realist Horror and Reflexivity', in *Post Script: Essays in Film and The Humanities*, vol. 21, no. 3, pp. 32–45.

Jackson, Neil (2016) 'Introduction: Shot, Cut and Slaughtered: The Cultural Mythology of Snuff', in Neil Jackson, Shaun Kimber, Johnny Walker and Thomas Joseph Watson (eds), *Snuff: Real Death and Screen* Media, Bloomsbury Academic, London and New York, pp. 1–22.

Jacoby, Jeff (2014) 'Why Beheading? Theology and History Play into the Use of an Old Horror in Warfare', *The Boston Globe*, online, 12 September, https://www.bostonglobe.com/opinion/2014/09/21/why-isis-emphasizes-beheading/Azrb65gWaiVfbz8aTiE8DI/story.html (accessed 25 October 2021).

Jarvis, Lee (2011) '9/11 Digitally Remastered? Internet Archives, Vernacular Memories and WhereWereYou.org', in *Journal of American Studies*, vol. 45, no. 4, pp. 793–814.

Jauregui, Carolina Gabriela (2004) '"Eat it Alive and Swallow it Whole!" Resavoring *Cannibal Holocaust* as a Mockumentary', *Invisible Culture: An Electronic Journal for Visual Culture*, 7, online, https://ivc.lib.rochester.edu/eat-it-alive-and-swallow-it-whole-resavoring-cannibal-holocaust-as-a-mockumentary/ (accessed 25 October 2021).

Jeffries, Adrienne (2013) 'Should you Go to Jail for Posting Video of a Real Murder?', *The Verge*, online, 16 October, https://www.theverge.com/2013/10/16/4841522/bestgore-corrupting-public-morals-mark-marek-luka-magnotta (accessed 25 October 2021).

Jeffries, Stuart (2017) '"We're All Car Crash Snoopers Now": The Truth About the TV True-Crime Wave', *The Guardian*, online, 4 March, https://www.theguardian.com/tv-and-radio/2017/mar/04/serial-jinx-making-murderer-rillington-place (accessed 25 October 2021).

Jenkins, Henry (2013) *Textual Poachers: Television Fans and Participatory Culture*. 20th Anniversary Edition, Routledge, Abingdon and New York.

Jenkins, Philip (2000) *Mystics and Messiahs: Cults and New Religions in American History*, Oxford University Press, Oxford.

Johnston Kohl, Laura (2010) *Jonestown Survivor: An Insider's Look*, iUniverse, New York.

Jones, Steve (2013) *Torture Porn: Popular Horror after Saw*, Palgrave Macmillan, Basingstoke.

Jones, Steve (2017) 'Cartesianism and Intersubjectivity in Paranormal Activity and the Philosophy of Mind', in *Film-Philosophy*, vol. 21, no. 1, pp. 1–19.

Jorgensen, Danny L. (1980) 'The Social Construction and Interpretation of Deviance: Jonestown and the Mass Media', *Deviant Behaviour*, vol. 1, no. 3–4, pp. 309–32.

Joubert, Luke (2016) 'You Are Not Ready for New French Extremity Films', *Medium*, online, 28 August, https://medium.com/@lukejoubert/you-are-not-ready-for-new-french-extremity-36e6bf5ae9c0 (accessed 11 April 2019).

Jowett, Lorna And Stacey Abbott (2013) *TV Horror: Investigating the Darker Side of the Small Screen*, I. B. Tauris, London.

Junod, Tom (2021) 'The Falling Man', *Esquire*, online, 9 September, https://www.esquire.com/news-politics/a48031/the-falling-man-tom-junod/ (accessed 25 October 2021).

Kaes, Anton (2011) *Shell Shock Cinema: Weimar Culture and the Wounds of War*, Princeton University Press, Princeton.

Kain, Erik (2016) '"The Walking Dead" Season 7, Episode 1 Review: The Wrath of Negan', *Forbes*, online, 23 October, https://www.forbes.com/sites/erikkain/2016/10/23/the-walking-dead-season-7-episode-1-review-the-wrath-of-negan/?sh=461f2eca77a6 (accessed 25 October 2021).

Kaplan, E. Ann (2003) 'A Camera and a Catastrophe: Reflections on Trauma and the Twin Towers', in Judith Greenberg (ed.), *Trauma at Home: After 9/11*, University of Nebraska Press, Lincoln, pp. 95–106.

Kaplan, E. Ann (2005) *Trauma Culture: The Politics of Terror and Loss in Media and Literature*, Rutgers University Press, New Brunswick, NJ.

Kaplan, E. Ann (2005) 'Introduction: 9/11 and "Disturbing Remains"' in E. Ann Kaplan (ed.), *Trauma Culture: The Politics of Terror and Loss in Media and Literature*, Rutgers University Press, New Brunswick, NJ, pp. 1–23.

Kavka, Misha (2012) *Reality TV*, Edinburgh University Press, Edinburgh.

Keetley, Dawn (2020) *Jordan Peele's Get Out: Political Horror*, Ohio State Press, Columbus.

Kellner, Douglas (1995) *Media Culture: Cultural Studies, Identity and Politics Between the Modern and the Postmodern*, Routledge, Abingdon and New York.

Kellner, Douglas (2004) 'Media Culture and the Triumph of the Spectacle', in Geoff King (ed.), *The Spectacle of the Real: From Hollywood to 'Reality' TV and Beyond*, Intellect, Bristol, pp. 23–36.

Kellner, Douglas (2010) *Cinema Wars: Hollywood Film and Politics in the Bush-Cheney Era*, Wiley Blackwell, Oxford.

Kent, Sara-Aisha (2021) 'Night Stalker Slammed by Netflix Viewers for Graphic and Bloody Crime Scene Reconstructions', *Mirror*, online, 15 January, https://www.mirror.co.uk/tv/tv-news/netflix-users-terrified-night-stalker-23323216 (accessed 9 March 2022).

Kerner, Aaron Michael (2015) *Torture Porn in the Wake of 9/11: Horror, Exploitation, and the Cinema of Sensation*, Rutgers University Press, New Brunswick, NJ.

Kilborn, Richard (2003) *Staging the Real: Factual TV Programming in the Age of Big Brother*, Manchester University Press, Manchester.

King, Geoff (2005) 'Introduction: The Spectacle of the Real', in Geoff King (ed.), *The Spectacle of the Real: From Hollywood to 'Reality' TV and Beyond*, Intellect, Bristol, pp. 13–21.

King, Geoff (2005) '"Just Like a Movie?": 9/11 and Hollywood Spectacle', in Geoff King (ed.), *The Spectacle of the Real: From Hollywood to 'Reality' TV and Beyond*, Intellect, Bristol, pp. 47–58.

King, Homay (2011) 'The Host Versus Cloverfield', in Aviva Briefel and Sam J. Miller (eds), *Horror After 9/11: World of Fear, Cinema of Terror*, University of Texas Press, Austin, pp. 124–41.

Kirk, Neal (2015) 'Networked Spectrality: In Memorium, Pulse, and Beyond', in Linnie Blake and Xavier Aldana Reyes (eds), *Digital Horror: Haunted Technologies, Network Panic and the Found Footage Phenomenon*, I. B. Tauris, London, pp. 54–65.

Kohn, Eric (2018) 'Timur Bekmambetov Is Done With Hollywood and Only Wants to Make Movies on Computer Screen', *Indiewire*, online, 1 August, https://www.indiewire.com/2018/08/timur-bekmambetov-screenlife-interview-searching-unfriended-1201989768/ (ccessed 15 October 2021).

Köhne, Julia B., Michael Elm and Kobi Kabalek (2014) *The Horrors of Trauma in Cinema: Violence Void Visualization*, Cambridge Scholars Publishing, Cambridge.

Koven, Mikel J. (2007) '*Most Haunted* and the Convergence of Traditional Belief and Popular Television', in *Folklore*, vol. 118, no. 2, pp. 183–202.

Kracauer, Siegfried (2004 [1947]) *From Caligari to Hitler: A Psychological History of the German Film*, Revised and expanded edition, Princeton University Press, Princeton.

Krause, Charles A. (1978) 'Survivor: "They Started with the Babies"', *The Washington Post*, online, 21 November, https://www.washingtonpost.com/archive/politics/1978/11/21/survivor-they-started-with-the-babies/ec559372-be60-4355-a5fc-f5e306370992/ (accessed 25 October 2021).

Krautschick, Lars R. (2012) 'Attacks on "Safe Zones": How Hollywood Horror Infiltrates Private Spheres', in *Synaesthesia: Communication Across Cultures Communications Journal*, vol. 1, no. 3, pp. 1–25.

Kubai, Andy L. (2016) 'Found Footage is Stagnating in the Smartphone Age', *Screen Rant*, online, 21 September, https://screenrant.com/blair-witch-found-footage-smartphones/ (accessed 25 October 2021).

LaCapra, Dominick (1997) 'Lanzmann's "Shoah": "Here There Is No Why"', in *Critical Inquiry*, vol. 23, no. 2, pp. 231–69.

Lambie, Ryan (2014) 'Ti West interview: *The Sacrament*, documentary horror & more', *Den of Geek*, online, 6 June, https://www.denofgeek.com/movies/ti-west/30803/ti-west-interview-the-sacrament-documentary-horror-more (accessed 25 October 2021).

Larsen, Katherine and Lynn S. Zubernis (2012) *Fandom At The Crossroads: Celebration, Shame and Fan/Producer Relationships*, Cambridge Scholars, Newcastle-Upon-Tyne.
Lattanzio, Ryan (2020) '"*Spree*" Review: Joe Keery is a Serial-Killing, Wannabe Influencer in this Nihilistic Satire', *Indiewire*, online, 13 August, https://www.indiewire.com/2020/08/spree-review-joe-keery-nihilistic-social-media-satire-1234579629/ (accessed 25 October 2021).
Lavender-Smith, Jordan (2009) 'Irony Inc: Parodic-Doc Horror and *The Blair Witch Project*', in Iain Robert Smith (ed.), *Cultural Borrowings: Appropriation, Reworking, Transformation*, Scope, Nottingham, pp. 169–85.
Laycock, Joseph (2013) '"Where Do They Get These Ideas?" Changing Ideas of Cults in the Mirror of Popular Culture', in *Journal of the American Academy of Religion*, vol. 18, no. 1, pp. 80–106.
Layton, Deborah (1999) *Seductive Poison: A Jonestown Survivor's Story of Life and Death in the Peoples Temple*, Anchor Books, New York.
Lázaro-Reboll, Antonio (2017) 'Generating Fear: From Fantastic Factory (2000–2005) to [REC] (2007–2014)', in Jorge Marí (ed.), *Tracing the Borders of Spanish Horror Cinema and Television*, Routledge, Abingdon and New York, pp. 161–89.
Lee, Benjamin (2015) 'Not Coming Soon: The Films Still Stuck in Purgatory', *The Guardian*, online, 2 June, https://www.theguardian.com/film/filmblog/2015/jun/02/not-coming-soon-david-o-russell-accidental-love (accessed 25 October 2021).
Lee, Benjamin (2016) '*Blair Witch* Review – Found-Footage Sequel Brings Horror of Deja-vu', *The Guardian*, online, 12 September, https://www.theguardian.com/film/2016/sep/12/blair-witch-review-horror-sequel (accessed 25 October 2021).
Lee-Wright, Peter. (2010) *The Documentary Handbook*, Routledge, Abingdon and New York.
Lewis, Helen (2021) 'Where are the Iconic Images of the COVID-19 Pandemic', *The Atlantic*, online, 24 February, https://www.theatlantic.com/international/archive/2021/02/where-are-iconic-images-covid-19-pandemic/618036/ (accessed 25 October 2021).
Lewis, Isobel (2020) '*Megan is Missing*: TikTok Users Left 'Traumatised' After Watching Controversial 2011 Horror Film for the First Time', *The Independent*, online, 16 November, https://www.independent.co.uk/arts-entertainment/films/news/megan-is-missing-tiktok-michael-goi-b1723530.html (accessed 20 October 2021).
Lewis, Rebecca (2020) '"This Is What the News Won't Show You": YouTube Creators and the Reactionary Politics of Micro-celebrity', in *Television and New Media*, vol. 21, no. 2, pp. 201–17.
Leyda, Julia (2014) 'Demon Debt: Paranormal Activity as Recessionary Post-Cinematic Allegory', *Jump Cut: A Review of Contemporary Media*, 56, online, https://www.ejumpcut.org/archive/jc56.2014-2015/LeydaParanormalActivity/text.html (accessed 25 October 2021).
Liénard-Yeterian, Marie and Agnieszka Soltyzik Monnet (2015) 'The Gothic in an Age of Terror(ism)', in *Gothic Studies*, vol. 17, no. 2, pp. 1–11.
Lillebuen, Steve (2012) 'The Sick Fascination With a Death Video', *CNN*, online, 6 June, http://edition.cnn.com/2012/06/06/opinion/lillebuen-killing-video/ (accessed 25 October 2021).
Littleton, Cynthia (2016) 'CNN Marks 15th Anniversary of 9/11 With Deal for Landmark Documentary', Digital Archive Plan, *Yahoo News*, online, 8 September, https://uk.news.yahoo.com/cnn-9-11-documentary-footage-gets-updates-15-203902813.html (accessed 25 October 2021).

Lizzlexsizzle (2010) [Twitter], online, 8 December, https://twitter.com/lizzlexsizzle/status/12614598171566080 (accessed 27 October 2021).

Lodge, Guy (2016) 'Toronto Film Review: "*Blair Witch*"', *Yahoo News*, online, 12 September, https://uk.sports.yahoo.com/news/toronto-film-review-blair-witch-040059865.html (accessed 25 October 2021).

Lowell, Percival (1906) 'First Photographs of the Canals of Mars', in *Proceedings of the Royal Society of London, Series A, Containing Papers of a Mathematical and Physical Character*, vol. 77, no. 515, pp. 132–5.

Lowenstein, Adam (2004) 'Allegorizing Hiroshima: Shindo Kaneto's Onibaba as Trauma Text', in E. Ann Kaplan and Ban Wang (eds), *Trauma and Cinema: Cross-Cultural Explorations*, Hong Kong University Press, Hong Kong, pp. 145–61.

Lowenstein, Adam (2005) *Shocking Representations: Historical Trauma, National Cinema and the Modern Horror Film*, Columbia University Press, New York.

Luft, Benjamin J. (2011) *We're Not Leaving: 9/11 Responders Tell Their Stories of Courage, Sacrifice and Renewal*, Greenpaint Press, New York.

Lukas, Scott A. and John Marmysz (2010) *Fear, Cultural Anxiety, and Transformation: Horror, Science Fiction, and Fantasy Films Remade*, Lexington Books, Plymouth.

Lyman, Rick (2001) 'Horrors! Time for an Attack of the Metaphors?', *The New York Times*, online, 23 October, https://www.nytimes.com/2001/10/23/movies/horrors-time-for-an-attack-of-the-metaphors-from-bug-movies-to-bioterrorism.html (accessed 25 October 2021).

Lyne, Charlie (2015) 'End of Watch: Enough With the Found Footage Movies', *The Guardian*, online, 23 November, https://www.theguardian.com/film/2012/nov/23/end-of-watch-found-footage (accessed 25 October 2021).

Lyon, David (2007) *Surveillance Studies: An Overview*, Polity Press, Cambridge.

MacDonald, Cheyenne (2016) 'Would YOU Resurrect Your Dead Friend as an AI? Try out "Memorial" Chatbot App – and You Can Even Talk to a Virtual Version of Prince', *Daily Mail*, online, 7 October, https://www.dailymail.co.uk/sciencetech/article-3826208/Would-resurrect-dead-friend-AI-Try-memorial-chatbot-app-talk-virtual-version-Prince.html (accessed 25 October 2021).

Maddrey, Joseph (2004) *Nightmares in Red, White, and Blue: The Evolution of the American Horror Film*, McFarland, Jefferson.

Maelstrom (2018) 'Entertainment and Voyeurism: Our Obsession with True Crime, and the Lines We're Eager to Blur', *Maelstrom*, online, 18 July, https://www.maelllstrom.com/musings/2018/7/18/entertainment-and-voyeurism-what-our-obsession-with-true-crime-reveals-about-the-lines-were-eager-to-blur (accessed 25 October 2021).

Makin, Kirk (2000) 'Torture Tapes Left Lawyer Traumatized', *The Globe and Mail Canada*, online, 18 April, https://www.theglobeandmail.com/news/national/torture-tapes-left-lawyer-traumatized/article18422428/ (accessed 25 October 2021).

Mandell, Jonathan (2001) 'ART/ARCHITECTURE; History is Impatient to Embrace Sept. 11', *The New York Times*, online, 18 November, https://www.nytimes.com/2001/11/18/arts/art-architecture-history-is-impatient-to-embrace-sept-11.html (accessed 25 October 2021).

Mann, Craig I. (2020) *Phases of the Moon: A Cultural History of the Werewolf Film*, Edinburgh University Press, Edinburgh.

Marchman-McNeely, Kelli (2017) '"The Poughkeepsie Tapes" Finally Seeing Release After 10 Years of Controversy', *Horror Fuel*, online, 16 October, https://horrorfuel.com/2017/10/16/poughkeepsie-tapes-finally-seeing-release-10-years-controversy/ (accessed 25 October 2021).

Markert, John (2011) *Post-9/11 Cinema: Through A Lens Darkly*, Scarecrow Press, Lanham, MD.
Markovitz, Jonathan (2004) 'Reel Terror Post 9/11', in Wheeler Winston Dixon (ed.), *Film and Television After 9/11*, Southern Illinois University Press, Carbondale, pp. 201–25.
Marsh, Jenni and Tara Mulholland (2019) How the Christchurch Terrorist Attack was Made for Social Media', *CNN*, online, 15 March, https://edition.cnn.com/2019/03/15/tech/christchurch-internet-radicalization-intl/index.html (accessed 25 October 2021).
Martinson, Jane (2015) 'The Virtues of Vice: How Punk Magazine was Transformed into Media Giant', *The Guardian*, online, 1 January, https://www.theguardian.com/media/2015/jan/01/virtues-of-vice-magazine-transformed-into-global-giant (accessed 25 October 2021).
Marwick, Alice E. (2013) *Status Update: Celebrity, Publicity, and Branding in the Social Media Age*, Yale University Press, New Haven.
Mason, Paul (2012) 'Global Unrest: How the Revolution Went Viral', *The Guardian*, online, 3 January, https://www.theguardian.com/world/2012/jan/03/how-the-revolution-went-viral (accessed 25 October 2021).
Matharu, Hardeep (2016) 'Donald Trump Reiterates Desire to Murder Terrorists' Families', *The Independent*, online, 4 March, https://www.independent.co.uk/news/world/americas/donald-trump-reiterates-desire-murder-terrorists-families-a6912496.html (accessed 25 October 2021).
McCartney, Jenny (2007) 'Make it Stop', *The Telegraph*, online, 1 July, https://www.telegraph.co.uk/culture/3666245/Make-it-stop.html (accessed 25 October 2021).
McCollum, Victoria (2016) *Post-9/11 Heartland Horror: Rural Horror Films in an Age of Urban Terrorism*, Routledge, Abingdon and New York.
McCollum, Victoria (2019) *Make America Hate Again: Trump-Era Horror and The Politics of Fear*, Routledge, Abingdon and New York.
McGrath, Patrick (2005) *Ghost Town: Tales of Manhattan Then and Now*, Bloomsbury, London and New York.
McKenna, Mark (2020) *Nasty Business: The Marketing and Distribution of the Video Nasties*, Edinburgh University Press, Edinburgh.
McMurdo, Shellie (2019) '"It's a Filthy Goddamn Helpless World": Reimagining Columbine, Tate Langdon, and the Spectre of School Shooters', in *European Journal of American Culture*, vol. 38, no. 1, pp. 57–69.
McRobert, Neil (2015) 'Mimesis of Media: Found Footage Cinema and the Horror of the Real', in *Gothic Studies*, vol. 17, no. 2, pp. 137–50.
McRoy, Jay (2008) *Nightmare Japan: Contemporary Japanese Horror Cinema*, Rodopi, Amsterdam.
McSweeney, Terence (2017) *American Cinema in the Shadow of 9/11*, Edinburgh University Press, Edinburgh.
Mee, Laura (2022) *Reanimated: The Contemporary American Horror Remake*, Edinburgh University Press, Edinburgh.
Merrill Jr, Will G. (2011) *9/11 Ordinary People: Extraordinary Heroes: NYC – The First Battle in the War against Terror*, Createspace, Scotts Valley, CA.
Merry, Stephanie (2015) '"*Unfriended*" Takes Place Entirely on a Computer Screen. Does it Work?', *The Washington Post*, online, 20 April, https://www.washingtonpost.com/news/arts-and-entertainment/wp/2015/04/20/unfriended-takes-place-entirely-on-a-computer-screen-does-it-work/ (accessed 20 October 2021).
Meslow, Scott (2012) '12 Years After "*Blair Witch*", When Will the Found-Footage Horror

Fad End?', *The Atlantic*, online, 6 January, https://www.theatlantic.com/entertainment/archive/2012/01/12-years-after-blair-witch-when-will-the-found-footage-horror-fad-end/250950/ (accessed 25 October 2021).

Middleton, Jason (2010) 'The Subject of Torture: Regarding the Pain of Americans in *Hostel*', in *Cinema Journal*, vol. 49, no. 4, pp. 1–24.

Miller, Prairie (2008) 'The George Romero *Diary of the Dead* Interview', *News Blaze*, online, 14 February, https://newsblaze.com/entertainment/interviews/the-george-romero-diary-of-dead-interview_4004/ (accessed 25 October 2021).

Misra, Ria (2014) 'The Inherent Problem With Found Footage Movies', *Gizmodo*, online, 18 November, https://io9.gizmodo.com/the-inherent-problem-with-found-footage-movies-1660340336 (accessed 25 October 2021).

Monnet, Agnieszka Soltysik (2015) 'Night Vision in the Contemporary Horror Film', in Linnie Blake and Xavier Almada Reyes (eds), *Digital Horror: Haunted Technologies, Network Panic, and The Found Footage Phenomenon*, I. B. Tauris, London, pp. 123–36.

Moore, Rebecca (2000) 'Is the Canon on Jonestown Closed?', in *Nova Religio: The Journal of Alternative and Emergent Religions*, vol. 4, no. 1, pp. 7–27.

Moore, Rebecca (2003) 'Drinking the Kool-Aid: The Cultural Transformation of a Tragedy', in *Nova Religio: The Journal of Alternative and Emergent Religions*, vol. 7, no. 2, pp. 92–100.

Moore, Rebecca (2011) 'The Stigmatized Deaths in Jonestown: Finding a Locus for Grief', *Death Studies*, vol. 35, no. 1, pp. 42–58.

Moore, Robert (2016) 'Donald Trump Promises "Impenetrable and Beautiful" Mexico Wall', *ITV*, online, 1 September, https://www.itv.com/news/2016-09-01/donald-trump-promises-impenetrable-and-beautiful-mexico-wall (accessed 20 October 2021).

Moran, Caitlin (2009) 'It Took 1 Min 47 Seconds for my Memory to Become Host to a Horror That Will Never Go', *The Times*, online, 12 January, https://www.thetimes.co.uk/article/it-took-1-min-47-seconds-for-my-memory-to-become-host-to-a-horror-that-will-never-go-xzmvppqggh3 [accessed 25 October 2021).

Morgan, Matthew J. (2009) *The Impact of 9/11 on Politics and War: The Day That Changed Everything?* Palgrave Macmillan, Basingstoke.

Morgan, Matthew J. and Robert J. Sternberg (2010) *The Impact of 9/11 on Psychology and Education: The Day that Changed Everything?* Palgrave Macmillan, Basingstoke.

Morgan, Sally J. (2001) 'Heritage Noire: Truth, History, and Colonial Anxiety in *The Blair Witch Project*', in *International Journal of Heritage Studies*, vol. 7, no. 2, pp. 137–48.

Moss, Stephanie (2004) '*Dracula* and *The Blair Witch Project*: The Problem with Scientific Empiricism', in Sarah Lynn Higley and Jeffrey Andrew Weinstock (eds), *Nothing That Is: Millennial Cinema and The Blair Witch Controversies*, Wayne State University Press, Detroit, pp. 197–216.

Munger, Sean (2013) 'What a Nightmare Sounds Like: The Jonestown "Death Tape"', *Sean Munger*, 18 November, https://www.seanmunger.com/blog/what-a-nightmare-sounds-like-the-jonestown-death-tape (accessed 25 October 2021).

Murley, Jean (2008) *The Rise of True Crime: 20th Century Murder and American Popular Culture*, Prager, Santa Barbara.

Murray, Noel (2017) 'Review: Despite Novel Perspective, the Found-Footage Horror of "*The Gracefield Incident*" Delivers Nothing New', *Los Angeles Times*, online, 20 July, https://www.latimes.com/entertainment/movies/la-et-mn-capsule-gracefield-incident-review-20170720-story.html (accessed 25 October 2021).

Murray, Susan and Ouellette, Laurie (2004) *Reality TV: Remaking Television Culture*, New York University Press, New York.

Nayman, Adam (2020) 'Zoom-bombing With the Astral Plane', *BFI*, online, 1 October, https://www.bfi.org.uk/sight-and-sound/reviews/host-zoom-video-call-covid-lockdown-horror-rob-savage (accessed 25 October 2021).
Ndalianis, Angela (2012) *The Horror Sensorium: Media and the Senses*, McFarland, Jefferson.
Ndalianis, Angela (2015) 'Genre, Culture and the Semiosphere: New Horror Cinema and Post-9/11', in *International Journal of Cultural Studies*, vol. 18, no. 1, pp. 1–17.
Nees, Michael (2015) 'Hearing Ghost Voices Relies on Pseudoscience and Fallibility of Human Perception', *The Conversation*, online, 30 October, https://theconversation.com/hearing-ghost-voices-relies-on-pseudoscience-and-fallibility-of-human-perception-48160 (accessed 25 October 2021).
Newman, Kim (2014) 'Unearthly Strangers', in James Bell (ed.), *Sci-Fi: Days of Fear and Wonder*, BFI, London.
Nichols, Bill (1991) *Representing Reality: Issues and Concepts in Documentary*, Indiana University Press, Indianapolis.
Nichols, Bill (1994) *Blurred Boundaries: Questions of Meaning in Contemporary Culture*, Indiana University Press, Indianapolis.
Nichols, Bill (2001) *Introduction to Documentary*, Indiana University Press, Indianapolis.
Nichols, Bill (2017) *Introduction to Documentary*, 3rd Edition, Indiana University Press, Indianapolis.
Nichols, William J. (2017) 'The Medium is the Monster: Metadiscourse and the Horrors of post-11 M Spain in the *[Rec]* Tetralogy', in Jorge Marí (ed.), *Tracing the Borders of Spanish Horror Cinema and Television*, Routledge, Abingdon and New York, pp. 190–211.
Niessen, Niels (2011) 'Lives of Cinema: Against its "death"', in *Screen*, vol. 52, no. 3, pp. 307–26.
Nugent, John Peer (1979) *White Night: The Untold Story of What Happened Before – and Beyond – Jonestown*, Rawson, Wade Publishers, New York.
O'Carroll, Lisa (2002) '9/11 makers "refused to film the dying"', *The Guardian*, online, 12 September, https://www.theguardian.com/media/2002/sep/12/september11200 1.usnews (accessed 25 October 2021).
O'Keefe, Meghan (2014) 'Found Footage Films: Should They Stay Lost?', *Decider*, online, 2 July, http://www.decider.com/2014/07/02/found-footage-films-to-stream (accessed 25 October 2021).
O'Malley, Sheila (2020) '*Spree*', *Roger Ebert*, online, 14 August, https://www.rogerebert.com/reviews/spree-movie-review-2020 (accessed 25 October 2021).
Olsen, Mark (2014) 'Ti West's "*The Sacrament*" finds horror in a realistic cult tale', *Los Angeles Times*, online, 31 May, https://www.latimes.com/entertainment/movies/la-et-mn-ca-indie-focus-the-sacrament-20140601-story.html (accessed 25 October 2021).
Onstad, Katrina (2008) 'Horror Auteur is Unfinished With the Undead', *The New York Times*, online, 10 February, https://www.nytimes.com/2008/02/10/movies/10onst.html (accessed 25 October 2021).
Palmer, Alex (2018) 'Chart of the Day: How Hollywood Became Hooked on the "Jump Scare"', *ABC*, online, 8 August, https://www.abc.net.au/news/2018-08-08/chart-of-the-day-hollywood-is-hooked-on-the-jump-scare/10082264?nw=0&r=HtmlFragment (accessed 25 October 2021).
Pease, Donald E. (2007) 'Between the Homeland and Abu Ghraib: Dwelling in Bush's Biopolitical Settlement', in Ashley Dawson and Malini Johar Schueller (eds), *Exceptional State: Contemporary US Culture and the New Imperialism*, Duke University Press, Durham, NC and London, pp. 60–87.

Penenberg, Adam L. (2001) 'The Surveillance Society', *Wired*, online, 1 December, https://www.wired.com/2001/12/surveillance/ (accessed 25 October 2021).

Perrie, Stewart (2017) 'Serial Killer Movie that was Banned from Theatres is Released on DVD', *Lad Bible*, online, 12 October, https://www.ladbible.com/entertainment/film-and-tv-serial-killer-movie-that-was-banned-from-theatres-is-released-on-dvd-2017 1012 (accessed 25 October 2021).

Persily, Nathaniel (2017) 'The 2016 U.S Election: Can Democracy Survive the Internet', in *Journal of Democracy*, vol. 28, no. 2, pp. 63–76.

Petley, Julian (2005) '*Cannibal Holocaust* and the Pornography of Death', in Geoff King (ed.), *The Spectacle of the Real: From Hollywood to 'Reality' TV and Beyond*, Intellect, Bristol, pp. 173–85.

Petley, J. (2016) 'The Way to Digital Death', in Neil Jackson, Shaun Kimber, Johnny Walker and Thomas Joseph Watson (eds), *Snuff: Real Death and Screen Media*, Bloosmbury Academic, London and New York, pp. 23–45.

Pfeifer, Joseph (2021) *Ordinary Heroes: A Memoir of 9/11*, Portfolio Press, New York.

Phillips, Kendall R. (2005) *Projected Fears: Horror Films and American Culture*, Praegar, San Diego.

Phillips, Kendall R. (2021) *A Cinema of Hopelessness: The Rhetoric of Rage in 21st Century Popular Culture*, Palgrave Macmillan, Cham.

Phillips, Whitney (2015) *This Is Why We Can't Have Nice Things: Mapping the Relationship between Online Trolling and Mainstream Culture*, MIT Press, London.

Phipps, Keith (1999) '*The Blair Witch Project*', *AV Club*, online, 16 July, https://film.avclub.com/the-blair-witchproject-1798192100 (accessed 25 October 2021).

Phipps, Keith and Scott Tobias (2014) 'The Present and Future of Found-Footage Horror', *The Dissolve*, online, 30 October, https://thedissolve.com/features/movie-of-the-week/804-the-present-and-future-of-found-footage-horror/ (accessed 25 October 2021).

Picciotto, Richard 'Pitch' (2003) *Last Man Down: The Fireman's Story: The Heroic Account of How Pitch Picciotto Survived the Collapse of the Twin Towers and Led his Men to Safety*, Orion, London.

Pile, Steve. (2005) *Real Cities: Modernity, Space and the Phantasmagorias of City Life*, Sage, London.

Poole, W. Scott (2018) *Wasteland: The Great War and the Origins of Modern Horror*, Counterpoint, Berkeley.

Prigge, Matt (2015) '"The Gallows" Suggests Found Footage Horror is Dead', *Metro*, online, 9 July, https://www.metro.us/the-gallows-suggests-found-footage-horror-is-dead/ (accessed 25 October 2021).

Prince, Stephen (2009) *Firestorm: American Film in the Age of Terrorism*, Columbia University Press, New York.

Prividera, Laura C. and John W. Howard III (2006) 'Masculinity, Whiteness, and the Warrior Hero: Perpetuating the Strategic Rhetoric of U.S Nationalism and the Marginalization of Women', in *Women and Language*, vol. 29, no. 2, pp. 29–37.

Pueyo, Victor (2017) 'After the End of History: Horror Cinema in Neoliberal Spain 2002-2013' in Jorge Marí (ed.), *Tracing the Borders of Spanish Horror Cinema and Television*, Routledge, Abingdon and New York, pp. 141–60.

Purdy, Chris (2013) 'Gore Site Owner Charged for Posting Dismemberment Video in Luka Magnotta Case', *The Globe and Mail*, online, 17 July, https://www.theglobeandmail.com/news/national/gore-site-owner-charged-for-posting-dismemberment-video-in-luka-magnotta-case/article13282060/ (accessed 25 October 2021).

Pyszczynski, Thomas A., Jeff Greenberg and Sheldon Solomon (2003) *In the Wake of*

9/11: *The Psychology of Terror*, American Psychological Association, Washington, DC.
Raimondo, Matthew J. (2014) 'Frenetic Aesthetics: Observational Horror and Spectatorship', in *Horror Studies*, vol. 5, no. 1, pp. 65–84.
Randall, Martin (2011) *9/11 and the Literature of Terror*, Edinburgh University Press, Edinburgh.
Raudive, Konstantin (1971) *Break Through: Electronic Communication with the Dead May Be Possible*, Zebra Books, New York.
Rehak, Bob (2011) 'Adapting Watchmen after 9/11', in *Cinema Journal*, vol. 51, no. 1, pp. 154–9.
Reiterman, Tim (2008) *Raven: The Untold Story of the Rev. Jim Jones and His People*, Penguin Group, New York.
Reith, Terry (2016) 'Mark Marek, who Posted Magnotta Murder Video, Pleads Guilty to Corrupting Morals', *CBC*, online, 25 January, https://www.cbc.ca/news/canada/edmonton/marek-trial-opens-1.3416408 (accessed 25 October 2021).
Remnick, David (2016) 'Obama Reckons with a Trump Presidency', *The New Yorker*, online, 18 November, https://www.newyorker.com/magazine/2016/11/28/obama-reckons-with-a-trump-presidency (accessed 25 October 2021).
Reyes, Xavier Aldana (2013) 'Violence and Mediation: The Ethics of Spectatorship in the Twenty-First Century Horror Film', in Graham Matthews and Sam Goodman (eds), *Violence and the Limits of Representation*, Palgrave Macmillan, London, pp. 145–60.
Reyes, Xavier Aldana (2015a) 'Reel Evil: A Critical Reassessment of Found Footage Horror', in *Gothic Studies*, vol. 17, no. 2, pp. 122–36.
Reyes, Xavier Aldana (2015b) 'The *[Rec]* Films: Affective Possibilities and Stylistic Limitations of Found Footage', in Linnie Blake and Xavier Aldana Reyes (eds), *Digital Horror: Haunted Technologies, Network Panic, and The Found Footage Phenomenon*, I. B. Tauris, London, pp. 149–60.
Reynolds, Eileen (2016) 'On 9/11, Women Were Heroes Too', *NYU*, online, 9 September, https://www.nyu.edu/about/news-publications/news/2016/september/fdny-captain-brenda-berkman-on-9-11.html (accessed 25 October 2021).
Rhodes, Gary D. (2002) 'Mockumentaries and the Production of Realist Horror', *Post Script: Essays in Film and the Humanities*, vol. 21, no. 3, pp. 46–60.
Rice, Condoleezza (2001) 'New Counter-terrorism and Cyberspace Security Positions Announced', *The White House*, online, 9 October, https://georgewbush-whitehouse.archives.gov/news/releases/2001/10/text/20011009-4.html (accessed 25 October 2021).
Richardson, James D. (2014) 'The Phrase "Drank the Kool-Aid" is Completely Offensive. We Should Stop Saying it Immediately', *The Washington Post*, online, 18 November, https://www.washingtonpost.com/posteverything/wp/2014/11/18/the-phrase-drank-the-koolaid-is-completely-offensive-we-should-stop-saying-it-immediately/ (accessed 25 October 2021).
Riegler, Thomas (2016) 'The Trauma of Terrorism: Post-9/11 Hollywood Cinema', in Adriana Martins, Alexandra Lopes and Mónica Dias (eds), *Mediations of Disruption in Post-Conflict Cinema*, Palgrave Macmillan, London, pp. 111–22.
Roper, Matt (2012) 'The Spooky Truth: *Most Haunted* Exposed as a Fake by Star that Claims Derek Acorah Show Features "Showmanship and Dramatics"', *Mirror*, online, 15 May, https://www.mirror.co.uk/tv/tv-news/most-haunted-exposed-fake-star-833433 (accessed 25 October 2021).
Roscoe, Jane (2000) '*The Blair Witch Project*: Mockumentary Goes Mainstream', *Jump

*Cut*, Online, 43, pp. 3–8, http://www.ejumpcut.org/archive/onlinessays/JC43folder/BlairWitch.html (accessed 25 October 2021).

Rose, Lloyd (1999) 'Documentary Style Aids "Blair Witch"', *The Washington Post*, online, 16 July, https://www.washingtonpost.com/wp-srv/style/longterm/movies/videos/blairwitchprojectrose.htm (accessed 25 October 2021).

Rosen, Jay (2006) 'The People Formerly Known as the Audience', *Press Think: Ghost of Democracy in the Media Machine*, online, 27 June, http://archive.pressthink.org/2006/06/27/ppl_frmr.html (accessed 1 October 2016).

Rosenberg, Eli and Liam Stack (2017) 'One Dead and 22 Injured as Car Rams into Pedestrians in Times Square', *The New York Times*, online, 18 May, https://www.nytimes.com/2017/05/18/nyregion/times-square-crash.html (accessed 25 October 2021).

Rothenberg Gritz, Jennie (2011) 'Drinking the Kool-Aid: A Survivor Remembers Jim Jones', *The Atlantic*, online, 18 November, https://www.theatlantic.com/national/archive/2011/11/drinking-the-kool-aid-a-survivor-remembers-jim-jones/248723/ (accessed 25 October 2021).

Rowan-Legg, Shelagh M. (2013) 'Don't Miss a Bloody Thing: [REC] and the Spanish Adaptation of Found Footage Horror', in *Studies in Spanish and Latin American Cinemas*, vol. 10, no. 2, pp. 213–23.

Rowat, Alison (2013) 'Eli Roth Interviewed by Alison Rowat', *Herald Scotland*, online, 30 May, https://www.heraldscotland.com/life_style/arts_ents/13107047.eli-roth-interviewed-alison-rowat/ (accessed 25 October 2021).

Roy, Ryan (2014) *Jonestown: A Novel*, Living Art Publications, Oklahoma.

Russell, Catherine (1994) *Narrative Mortality: Death, Closure and New Wave Cinemas*, University of Minnesota Press, Minneapolis and London.

Russell, Catherine (1999) *Experimental Ethnography: The Work of Film in the Age of Video*, Duke University Press, Durham and London.

Saliba, John A. (1995) *Understanding New Religious Movements*, William B. Eerdmans Publishing Company, Grand Rapids, MI.

Samuels, Stuart (1979) 'The Age of Conspiracy and Conformity: Invasion of the Body Snatchers', in John E. O'Connor and Martin A. Jackson (eds), *American History/American Film: Interpreting the Hollywood Image*, Frederick Ungar, New York, pp. 198–207.

Sawczuk, Tomasz (2020) 'Taking Horror as you Find it: From Found Manuscripts to Found Footage Aesthetics', in *Text Matters: A Journal of Literature, Theory and Culture*, no. 10, pp. 223–35.

Sayad, Cecilia (2016) 'Found-Footage Horror and the Frame's Undoing', in *Cinema Journal*, vol. 55, no. 2, pp. 43–66.

Schager, Nick (2016) 'Review: "London Has Fallen" Starring Gerard Butler, Aaron Eckhart, Morgan Freeman, Angela Bassett, Robert Forster, More', *Indiewire*, online, 2 March, https://www.indiewire.com/2016/03/review-london-has-fallen-starring-gerard-butler-aaron-eckhart-morgan-freeman-angela-bassett-robert-forster-more-265894/ (accessed 25 October 2021).

Schedeen, Jesse (2012) 'Drop the Camera and Run!', *IGN*, 2 February, http://uk.ign.com/articles/2012/02/02/drop-the-camera-and-run (accessed 25 October 2021).

Scheeres, Jesse (2012) *A Thousand Lives: The Untold Story of Jonestown*, Free Press, New York.

Scheeres, Jesse. (2018) 'Op-Ed: Jonestown Victims Drew Public Scorn, but Now We Know the Story of their Betrayal', *Los Angeles Times*, online, 16 November, https://www.latimes.com/opinion/op-ed/la-oe-scheeres-jonestown-20181116-story.html (accessed 25 October 2021).

Schmid, David (2005) *Natural Born Celebrities: Serial Killers in American Culture*, University of Chicago Press, Chicago.
Schneider, Steven Jay (2004) 'Architectural Nostalgia and the New York City Skyline on Film', in Wheeler Winston Dixon (ed.), *Film and Television After 9/11*, Southern Illinois University Press, Carbondale, pp. 29–41.
Schopp, Andrew (2004) 'Transgressing the Safe Space: Generation X Horror in *The Blair Witch Project* and *Scream*', in Sarah Lynn Higley and Jeffrey Andrew Weinstock (eds), *Nothing That Is: Millennial Cinema and the Blair Witch Controversies*, Wayne State University, Detroit, pp. 125–43.
Schreier, Margrit (2004) '"Please Help Me; All I Want to Know is: Is it Real or Not?": How Recipients View the Reality Status of Blair Witch Project', in *Poetics Today*, vol. 25, no. 2, pp. 305–34.
Sconce, Jeffrey (2000) *Haunted Media: Electronic Presence from Telegraphy to Television*, Duke University Press, Durham, NC and London.
Scurfield, Raymond Monsour (2004) *A Vietnam Trilogy: Veterans and Post Traumatic Stress, 1968, 1989, 2000*, Algora, New York.
Seaton, A. V. (1996) 'Guided by the Dark: From Thanatopsis to Thanatourism', in *International Journal of Heritage Studies*, vol. 2, no. 4, pp. 234–44.
Seguin, Jean-Claude (2017) '"I Am an Eye, I Am a Mechanical Eye . . .": (The *[REC]* Series)', in Jorge Marí (ed.), *Tracing the Borders of Spanish Horror Cinema and Television*, Routledge, Abingdon and New York, pp. 212–31.
Seitz, Dan (2012) 'Five Reasons Why Found Footage Movies Mostly Don't Work', *Proxx*, online, 19 April, https://uproxx.com/viral/five-reasons-why-found-footage-movies-mostly-dont-work/ (accessed 25 October 2021).
Sélavy, Virginie (2014) '*The Sacrament*: Interview with Ti West', *Electric Sheep Magazine*, online, 5 May, http://www.electricsheepmagazine.co.uk/features/2014/06/05/the-sacrament-interview-with-ti-west/ (accessed 25 October 2021).
Seltzer, Mark (1997) 'Wound Culture: Trauma in the Pathological Public Sphere', in *October*, no. 80, pp. 3–26.
Seltzer, Mark (1998) *Serial Killers: Death and Life in America's Wound Culture*, Routledge, Abingdon and New York.
Senft, Theresa M. (2001) *Camgirls: Celebrity and Community in the Age of Social Networks*, Peter Lang, New York.
Sharrett, Christopher (2014) 'The Horror Film as Social Allegory (And How it Comes Undone)', in Harry M. Benshoff (ed.), *A Companion to the Horror Film*, Wiley Blackwell, Chichester, pp. 56–72.
Shaviro, Steven (2010) *Post-Cinematic Affect*, 0-Books, Ropley.
Shaviro, Steven (2017) 'The Glitch Dimension: Paranormal Activity and the Technologies of Vision', in Martine Baugnet, Allen Cameron and Arild Fetveit (eds), *Indefinite Visions: Cinema and the Attractions of Uncertainty*, Edinburgh University Press, Edinburgh, pp. 316–33.
Sherwin, Adam (2016) 'London has Fallen Movie Condemned as Racist 'Terrorsploitation' for Donald Trump Era', *The Independent*, online, 3 March, https://www.independent.co.uk/arts-entertainment/films/news/london-has-fallen-movie-condemned-as-racist-terrorsploitation-for-donald-trump-era-a6909596.html (accessed 25 October 2021).
Shortell, David (2015) 'Marcy Borders, Survivor Known as 'Dust Lady' in Iconic 9/11 Photo, Dies at 42', *CNN*, online, 27 August, https://edition.cnn.com/2015/08/26/us/9-11-survivor-dust-lady-dies/index.html (accessed 25 October 2021).
Sims, David (2019) 'Dragged Across Concrete and the Sloppy Provocations of S. Craig Zahler', *The Atlantic*, online, 25 March, https://www.theatlantic.com/entertainment

/archive/2019/03/s-craig-zahler-dragged-across-concrete-films/585424/ (accessed 25 October 2021).

Singular, Stephen and Joyce Singular (2015) *The Spiral Notebook: The Aurora Theater Shooter and the Epidemic of Mass Violence Committed by American Youth*, Counterpoint, Berkeley.

Sisco King, Claire (2011) *Washed in Blood: Male Sacrifice, Trauma, and the Cinema*, Rutgers University Press, New Brunswick, NJ.

Skal, David J. (1994) *The Monster Show: A Cultural History of Horror*, Plexus, London.

Smith, Jonathan Z. (1982) *Imagining Religion: From Babylon to Jonestown*, University of Chicago Press, Chicago.

Smith, Kyle (2016) 'Poor Blair Witch – She Deserves a Better Movie', *The New York Post*, online, 15 September, https://nypost.com/2016/09/15/poor-blair-witch-she-deserves-a-better-movie/ (accessed 25 October 2021).

Smith, Neil (2008) 'Zombie Maestro Lays Down the Lore', *BBC*, online, 7 March, http://news.bbc.co.uk/1/hi/entertainment/7280793.stm (accessed 25 October 2021).

Smith, Paige (2018) 'This Is Your Brain on True Crime Stories', *Huffington Post*, online, 4 May, https://www.huffingtonpost.co.uk/entry/psychological-reasons-you-love-true-crime-stories_us_5ac39559e4b09712fec4b143 (accessed 25 October 2021).

Sneider, Jeff (2020) '"*Spree*" Review: Joe Keery Leads This "American Psycho" for the Digital Age Sundance 2020', *Collider*, online, 26 January, https://collider.com/spree-review-joe-keery/ (accessed 25 October 2021).

Sobchack, Vivian (2004) *Carnal Thoughts: Embodiment and Moving Image Culture*, University of California Press, Berkeley.

Somma, Brandon (2012) 'What Happened?: "*The Poughkeepsie Tapes*"', *The Artifice*, online, 1 December, https://the-artifice.com/the-poughkeepsie-tapes/ (accessed 25 October 2021).

Sontag, Susan (1977) *On Photography*, Farrar, Straus and Giroux, New York.

Sontag, Susan (2003) *Regarding the Pain of Others*, Penguin, London.

Stephen, Andrew (2007) 'The Poisonous Legacy of 9/11', *The New Statesman*, online, 4 June, https://www.newstatesman.com/uncategorized/2007/06/york-air-death-city-breathe (accessed 25 October 2021).

Stern, Dave A. (1999) *The Blair Witch Dossier*, Boxtree, London.

Stern, Marlow (2018) 'Mel Gibson's New Police Brutality Movie is a Vile, Racist Right-Wing Fantasy', *The Daily Beast*, online, 4 September, https://www.thedailybeast.com/mel-gibsons-new-police-brutality-movie-is-a-vile-racist-right-wing-fantasy (accessed 25 October 2021).

Sterritt, David (2004) 'Representing Atrocity: From the Holocaust to September 11', in Wheeler Winston Dixon (ed.), *Film and Television After 9/11*, Southern Illinois University Press, Carbondale, pp. 63–78.

Stuart, Keith (2019) 'The Sonic the Hedgehog Movie Trailer is a 200mph Slap in the Face', *The Guardian*, online, 30 April, https://www.theguardian.com/games/2019/apr/30/sonic-the-hedgehog-movie-trailer (accessed 25 October 2021).

Stubblefield, Thomas (2014) *9/11 and the Visual Culture of Disaster*, Indiana University Press, Bloomington.

Stuever, Hank (2013) 'HBO's "Vice": Journo-tourism for Hipsters', *The Washington Post*, online, 4 April, https://www.washingtonpost.com/entertainment/tv/hbos-vice-journo-tourism-for-hipsters/2013/04/04/9d8a5076-9cae-11e2-9bda-edd1a7fb557d_story.html (accessed 25 October 2021).

Surette, Ray (1994) 'Predator Criminals as Media Icons', in Gregg Barak (ed.), *Media*,

*Process, and the Social Construction of Crime*, Garland Publishing Inc., New York and London, pp. 131–58.

Swaine, Jon (2014) 'Vice's Shane Smith: "Young People are Angry and Leaving TV in Droves"', *The Guardian*, online, 2 March, https://www.theguardian.com/media/2014/mar/02/vice-media-shane-smith-north-korea (accessed 25 October 2021).

Swanson, Alexander (2015) 'Audience Reaction Movie Trailers and the Paranormal Activity Franchise', in *Transformative Works & Cultures*, no. 18, pp. 1–27.

Swanson, Anna (2021) 'TIFF 2021: "Dashcam" is an Abysmal Low-Point for Found Footage', *Film School Rejects*, online, 12 September, https://filmschoolrejects.com/dashcam-review/ (accessed 27 October 2021).

Sweney, Mark (2014) 'ITV and BBC Told to Learn Lessons from Graphic Lee Rigby Murder Coverage', *The Guardian*, online, 6 January, https://www.theguardian.com/media/2014/jan/06/itv-bbc-lee-rigby-murder-coverage (accessed 25 October 2021).

Tal, Kalí (1996) *Worlds of Hurt: Reading the Literatures of Trauma*, Cambridge University Press, Cambridge.

Tanguay, Liane (2013) *Hijacking History: American Culture and the War on Terror*, McGill-Queen's University Press, Montreal.

Tanz, Jason (2007) '"The Snarky Vice Squad is Ready to be Taken Seriously". Seriously', *Wired*, online, 18 October, https://www.wired.com/2007/10/ff-vice/ (accessed 25 October 2021).

Tapp, Tom (2021) '9/11 Programming Schedule Leading up to 20th Anniversary of the Attacks: How to Watch on TV, Streaming & Online', *Deadline*, online, 2 September, https://deadline.com/2021/09/9-11-20th-anniversary-programs-specials-how-to-watch-tv-streaming-1234816716/ (accessed 25 October 2021).

Telotte, J. P. (2001) '*The Blair Witch Project* Project: Film and the Internet', in *Film Quarterly*, vol. 54, no. 3, pp. 32–9.

Tharpe, Frazier (2012) 'The 7 Worst Justifications for Found Footage in Movies', *Complex*, online, 20 October, https://www.complex.com/pop-culture/2012/10/7-worst-justifications-found-footage-movies/ (accessed 25 October 2021).

The Skinny (2014) 'Ti West on The Sacrament – The Skinny Magazine', *YouTube*, online, 23 June, https://www.youtube.com/watch?v=27LDF7c0FdY (accessed 25 October 2021).

TheSomebodytoknow (2012) 'My Story: Struggling, Bullying, Suicide, Self Harm', *YouTube*, online, 8 September. https://www.youtube.com/watch?v=vOHXGNx-E7E&bpctr=1564228515 (accessed 25 October 2021).

Thompson, Kirsten Moana (2007) *Apocalyptic Dread: American Film at the Turn of the Millennium*, State of New York Press, Albany.

Tiffany, Joel (1857) 'Telegraphic Meeting', in *Tiffany's Monthly*, no. 3, pp. 142–3.

Travers, Peter (2016) '"*Blair Witch*" Review: D.O.A. Horror Sequel Loses Its Scares in the Woods', *Rolling Stone*, online, 16 September, https://www.rollingstone.com/movies/movie-reviews/blair-witch-review-d-o-a-horror-sequel-loses-its-scares-in-the-woods-123276/ (accessed 25 October 2021).

Travers, Peter (2018) '"Searching" Review: High-Tech Thriller Delivers Old-Fashioned Chills', *Rolling Stone*, online, 22 August, https://www.rollingstone.com/movies/movie-reviews/searching-movie-review-713128/ (accessed 25 October 2021).

Treaster, Joseph B. (1978) 'A Cult Mother Led Children to Death', *The New York Times*, online, 5 December, https://www.nytimes.com/1978/12/05/archives/a-cult-mother-led-children-to-death-witnesses-initially-unaware-of.html (accessed 25 October 2021).

Tucker, Jennifer (2005) *Nature Exposed: Photography as Eyewitness in Victorian Science*, John Hopkins University Press, Baltimore.
Tucker, Ken (2002) 'The "9/11" Film is Startling, but Flawed', *Entertainment Weekly*, online, 12 March, https://ew.com/article/2002/03/12/911-film-startling-flawed/ (accessed 25 October 2021).
Tudor, Andrew (1989) *Monsters and Mad Scientists: A Cultural History of the Horror Movies*, Blackwell, Oxford.
Tudor, Andrew (1997) 'Why Horror? The Peculiar Pleasures of a Popular Genre', in *Cultural Studies*, vol. 11, no. 3, pp. 443–63.
Turek, Ryan (2009) 'Exclusive Interview: Rec & Rec 2's Javier Botet', *Coming Soon*, online, 11 October, https://www.comingsoon.net/horror/news/715441-exclusive-intervi ew-rec-rec-2s-javier-botet (accessed 25 October 2021).
Turek, Ryan (2014) 'Editorial: Found Footage Horror is Supposedly Dead, ut it's Not', *Coming Soon*, online, 6 June, https://www.comingsoon.net/horror/news/741503-found-footage-horror-is-dead-but-its-not (accessed 25 October 2021).
Turner, Peter (2014) *The Blair Witch Project*, Auteur, Leighton Buzzard.
Turner, Peter (2019) *Found Footage Horror Films: A Cognitive Approach*, Routledge, Abingdon and New York.
Tziallas, Evangelos. (2014) 'Of Doppelgängers and Alter Egos: Surveillance Footage as Cinematic Double', in *Écranospherè*, no. 1, pp. 1–27.
Tzioumakis, Yannis (2006) *American Independent Cinema: An Introduction*, Rutgers University Press, New Brunswick, NJ.
VanArendonk, Kathryn (2018) 'The 8 Best True-Crime Parodies', *Vulture*, online, 3 August, https://www.vulture.com/article/the-8-best-true-crime-parodies.html (accessed 25 October 2021).
Van Bauwel, Sofie (2010) 'The Spectacle of the Real and Whatever Other Constructions', in Van Bauwel, Sofie and Carpentier, Nico (eds), *Trans-Reality Television: The Transgression of Reality, Genre, Politics and Audience*, Lexington Books, Plymouth, pp. 23–36.
Vejvoda, Jim (2013) 'Barry Levinson Talks About Making *The Bay*', *Ign*, online, 13 March, https://www.ign.com/articles/2013/03/13/barry-levinson-talks-about-making-the -bay (accessed 25 October 2021).
Vella, Nadia (2017) 'Serial Killer Film So Dark it was Banned has Been Re-Released', *The Horror Movies Blog*, online, 27 October, https://thehorrormoviesblog.com/2017/10 /27/serial-killer-film-dark-banned-re-released/ (accessed 25 October 2021).
Wada-Marciano, Mitsuyo. (2007) 'J-Horror: New Media's Impact on Contemporary Japanese Horror Cinema', in *Canadian Journal of Film Studies*, vol. 16, no. 2, pp. 23–48.
Waldman, Katy (2015) 'Is it Kosher to "Drink the Kool-Aid"?', *Slate*, online, 30 January, https://slate.com/human-interest/2015/01/is-the-phrase-drink-the-kool-aid-offens ive-because-of-jonestown.html (accessed 25 October 2021).
Wallace, Richard James (2021) 'Documentary Style as Post-Truth Monstrosity in the Mockumentary Horror Film', in *Quarterly Review of Film and Video*, vol. 38, no. 6, pp. 519–40.
Walliss, John and James Aston (2011) 'Doomsday America: The Pessimistic Turn of Post-9/11 Apocalyptic Cinema', in *Journal of Religion and Popular Culture*, vol. 23, no. 1, pp. 53–64.
Walliss, John and James Aston (2013) *To See the Saw Movies: Essays on Torture Porn and Post-9/11 Horror*, McFarland, Jefferson.
Walters, Ben (2007) 'A Guaranteed Premonition', *Film Quarterly*, vol. 61, no. 2, pp. 66–7.
Walters, Joanna (2016) '9/11 Health Crisis: Death Toll from Illness Nears Number Killed

on Day of Attacks', *The Guardian*, online, 11 September, https://www.theguardian.com/us-news/2016/sep/11/9-11-illnesses-death-toll (accessed 25 October 2021).

Warzel, Charlie (2019) 'The New Zealand Massacre was Made to Go Viral', *The New York Times*, online, 15 March, https://www.nytimes.com/2019/03/15/opinion/new-zealand-shooting.html (accessed 25 October 2021).

Watson, Keith (2016) 'Review: *Blair Witch*', *Slant Magazine*, online, 14 September, https://www.slantmagazine.com/film/blair-witch/ (accessed 25 October 2021).

Wax, Emily. (1999) 'The Dizzy Spell of *"Blair Witch Project"*', *The Washington Post*, online, 30 July, https://www.washingtonpost.com/archive/lifestyle/1999/07/30/the-dizzy-spell-of-blair-witch-project/7e4afd77-c9eb-42b3-a0f5-8c1b22e7a105/ (accessed 25 October 2021).

Wee, Valerie (2013) *Japanese Horror Films and their American Remakes: Translating Fear, Adapting* Culture, Routledge, Abingdon and New York.

Weigel, Moira (2016) 'Political Correctness: How the Right Invented a Phantom Enemy', *The Guardian*, online, 30 November, https://www.theguardian.com/us-news/2016/nov/30/political-correctness-how-the-right-invented-phantom-enemy-donald-trump (accessed 25 October 2021).

Weightman, Judith M. (1984) *Making Sense of the Jonestown Suicides*, Edwin Mellen Press Ltd, New York.

Weinstein, Bruce (2018) 'Two Great Reasons to Stop Saying "Drinking the Kool-Aid"', *Forbes*, online, 29 March, https://www.forbes.com/sites/bruceweinstein/2018/03/29/two-great-reasons-to-stop-saying-i-drank-the-kool-aid/ (accessed 25 October 2021).

Wessels, Emanuelle (2011) '"Where Were You When the Monster Hit?" Media Convergence, Branded Security Citizenship, and the Trans-media Phenomenon of *Cloverfield*', *Convergence: The International Journal of Research into New Media Technologies*, vol. 17, no. 1, pp. 69–83.

West, Amy (2005) '"Caught on Tape": A Legacy of Low-Tech Reality', in Geoff King (ed.), *The Spectacle of the Real: From Hollywood to 'Reality' TV and Beyond*, Intellect, Bristol, pp. 83–92.

Westwell, Guy (2014) *Parallel Lines: Post-9/11 American Cinema*, Wallflower Press, New York.

Wetmore Jr, Kevin (2012) *Post-9/11 Horror in American Cinema*, Continuum, New York and London.

White, Hayden (1992) 'Historical Emplotment and the Problem of Truth', in Saul Freidlander (ed.), *Probing the Limits of Representation: Nazism and the 'Final Solution'*, Harvard University Press, Massachusetts, pp. 37–53.

Widdicombe, Lizzie (2013) 'The Bad Boy Brand', *The New Yorker*, online, 8 April, https://www.newyorker.com/magazine/2013/04/08/the-bad-boy-brand (accessed 25 October 2021).

Wiest, Julie B. (2011) *Creating Cultural Monsters: Serial Murder in America*, CRC Press, Florida.

Wilder, Kelley Elizabeth (2009) *Photography and Science*, Reaktion, London.

Williams, Karen (2010) 'The Liveness of Ghosts: Haunting and Reality TV', in Maria de Pilar Blanco and Esther Peeren (eds), *Popular Ghosts: The Haunted Spaces of Everyday Culture*, Continuum, New York, pp. 149–61.

Williams, Linda (1991) 'Film Bodies: Gender, Genre, and Excess', in *Film Quarterly*, vol. 44, no. 4, pp. 2–13.

Williams, Mary Elizabeth. (1999) '*The Blair Witch Project*', *Salon*, online, 13 July, https://www.salon.com/1999/07/13/blair/ (accessed 25 October 2021).

Willis, Andy (2017) 'The Cultural Politics of Remaking Spanish Horror Films in the Twenty-First Century: *Quarantine* and *Come Out and Play*', in Iain Robert Smith and Constantine Verevis (eds), *Transnational Film Remakes* Edinburgh University Press, Edinburgh, pp. 54–65.

Winston, Brian (2000) *Lies, Damn Lies and Documentaries*, BFI, London.

Wolf, Mark J. P. (2000) *Abstracting Reality: Art, Communication and Cognition in the Digital Age*, University Press of America, Maryland.

Wood, Robin (1985) 'An Introduction to the American Horror Film', in Bill Nichols (ed.), *Movies and Methods vol. II*, University of California Press, Berkeley, pp. 195–220.

Worland, Rick (2006) *The Horror Film: An Introduction*, Wiley Blackwell, Chichester.

Wortham, Jenna (2010) 'As Facebook Users Die, Ghosts Reach Out', *The New York Times*, online, 17 July, https://www.nytimes.com/2010/07/18/technology/18death.html?_r=0 (accessed 25 October 2021).

Wright, Lawrence (2007) *The Looming Tower: Al Qaeda and the Road to 9/11*, Penguin, London.

Yanni, Carla (2007) *The Architecture of Madness: Insane Asylums in the United States*, University of Minneapolis Press, Minneapolis and London.

Zimmer, Catherine (2011) 'Caught on Tape? The Politics of Video in the New Torture Film', in Aviva Briefel and Sam J. Miller (eds), *Horror After 9/11: World of Fear, Cinema of Terror*, University of Texas Press, Austin, pp. 83–106.

Zimmerman, Amy (2017) 'What Pop Culture's Obsession With Cults Says About Us', *Daily Beast*, online, 5 October, https://www.thedailybeast.com/what-pop-cultures-obsession-with-cults-says-about-us (accessed 25 October 2021).

Zoellner, Danielle (2020) 'Bianca Devin's Murder: Man Admits Killing Instagram Star After Posting Gruesome Images Online', *The Independent*, online, 11 February, https://www.independent.co.uk/news/world/americas/bianca-devins-murder-brandon-clark-guilty-new-york-instagram-a9328416.html (accessed 25 October 2021).

# Found footage filmography and other media

*21 Days* (Kathleen Behun, 2014, USA)
*A Ride in the Park* (Eduardo Sánchez and Gregg Hale, 2013, USA)
*Afflicted* (Derek Lee and Clif Prowse, 2013, Canada)
*Alien Abduction* (Matty Beckerman, 2014, USA)
*American Horror Story: Roanoake* (FX, 2016, USA)
*Anatomy* [Videogame] (Developed by Kitty Horror Show, 2017, USA)
*Apartment 143* (Carles Torrens, 2011, Spain)
*Apollo 18* (Gonzalo López-Gallego, 2011, USA/Canada)
*Area 51* (Oren Peli, 2015, USA)
*As Above, So Below* (John Erick Dowdle, 2014, USA)
*The Atticus Institute* (Chris Sparling, 2015, USA)
*August Underground* (Fred Vogel, 2001, USA)
*August Underground's Mordem* (Fred Vogel, Killjoy, Cristie Whiles, Jerami Cruise, Michael Todd Schneider, 2003, USA)
*August Underground's Penance* (Fred Vogel, 2007, USA)
*The Backrooms (Found Footage)* (Kane Pixels, 2022, USA)
*The Bay* (Barry Levinson, 2012, USA)
*Be My Cat: A Film for Anne* (Adrian Tofei, 2015, Romania)
*Behind the Mask: The Rise of Leslie Vernon* (Scott Glosserman, 2006, USA)
*The Black Tapes* [Podcast] (Paul Bae and Terry Miles, 2015–2017, USA)
*The Blackwell Ghost* (Turner Clay, 2017, USA)
*Blair Witch* (Adam Wingard, 2016, USA)
*Blair Witch* [Videogame] (developed by Bloober Team, 2019, Poland)
*The Blair Witch Project* (Eduardo Sánchez and Daniel Myrick, 1999, USA)
*Bounty* (Kevin Kangas, 2009, USA)
*Butterfly Kisses* (Erik Kristopher Myers, 2018, USA)
*Cannibal Holocaust* (Ruggero Deodato, 1980, Italy)
*Closed Circuit Extreme* (Giorgio Amato, 2012, Italy)
*Cloverfield* (Matt Reeves, 2008, USA)
*The Conspiracy* (Christopher MacBride, 2012, Canada)
*Crowsnest* (Brenton Spencer, 2012, Canada)
*The Crying Dead* (Hunter G. Williams, 2011, USA)
*Curse of the Blair Witch* (Eduardo Sánchez and Daniel Myrick, 1999, USA)
*Delivery: The Beast Within* (Brian Netto, 2013, USA)

*The Den* (Zachary Donohue, 2013, USA)
*The Devil Inside* (William Brent Bell, 2012, USA)
*The Devil's Doorway* (Aislinn Clarke, 2018, Ireland)
*Devil's Due* (Matt Bettinelli-Olpin and Tyler Gillett, 2014, USA)
*Devil's Trail* (Henrique Couto, 2017, USA)
*Diary of the Dead* (George A. Romero, 2007, USA)
*Digging Up the Marrow* (Adam Green, 2014, USA)
*District 9* (Neill Blomkamp, 2009, South Africa/USA/New Zealand/Canada)
*The Dyatlov Pass Incident* (Renny Harlin, 2013, Russia/Finland)
*The Empty Wake* (Simon Barrett, 2021, USA)
*Exhibit A* (Dom Rotheroe, 2007, UK)
*Followers* (Ryan Justice, 2017, USA)
*Found Footage 3D* (Stephen DeGennaro, 2016, USA)
*Ghostwatch* (Lesley Manning, BBC, 1992, UK)
*Gonjiam: Haunted Asylum* (Beom-sik Jeong, 2018, South Korea)
*Grave Encounters* (Colin Minihan and Stuart Ortiz, 2011, Canada)
*Greystone Park* (Sean Stone, 2012, USA)
*Hate Crime* (James Cullen Bressack, 2012, USA)
*Head Cases: Serial Killers in the Delaware Valley* (Anthony Spadaccini, 2013, USA)
*Hell House LLC* (Stephen Cognetti, 2015, USA)
*Hell House II: The Abaddon Hotel* (Stephen Cognetti, 2018, USA)
*Hell House III: Lake of Fire* (Stephen Cognetti, 2019, USA)
*Hollows Grove* (Craig Efros, 2014, USA)
*Home Movie* (Christopher Denham, 2008, USA)
*Horror in the High Desert* (Dutch Marich, 2021, USA)
*Host* (Rob Savage, 2020, UK)
*The Houses October Built* (Bobby Roe, 2014, USA)
*The Hunted* (Josh Stewart, 2013, USA)
*I Am Alone* (Robert A. Palmer, 2015, USA)
*In Memorium* (Amanda Gusack, 2005, USA)
*Invasion* (Albert Pyun, 2005, USA)
*Jeruzalem* (Doron Paz and Yoav Paz, 2015, Israel)
*Lake Mungo* (Joel Anderson, 2008, Australia)
*The Last Broadcast* (Stefan Avalos and Lance Weiler, 1998, USA)
*The Last Exorcism* (Daniel Stamm, 2010, France/USA)
*The Last Horror Movie* (Julian Richards, 2003, UK)
*The Legend of Boggy Creek* (Charles B. Pierce, 1972, USA)
*Long Pigs* (Nathan Hynes and Chris Power, 2007, Canada)
*The Lost Coast Tapes* (Corey Grant, 2012, USA)
*The Lost Footage of Leah Sullivan* (Burt Grinstead, 2018, USA)
*Lunapolis* (Matthew Avant, 2010, USA)
*The McPherson Tape* (Dean Alioto, 1989, USA)
*Man Bites Dog* (Rémy Belvaux, André Bonzel and Benoît Poelvoorde, 1992, Belgium)
*Marble Hornets* (Joseph DeLage and Troy Wagner, 2009–14, USA)
*Megan Is Missing* (Michael Goi, 2011, USA)
*The Mitchell Tapes* (Thomas S. Nichol, 2010, USA)
*The Monster Project* (Victor Mathieu, 2017, USA)
*Mr. Jones* (Karl Mueller, 2013, USA)
*Muirhouse* (Tanzeal Rahim, 2012, Australia)
*Murder Box* (Gerald Varga, 2018, Canada)

*Murder in the Heartland: The Search for Video X* (James D. Mortellaro, 2003, USA)
*Night Stalkers: Paranormal Investigators* (Wayne Poe, 2017, USA)
*Noroi: The Curse* (Kôji Shiraishi, 2005, Japan)
*Occult* (Kōji Shiraishi, 2009, Japan)
*Out of the Shadows* (Allen Kellogg, 2017, USA)
*Outlast* [Videogame] (Developed by Red Barrels, 2014, Canada)
*Outlast 2* [Videogame] (Developed by Red Barrels, 2017, Canada)
*Outlast: Whistleblower* [Videogame] (Developed by Red Barrels, 2014, Canada)
*Paranormal Activity* (Oren Peli, 2007, USA)
*Paranormal Activity 2* (Tod Williams, 2010, USA)
*Paranormal Activity 3* (Henry Joost and Ariel Schulman, 2011, USA)
*Paranormal Activity 4* (Henry Joost and Ariel Schulman, 2012, USA)
*Paranormal Activity: The Marked Ones* (Christopher Landon, 2014, USA)
*Paranormal Activity: The Ghost Dimension* (Gregory Plotkin, 2015, USA)
*Paranormal Activity: Next of Kin* (William Eubank, 2021, USA)
*Penance* (Jake Kennedy, 2009, USA)
*Phase 1, Clinical Trials* (Adam Wingard, 2013, USA)
*Phoenix Forgotten* (Justin Barber, 2017, USA)
*The Phoenix Incident* (Keith Arem, 2015, USA)
*The Poughkeepsie Tapes* (John Erick Dowdle, 2007, USA)
*Quarantine* (John Erick Dowdle, 2008, USA)
*[Rec]* (Jaume Balagueró and Paco Plaza, 2007, Spain)
*[Rec] 2* (Jaume Balagueró and Paco Plaza, 2009, Spain)
*Rec: Shutter* [Videogame] (Steelkrill Studio, 2012, USA)
*Reel Evil* (Danny Draven, 2012, USA)
*Resident Evil VII: Biohazard* [Videogame] (Capcom, 2017, Japan)
*The River* (ABC, 2012, USA)
*RWD* (Matt Stuertz, 2015, USA)
*The Sacrament* (Ti West, 2013, USA)
*Sanatorium* (Brant Sersen, 2013, USA)
*Savageland* (Phil Guidry, Simon Herbert and David Whelan, 2016, USA)
*The Sick Thing That Happened to Emily When She Was Younger* (Joe Swanberg, 2012, USA)
*Sickhouse* (Hannah MacPherson, 2016, USA)
*Skew* (Sevé Schlenz, 2011, Canada)
*Slumber Party Alien Abduction* (Jason Eisner, 2013, USA/Canada)
*The Speak* (Anthony Pierce, 2011, USA)
*Spree* (Eugene Kotlyarenko, 2020, USA)
*Survive The Hollow Shoals* (Jonathon Klimek, 2018, USA)
*The Taking of Deborah Logan* (Adam Robitel, 2014, USA)
*They're Watching* (Jay Lender and Micah Wright, 2016, USA/Romania)
*Tontine Massacre: The Fiji Tapes* (Ezna Sands, 2010, USA)
*Trollhunter* (André Øvredal, 2010, Norway)
*Tuesday the 17th* (Glenn McQuaid, 2012, USA)
*The Tunnel* (Carlo Ledesma, 2011, Australia)
*The Unfolding* (Eugene McGing, 2016, UK)
*Unfriended* (Levan Gabriadze, 2014, USA/Russia)
*Unfriended: Dark Web* (Stephen Susco, 2018, USA/Russia)
*The Upper Footage* (Justin Cole, 2013, USA)
*V/H/S* (Matt Bettinelli-Olpin, David Bruckner, Tyler Gillett, Justin Martinez, Glenn

McQuaid, Radio Silence, Joe Swanberg, Chad Villella, Ti West, Adam Wingard, 2012, USA)
*V/H/S: 94* (Simon Barrett, Steven Kostanski, Chloe Okuno, Ryan Prows, Jennifer Reeder, Timo Tjahjanto, 2021, USA/Indonesia)
*V/H/S/2* (Simon Barrett, Jason Eisener, Gareth Evans, Gregg Hale, Eduardo Sánchez, Timo Tjahjanto, Adam Wingard, 2013, USA/Canada/Indonesia)
*V/H/S: Viral* (Justin Benson, Gregg Bishop, Todd Lincoln, Aaron Moorhead, Marcel Sarmiento, Nacho Vigalondo, 2014, USA/Spain)
*Video Palace* [Podcast] (Ben Rock, 2018, USA)
*The Visit* (M. Night Shyamalan, 2015, USA)
*Willow Creek* (Bobcat Goldthwait, 2013, USA)
*WNUF Halloween Special* (Chris LaMartina, 2013, USA)

# Filmography

*#Horror* (Tara Subkoff, 2015, USA)
*11'09"01 September 11* (Samira Makmalbaf, Claude Lelouch, Youssef Chahine, Danis Tanović, Idrissa Ouédraogo, Ken Loach, Alejandro González Iñárritu, Amos Gitai, Mira Nair, Sean Penn, Shōhei Imamura, 2002, UK/France/Egypt/Japan/Mexico/USA/Iran)
*102 Minutes That Changed America* (Nicole Rittenmeyer and Seth Skundrick, 2008, USA)
*28 Weeks Later* (Juan Carlos Fresnadillo, 2007, UK)
*9/11* (Jules Naudet, Gédéon Naudet, and James Hanlon, 2002, USA/France)
*9/11: Day That Changed the World* (Leslie Woodhead, 2011, UK)
*9/11: The Falling Man* (Henry Singer, 2006, UK)
*A Serbian Film* (Srdan Spasojević, 2010, Serbia)
*American Horror Story: Asylum* (FX, 2012–13, USA)
*American Horror Story: Cult* (FX, 2017, USA)
*The Amityville Horror* (Stuart Rosenberg, 1979, USA)
*The Amityville Horror* (Andrew Douglas, 2005, USA)
*Angel Has Fallen* (Ric Roman Waugh, 2019, USA)
*Antrum* (David Amito and Michael Laicini, 2018, Canada)
*Appropriate Adult* (Neil McKay, 2011, UK)
*Archive 81* (Netflix, 2022)
*Armageddon* (Michael Bay, 1998, USA)
*Audrie & Daisy* (Bonni Cohen and Jon Shenk, 2016, USA)
*The Bat Whispers* (Roland West, 1930, USA)
*Behind Enemy Lines* (John Moore, 2001, USA)
*Beyond the Gates* (Jackson Stewart, 2016, USA)
*Black Hawk Down* (Ridley Scott, 2001, USA)
*Black Mirror* (Channel 4/Netflix, 2011, UK)
*Bone Tomahawk* (S. Craig Zahler, 2015, USA)
*Book of Shadows: Blair Witch 2* (Joe Berlinger, 2000, USA)
*Brawl in Cell Block 99* (S. Craig Zahler, 2017, USA)
*The Cabinet of Dr. Caligari* (Robert Wiene, 1920, Germany)
*Captivity* (Roland Joffe, 2007, Russia/USA/Canada)
*Cherry Falls* (Geoffrey Wright, 2000, USA)
*Chronicle* (Josh Trank, 2012, USA)
*Collateral Damage* (Andrew Davis, 2002, USA)

*The Core* (Shudder, 2017–18, UK)
*The Crazies* (Breck Eisner, 2010, USA)
*Criminal Minds* (CBS, 2005–20, USA)
*Cropsey* (Joshua Zeman and Barbara Branaccio, 2009, USA)
*Dahmer* (David Jacobson, 2002, USA)
*Dawn of the Dead* (Zack Snyder, 2004, USA)
*Deathdream* (Bob Clark, 1974, USA)
*Deep Impact* (Mimi Leder, 1998, USA)
*Demon House* (Zak Bagans, 2018, USA)
*Detour* (Severin Eskeland, 2009, Norway)
*The Devil's Rejects* (Rob Zombie, 2005, USA)
*Dog The Bounty Hunter* (A&E, 2004–12, USA)
*Don't F**k With Cats: Hunting an Internet Killer* (Mark Lewis, 2019, UK/USA)
*Dragged Across Concrete* (S. Craig Zahler, 2018, USA)
*Dreamcatcher* (Jacob Johnston, 2003, USA)
*Earth to Echo* (Dave Green, 2014, USA)
*Earthquake* (Mark Robson, 1974, USA)
*Ed Gein: Butcher of Plainfield* (Michael Fifer, 2007, USA)
*End of Watch* (David Ayer, 2012, USA)
*Evidence* (Olatunde Osunsanmi, 2013, USA)
*Extreme Makeover* (ABC, 2002–7, USA)
*Extreme Paranormal* (A&E, 2009, USA)
*Extremely Wicked, Shockingly Evil and Vile* (Joe Berlinger, 2019, USA)
*Faces of Death* (Conan Le Cilaire, 1978, USA)
*Fight Club* (David Fincher, 1999, USA)
*Final Destination* (James Wong, 2000, USA)
*The First Purge* (Gerard McMurray, 2018, USA)
*The Found Footage Phenomenon* (Sarah Appleton and Phillip Escott, 2021, UK)
*Gacy* (Clive Saunders, 2003, USA)
*Get Out* (Jordan Peele, 2017, USA)
*Ghost Adventures* (Travel Channel, 2008–, USA)
*Ghost Brothers* (TLC, 2016–17, USA)
*Ghost Hunters* (SciFi/Syfy/A&E/Discovery+, 2004–6, USA)
*The Girly Ghosthunters* (Space, 2005, Canada)
*Gojira/Godzilla* (Ishirō Honda, 1954, Japan)
*Halloween* (David Gordon Green, 2018, USA)
*Halloween III: Season of the Witch* (Tommy Lee Wallace, 1982, USA)
*Häxan* (Benjamin Christensen, 1922, Sweden/Denmark)
*Hiroshima Mon Amour* (Alain Resnais, 1959, France/Japan)
*Horsemen* (Jonas Akerlund, 2009, USA)
*Hostel* (Eli Roth, 2005, USA)
*Hostel: Part II* (Eli Roth, 2007, USA)
*Hostel: Part III* (Scott Spiegel, 2011, USA)
*House on Haunted Hill* (William Malone, 1999, USA)
*The Human Centipede: First Sequence* (Tom Six, 2009, Netherlands)
*I Know What You Did Last Summer* (Jim Gillespie, 1997, USA)
*Illegal Border Crossing Park* (Eddie Moretti and Shane Smith, 2010, Canada)
*In the Jungle: The Making of Cannibal Holocaust* (Michéle De Angelis, 2003, Italy)
*Independence Day* (Roland Emmerich, 1996, USA)
*Invasion of the Body Snatchers* (Don Siegel, 1956, USA)

*Invasion U.S.A.* (Joseph Zito, 1985, USA)
*The Invitation* (Karyn Kusama, 2015, USA)
*Jesus of Siberia* (Eddie Moretti and Shane Smith, 2012, Canada)
*Jigsaw* (Michael Spierig and Peter Spierig, 2017, Canada/USA)
*The Jonestown Haunting* (Andrew Jones, 2020, UK)
*Jonestown: The Life and Death of Peoples Temple* (Stanley Nelson, 2006, USA)
*Kairo* (Kiyoshi Kurosawa, 2001, Japan)
*Land of the Dead* (George A. Romero, 2005, USA)
*The Last House on the Left* (Wes Craven, 1972, USA)
*Little People, Big World* (TLC, 2006–, USA)
*London Has Fallen* (Babak Najafi, 2016, USA)
*The Long Road Back From Hell: Reclaiming Cannibal Holocaust* (Xavier Mendik, 2011, UK)
*Making a Murderer* (Moira Demos and Laura Ricciardi, 2015, USA)
*Men in Black II* (Barry Sonnenfeld, 2002, USA)
*Metropolis* (Fritz Lang, 1927, Germany)
*Mindhunter* (Netflix, 2017–19, USA)
*Missing in Action* (Joseph Zito, 1984, USA)
*The Mist* (Frank Darabont, 2007, USA)
*Most Haunted* (Living/Really/Youtube, 2002–, UK)
*Mulberry Street* (Jim Mickle, 2006, USA)
*My Friend Dahmer* (Marc Meyers, 2017, USA)
*Nanook of the North* (Robert J. Flaherty, 1922, USA)
*Night of the Living Dead* (George A. Romero, 1968, USA)
*Night Stalker: The Hunt for a Serial Killer* (Tiller Russell and James Carroll, 2021, USA)
*No Man of God* (Amber Sealey, 2021, USA)
*North Korean Labor Camps* (Eddie Moretti and Shane Smith, 2011, Canada)
*Nosferatu* (F. W. Murnau, 1922, Germany)
*Olympus Has Fallen* (Antoine Furqua, 2013, USA)
*Once Upon a Time in Hollywood* (Quentin Tarantino, 2019, USA/UK)
*Open Windows* (Nacho Vigalondo, 2014, USA/Spain)
*Paranormal Lockdown* (Destination America/TLC, 2016–, USA)
*Paranormal State* (A&E, 2007–11, USA)
*The Path* (Hulu, 2016–18, USA)
*Patriot Games* (Phillip Noyce, 1992, USA)
*Patriots Day* (Peter Berg, 2016, USA/Japan)
*Poltergeist* (Tobe Hooper, 1982, USA)
*Project X* (Nima Nourizadeh, 2012, USA)
*Psycho* (Alfred Hitchcock, 1960, USA)
*Pulse* (Jim Sonzero, 2006, USA)
*The Purge* (James DeMonaco, 2013, USA)
*The Purge: Anarchy* (James DeMonaco, 2014, USA)
*The Purge: Election Year* (James DeMonaco, 2016, USA)
*Quarantine 2: Terminal* (John Pogue, 2011, USA)
*Radioactive Beasts of Chernobyl* (Eddie Moretti and Shane Smith, 2007, Canada)
*REC 3: Génesis* (Paco Plaza, 2012, Spain)
*REC 4: Apocalypse* (Jaume Balagueró, 2014, Spain)
*Red State* (Kevin Smith, 2011, USA)
*Ring* (Hideo Nakata, 1998, Japan)
*The Ring* (Gore Verbinski, 2002, USA)

*The Ruins* (Carter Smith, 2008, USA/Australia)
*Rules of Engagement* (William Friedkin, 2000, USA)
*Saw* (James Wan, 2004, USA)
*Saw II* (Darren Lynn Bousman, 2005, Canada/USA)
*Saw III* (Darren Lynn Bousman, 2006, Canada/USA)
*Saw IV* (Darren Lynn Bousman, 2007, Canada/USA)
*Saw V* (David Hackl, 2008, Canada/USA)
*Saw VI* (Kevin Greutert, 2009, Canada/USA/Australia)
*Saw 3D: The Final Chapter* (Kevin Greutert, 2010, Canada/USA)
*Schindler's List* (Steven Spielberg, 1993, USA)
*Scream* (Wes Craven, 1996, USA)
*Scream* (Matt Bettinelli-Olpen and Tyler Gillett, 2022, USA)
*Scream 2* (Wes Craven, 1997, USA)
*Scream 3* (Wes Craven, 2000, USA)
*Scream 4* (Wes Craven, 2011, USA)
*Searching* (Aneesh Chaganty, 2018, USA)
*Serendipity* (Peter Chelsom, 2001, USA/Canada)
*Shoah* (Claude Lanzmann, 1985, France/UK)
*The Sixth Sense* (M. Night Shyamalan, 1999, USA)
*Sonic the Hedgehog* (Jeff Fowler, 2020, Japan/USA)
*Spiral: From the Book of Saw* (Darren Lynn Bousman, 2021, USA/Canada)
*The Strangers* (Bryan Bertino, 2008, USA)
*The Terror* (Roy Del Ruth, 1928, USA)
*The Titticut Follies* (Frederick Wiseman, 1967, USA)
*The Towering Inferno* (John Guillermin, 1974, USA)
*The Town That Dreaded Sundown* (Charles B. Pierce, 1976, USA)
*The Town That Dreaded Sundown* (Alfonzo Gomez-Rejon, 2014, USA)
*Turistas* (John Stockwell, 2006, USA)
*Turning Point: 9/11 and the War on Terror* (Brian Knappenberger, 2021, USA)
*United 93* (Paul Greengrass, 2006, USA)
*Urban Legend* (Jamie Blanks, 1998, USA)
*Videodrome* (David Cronenberg, 1983, Canada)
*Vlog* (Joshua Butler, 2008, USA)
*Volcano* (Mick Jackson, 1997, USA)
*Waco* (Paramount Network, 2018, USA)
*The Walking Dead* (AMC/Fox, 2010–22, USA)
*War of the Worlds* (Byron Haskin, 1953, USA)
*War of the Worlds* (Steven Spielberg, 2005, USA)
*We Were Soldiers* (Randall Wallace, 2002, USA)
*When A Stranger Calls* (Fred Walton, 1979, USA)
*When A Stranger Calls* (Simon West, 2006, USA)
*Willowbrook: The Last Great Disgrace* (Geraldo Rivera, 1972, USA)
*Windtalkers* (John Woo, 2002, USA)
*World Trade Center* (Oliver Stone, 2006, USA)
*World War Z* (Marc Forster, 2013, USA)
*Zero Day* (Ben Coccio, 2003, USA)
*Zoolander* (Ben Stiller, 2001, USA)

# Index

#Horror (2015), 183
11'09"01 September 11 (2002), 100
9/11 (2002), 19, 95, 111–12, 113–14, 117–18, 119, 120–2, 123, 125, 126–7
9/11: Day That Changed the World (2011), 95
9/11: The Falling Man (2006), 191n
21 Days (2014), 105
28 Weeks Later (2007), 103
102 Minutes That Changed America (2008), 95

Abbott, Stacey, 16, 17, 104, 122, 150
Afflicted (2013), 28
Alien Abduction (2014), 199
Aloi, Peg, 1, 38, 172
Altheide, David L., 98, 100
American Horror Story: Asylum (2012–13), 90n
American Horror Story: Cult (2017), 63–4
American Horror Story: Roanoake (2016), 165
Amityville Horror, The (1979/2005), 45
Anderson, Donald L., 130–1
Antrum (2018), 202
Apartment 143 (2011), 37, 105
Apollo 18 (2011), 28
Archive 81 (2022), 202
Area 51 (2015), 199
Armageddon (1998), 94
As Above, So Below (2014), 22n, 28, 113
Astley, Mark, 72

Atkinson, Rowland, 158
Atticus Institute, The (2015), 27
Audrie & Daisy (2016), 183
Aufderheide, Patricia, 26, 31
August Underground (film series), 70

Backrooms (Found Footage), The, 202
Barthes, Roland, 31, 166
Bat Whispers, The (1930), 150
Baudrillard, Jean, 139
Bay, The (2012), 7, 8, 9, 19, 28, 57, 104, 109, 110n, 129, 130–3, 137–41, 143–6
Be My Cat: A Film for Anne (2015), 70
Behind Enemy Lines (2001), 100
Behind the Mask: The Rise of Leslie Vernon (2006), 70
Benson-Allott, Caetlin, 25, 74
Berger, James, 120
Bernard, Mark, 16–17, 97–8, 109n, 144
Beyond The Gates (2016), 150
Biressi, Anita, 85, 86
Black Hawk Down (2001), 100
Black Mirror (2011–), 167n
Black Tapes, The (2015–17), 201
Blackwell Ghost, The (2017), 105
Blair Witch (2016), 1–2, 8, 39, 41n, 201
Blair Witch Project, The (1999), 1–2, 3, 7, 11, 20, 21n, 22n, 25, 39–40, 41n, 79, 88, 107, 127, 151, 158–62, 163, 164, 165, 166, 167, 168n, 171–2, 200, 201
Blake, Linnie, 5, 13, 16, 46–7, 60, 99, 103, 126, 142, 196

Bolter, Jay David, 103–4
*Bone Tomahawk* (2015), 110n
*Book of Shadows: Blair Witch 2* (2000), 21n
Bordwell, David, 7
*Bounty* (2009), 67
Bowen, A. J., 56
*Brawl in Cell Block 99* (2017), 110n
Briefel, Aviva, 96, 97, 104
Bronfen, Elisabeth, 15
Brottman, Mikita, 149
Butt, Aimen Khalid, 52
*Butterfly Kisses* (2018), 28

*Cabinet of Dr. Caligari, The* (1920), 15
*Cannibal Holocaust* (1980), 7, 25–6, 39, 88, 90n, 129, 130–1
*Captivity* (2007), 12
Carr, David, 52, 59
Caruth, Cathy, 14, 46–7
Castonguay, James, 161–2
Cavanaugh, Carole, 14–15, 65
censorship, 120–1, 122, 155, 171, 172
Chen, Guo-Ming, 156
Cherry, Brigid, 65n, 107, 138, 144–5
*Cherry Falls* (2000), 11
Chidester, David, 58–9
Christiansen, Steen, 105
*Chronicle* (2012), 200
*Closed Circuit Extreme* (2012), 105
Clover, Carol J., 162
*Cloverfield* (2008), 97, 102, 106, 107, 108, 160–1, 162–3, 166
Cole, Justin, 164–5
Colesky, Niels, 49
*Collateral Damage* (2002), 100
*Conspiracy, The* (2012), 9, 19, 104, 109, 110n, 129–31, 133, 136–7, 139–40, 142–3, 144, 145, 146
Corner, John, 29–30, 30, 67, 81
Costello, Sam, 45, 46, 51, 56
Craps, Stef, 119–20, 125
*Crazies, The* (2010), 103
*Criminal Minds* (2005–20), 61
*Cropsey* (2009), 40
*Crowsnest* (2012), 113
*Crying Dead, The* (2011), 86
*Curse of the Blair Witch* (1999), 158–9

*Dahmer* (2002), 45
Daniel, Adam, 4, 178, 198
Dargis, Manohla, 45
*Dawn of the Dead* (2004), 126
*Deathdream* (1974), 47
*Deep Impact* (1998), 94
*Delivery: The Beast Within* (2013), 67
*Demon House* (2018), 90n
*Den, The* (2013), 20, 169–70, 171–6, 183, 184, 186, 190, 191, 191n, 197
Deren, Maya, 31
*Detour* (2009), 104
*Devil Inside, The*, 163–4, 167
*Devil's Doorway, The* (2018), 10
*Devil's Due* (2014), 57
*Devil's Rejects, The* (2005), 12
*Devil's Trail* (2017), 67
*Diary of the Dead* (2007), 9, 19, 37–8, 90n, 104, 109, 110n, 129, 130–1, 132–3, 134–6, 138–42, 143–6, 198, 199
*Digging Up the Marrow* (2014), 28
*District 9* (2009), 10
Dixon, Winston Wheeler, 94, 96, 99, 100
Doka, Kenneth J., 60–1
*Don't F\*\*k With Cats: Hunting an Internet Killer* (2019), 69
Dovey, Jon, 30, 78
Dowdle, John Erick, 22n, 110n
*Dragged Across Concrete* (2018), 110n
*Dreamcatcher* (2003), 103
Durham Peters, John, 33
*Dyatlov Pass Incident, The* (2013), 113

*Earth to Echo* (2014), 200
*Earthquake* (1974), 94
Ebiri, Bilge, 64
*Ed Gein: Butcher of Plainfield* (2007), 45
Elsaesser, Thomas, 50, 103
*Empty Wake, The* (2021), 40
*End of Watch* (2012), 200
*Evidence* (2013), 9
*Exhibit A* (2007), 10
*Extreme Paranormal* (2009), 78
*Extremely Wicked, Shockingly Evil and Vile* (2019), 84

*Faces of Death* (1978), 76, 154
Faludi, Susan, 117–18, 141

Fetveit, Arild, 31
*Fight Club* (1999), 94
*Final Destination* (2000), 11
Fiske, John, 166
Flynn, Bernadette, 33
*Followers* (2017), 39, 106
Forrest, Jennifer, 127
*Found Footage 3D* (2016), 7, 21n
Freeman, Mark, 108, 145–6, 158
Friend, David, 107, 114
Frost, Laura, 16, 103, 109, 120, 122
Fuchs, Christian, 157

*Gacy* (2003), 45
*Get Out* (2017), 17
*Girly Ghosthunters, The* (2005), 78
*Ghost Adventures* (2008–), 78, 79–80
*Ghost Brothers* (2016–17), 78
*Ghostwatch* (1992), 150
*Gojira/Godzilla* (1954), 14–15
*Gonjiam: Haunted Asylum* (2018), 86
Grant, Barry Keith, 6, 7, 25, 34–5, 89
*Grave Encounters* (2011), 18, 19, 30, 38, 68, 77–83, 86–9, 90n, 197
Greenberg, Jeff, 93, 110n
*Greystone Park* (2012), 86
Gunning, Tom, 152

Hale, Mike, 78, 82
Hallam, Lindsay, 102, 169–70, 185
*Halloween* (film series), 84, 150
Hantke, Steffen, 11, 126
Hart, Adam Charles, 4, 11, 25, 150, 176, 189, 198
*Has Fallen* (film series), 101
*Hate Crime* (2012), 13, 90n
*Häxan* (1922), 41n
*Head Cases: Serial Killers in the Delaware Valley* (2013), 68
*Hell House* (film series), 28, 40, 198, 199
Heller-Nicholas, Alexandra, 3–4, 12, 25, 73, 161
Hess, Aaron, 155
Hight, Craig, 76
Higley, Sarah Lynn, 3, 38
Hill, Annette, 67, 81, 86, 87, 89
Hill, Katherine, 45
Hills, Matt, 161

*Hollows Grove* (2014), 68
*Home Movie* (2008), 191n
*Horror in the High Desert* (2021), 68
*Horsemen* (2009), 12
*Host* (2020), 8, 200–1
*Hostel* (film series), 12, 98, 172
*The Houses October Built, The* (2014), 199
Hubber, Duncan, 4–5
*Human Centipede: First Sequence, The* (2009), 12
Humphries, Reynold, 12
*Hunted, The* (2013), 67
Hutchings, Peter, 2, 11, 109n

*I Am Alone* (2015), 67
*I Know What You Did Last Summer* (1997), 11
*In Memorium* (2005), 153
*Independence Day* (1996), 94
*Invasion* (2005) 8, 29
*Invasion of the Body Snatchers* (1956), 17
*Invitation, The* (2015), 61

Jackson, Neil, 26, 176
Jacoby, Jeff, 154–5
Jarvis, Lee, 104, 155
Jenkins, Henry, 61, 161–2
*Jeruzalem* (2015), 10
*Jesus of Siberia* (2012), 65n
Jones, Steve, 3, 97, 104
*Jonestown Haunting, The* (2020), 63–4
Jowett, Lorna, 150
Junod, Tom, 114, 122

Kaes, Anton, 15
*Kairo* (2001), 149
Kaplan, E. Ann, 13, 107, 118, 120
Kattelman, Beth, 102
Kavka, Misha, 88
Kellner, Douglas, 34, 102
Kerner, Aaron Michael, 102
Kilborn, Richard, 83
King, Geoff, 73, 81, 94
King, Homay, 161
Kirk, Neal, 153
Koos, Leonard R., 127
Koven, Mikel, 89
Kracauer, Siegfried, 15

Krautschick, Lars R., 162

LaCapra, Dominick, 14
*Lake Mungo* (2008), 10
*Land of the Dead* (2005), 103
*Last Broadcast, The* (1998), 2, 27
*Last Exorcism, The* (2010), 27, 28, 38, 40, 162–3, 165, 167
*Last Horror Movie, The* (2003), 27
*Last House on the Left, The* (1972), 45, 48
Laycock, Joseph, 61, 62
Lee-Wright, Peter, 35
*Legend of Boggy Creek, The* (1972), 41n
Levinson, Barry, 110n, 131
*Long Pigs* (2007), 70
*Lost Coast Tapes*, 28
*Lost Footage of Leah Sullivan, The* (2018), 38
Lowell, Percival, 32
Lowenstein, Adam, 13, 14, 14–16, 44, 46, 47–8, 48, 60, 196–7
*Lunapolis* (2010), 28

McCollum, Victoria, 2, 16, 97
*McPherson Tape, The* (1989), 199
McRobert, Neil, 5, 8, 9, 138, 197
Maddrey, Joseph, 2
*Making a Murderer* (2015), 84
*Man Bites Dog* (1992), 70
*Marble Hornets* (2009–14), 165
Marwick, Alice E., 184
Mason, Paul, 156
Mee, Laura, 11, 109, 128n
*Megan is Missing* (2011), 201
*Men in Black II* (2002), 100
Meslow, Scott, 9, 201
*Metropolis*, 15
Middleton, Jason, 102
Miller, Sam J., 96, 97, 104
*Mist, The* (2007), 103
*Mitchell Tapes, The* (2010), 68
Monnet, Agnieszka Soltyzik 101, 102, 109, 112, 124
*Monster Project, The* (2017), 28
Moore, Rebecca, 60, 61, 62
Moran, Caitlin, 173
*Most Haunted* (2002–), 82–3
*Mr. Jones* (2013), 113
*Muirhouse* (2012), 27

*Mulberry Street* (2006), 103
Munger, Sean, 50
*Murder Box* (2018), 27
*Murder in the Heartland: The Search for Video X* (2003), 27

*Nanook of the North* (1922), 26
Naudet, Gédéon, 112, 113–14, 117, 118, 120–1, 123, 125, 126–7
Naudet, Jules *see* Naudet, Gédéon
Newman, Kim, 17
Nichols, Bill, 28–9, 30, 38, 56, 57, 58, 76, 197
*Night of the Living Dead* (1968), 116
*Night Stalker: The Hunt for a Serial Killer* (2021), 75
*Night Stalkers: Paranormal Investigators* (2017), 68
*Noroi: The Curse* (2005), 10
*Nosferatu*, 15
Nunn, Heather, 86

*Occult* (2009), 4
*Open Windows* (2014), 169–70
*Out of the Shadows* (2017), 28

*Paranormal Activity* (film series), 2, 3, 11, 21n, 29, 33–4, 36–7, 69, 105, 169, 172, 190, 198, 201
*Paranormal Lockdown* (2016–), 78
*Paranormal State* (2007–11), 78, 86
*Path, The* (2016–18), 62
*Patriots Day* (2016), 108
*Penance* (2009), 13
Penenberg, Adam, 105
Petley, Julian, 25, 154
*Phase 1, Clinical Trials* (2013), 8
Phillips, Kendall R., 11, 13, 104, 108, 130
*Phoenix Forgotten* (2017), 199
*Phoenix Incident, The* (2015), 28
Pile, Steve, 86
*Poltergeist* (1982), 150, 154, 179
Poole, W. Scott, 15, 16
*Poughkeepsie Tapes, The* (2007), 8, 18, 19, 22n, 28, 30, 68–76, 84, 85, 87–9, 90n, 200
Prince, Stephen, 102, 108
*Project X* (2012), 200
*Pulse* (2006), 149, 153

*Purge, The* (film series), 17, 102
Pyszcznski, Tom, 110n

*Quarantine* (2008), 10, 19, 22n, 57, 104, 106, 109, 110n, 111–27, 127n, 138, 199
*Quarantine 2: Terminal* (2011), 127n

Raimondo, Matthew J., 3, 6, 25, 28–9, 112, 181
Raudive, Konstantine, 183
*Rec* (2007), 19, 21n, 111, 112, 115, 117, 119, 120, 125–7
*Rec* (film series), 10, 113
*Red State* (2011), 61
*Reel Evil* (2012), 86
Remakes, 19, 111, 112–13, 125–6, 127, 128n
Reyes, Xavier Aldana, 5, 6, 75–6, 112, 160, 169
Rhodes, Gary D., 3, 6, 25, 35, 36, 149–50
Rice, Condoleezza, 107
*Ride in the Park, A* (2013), 8
*Ring* (1998), 150, 162
*Ring, The* (2002), 162
*River, The* (2012), 165
Rodgers, Thomas, 158
Romero, George A., 110n, 127, 135, 145
Roscoe, Jane, 6, 35–6, 158–9
Rosen, Jay, 156–7
Roth, Eli, 98, 109n
*Ruins, The* (2008), 12
Russell, Catherine, 173
*RWD* (2015), 57

*Sacrament, The* (2013), 7, 9, 14, 18, 28, 30, 42n, 43, 44–7, 48–51, 52–8, 59, 62–5, 197
Samuels, Stuart, 17
*Sanatorium* (2013), 86
*Savageland* (2016), 8, 28, 41n, 68, 193–5, 197
*Saw* (film series), 12, 104, 172, 182
Sayad, Cecilia, 8
*Schindler's List* (1993), 14
Schopp, Andrew, 106
Sconce, Jeffrey, 86, 150, 151, 151–3, 180, 181, 182
*Scream* (film series), 1, 11, 150, 182

*Searching* (2018), 190
Seaton, A. V., 90n
Seltzer, Mark, 76
Senft, Theresa M., 184
*Serbian Film, A* (2010), 74
*Serendipity* (2001), 100
Sharrett, Christopher, 12, 126
*Shoah* (1985), 14
shock websites, 154–5, 172, 178, 191n
*Sick Thing That Happened to Emily When She Was Younger, The* (2012), 190
*Sickhouse* (2016), 170, 191n
Sisco King, Claire, 13, 15
*Skew* (2011), 57
*Slumber Party Alien Abduction* (2013), 199
Sneider, Jeff, 185
Sobchack, Vivian, 57–8
Solomon, Sheldon, 110n
Sontag, Susan, 56, 105–6, 124, 137, 200
*Speak, The* (2011), 68
*Spree* (2020), 20–1, 128n, 166, 169–70, 171, 184–90, 191, 199
*Strangers, The* (2008), 12, 45, 102
Stubblefield, Thomas, 96, 106, 107
*Survive The Hollow Shoals* (2018), 67

*Taking of Deborah Logan, The* (2014), 28
Tal, Kalí, 14
*Terror, The* (1928), 150
*They're Watching* (2016), 67
Tiffany, Joel, 151
*Titticut Follies, The* (1967), 87
*Tontine Massacre: The Fiji Tapes*, 67
torture horror, 12–13, 97, 98, 102, 104, 171, 172
torture porn *see* torture horror
*Towering Inferno, The* (1974), 94
*Town That Dreaded Sundown, The* (1976/2014), 45
*Trollhunter* (2010), 10
Tucker, Jennifer, 32
Tudor, Andrew, 5, 16, 22n
*Tuesday the 17th* (2012), 88
*Tunnel, The* (2011), 4, 10, 113
*Turistas* (2006), 12
Turner, Peter, 3, 4
*Turning Point: 9/11 and the War on Terror* (2021), 95

Tzioumakis, Yannis, 17

*Unfolding, The* (2016), 105
*Unfriended* (2014), 8, 20, 166, 169–71, 173, 177–83, 184, 186, 190, 191, 196, 197, 201
*Unfriended: Dark Web* (2018), 195–6, 197
*United 93* (2006), 100, 108
*Upper Footage, The* (2013), 161, 164–5, 167, 200
*Urban Legend* (1998), 1

*V/H/S* (film series), 8, 190, 198, 201
Vice, 44, 49, 51–5, 56, 57, 59, 65n, 190
*Videodrome* (1983), 150
video games, 62, 158, 168n, 198
video nasties, 73–4
*Video Palace*, 201
*Visit, The* (2015), 39
*Vlog* (2008), 9
*Volcano* (1997), 94

*Waco* (2018), 62
Wada-Marciano, Mitsuyo, 167n
*Walking Dead, The* (2010–22), 12
Wallace, Richard James, 30

*War of the Worlds* (1953/2005), 94, 100
Weinstock, Jeffrey A., 3, 38
West, Amy, 35, 36, 83, 106, 114
West, Ti, 46, 51, 53, 59, 62, 64
Wetmore Jr, Kevin, 16, 96, 97, 102, 115–16, 153, 173
*When a Stranger Calls* (1979/2006), 126, 150
White, Hayden, 13–14
Wiest, Julie B., 85
Williams, Karen, 79, 81
Williams, Linda, 36
Willis, Andy, 125–6
*Willow Creek* (2013), 5, 28
*Willowbrook: The Last Great Disgrace* (1972), 87, 90n
*Windtalkers* (2002), 100
*WNUF Halloween Special* (2013), 90n
Wood, Robin, 45
*World Trade Center* (2006), 100
*World War Z* (2013), 103

*Zero Day* (2003), 200
Zimmer, Catherine, 16, 102, 104
*Zoolander* (2001), 100

EU representative:
Easy Access System Europe
Mustamäe tee 50, 10621 Tallinn, Estonia
Gpsr.requests@easproject.com